~ End ~

When my husband John and I first met Pastors Gary and Marilyn Skinner in 1984, our country of Uganda was recovering from the ravages of war. For the next 40 years, Watoto Church was to become the spiritual home we were yearning for. Gary and Marilyn have been exceptional spiritual models and leaders. The Godly values of integrity, honesty, justice, mercy, empathy, and hard work that the Skinners and Watoto Church instilled and nurtured in me, over the years, account for who I am today and have immensely contributed to my incredible career as a judge in Uganda and a judge at the International Court of Justice. This book is a testament to the potential of a mustard seed sown by the Skinners 40 years ago and is a must-read.

H.E. Julia Sebutinde
Vice President and Judge
The International Court of Justice, The Hague, Netherlands

Our partnership with Watoto has been very fruitful. The work they do with children is incredible. Many lives have been saved and transformed.

Joyce Meyer

We have had the immense honour of knowing Gary and Marilyn Skinner for over 20 years. Our lives collided miraculously in what can only be described as the kindness and providence of God. Across two decades, we have come to know them not merely in ministry and strategic partnership, but as loyal, faithful, and godly friends. They are Apostolic in nature and calling and have inspired multiplied thousands with their courage, capacity, and heart for what is paramount to God's heart. We are confident that this new book *Where Faith Lit the Way* will capture the ongoing legacy of their lives and will extend much needed wisdom and perspective to those who seek to journey similar roads. We are proud to call them friends, co-labourers in His Kingdom, and family.

Brian & Bobbie Houston,
Founders · Hillsong

Where Faith Lit the Way allows you to dive into captivating stories of both miraculous and everyday moments. Skinner's poignant work covering faith, family, and the vibrant Christian Church reminds you of God's unwavering faithfulness and His sovereign hand through every circumstance.

Rob Hoskins
President · One Hope

I have always been an admirer of the ministry of Gary and Marilyn Skinner. This book is an important contribution to understanding the responsibility of the church to be a transformative agent of change and development in our world. It is deeply rooted in biblical teaching and beautifully captures their clarity of vision and passionate determination to care for Uganda's most vulnerable children. In my view, what sets Watoto Church and Child-Care Ministries apart is the unwavering commitment to go beyond mere care, by providing family values, education, and empowerment to these children. Through their holistic approach, they aim to shape these young lives into future leaders who will catalyze the transformation of a nation. This book is a must-read for anyone seeking inspiration, and a call to action in making a lasting difference in the lives of the most vulnerable.

D. Murray Cornelius
Executive Director · Mission Global
The Pentecostal Assemblies of Canada

While only Heaven will truly be able to tell the whole miraculous account of what the ministry of Watoto has meant not only to the beautiful people of Uganda, but the whole world, it is a great blessing to hear the story from the heart and life of its founder and leader, Pastor Gary Skinner.

We have been deeply impacted and personally privileged to witness what God has built through the dedicated ministry of Gary and Marilyn and the magnificent team they have raised up throughout their 40-year history.

Watoto has truly been kissed by the favour and blessing of God and we know that in the years to come its impact and legacy will continue to grow from strength to strength to the glory of God.

Pastors John and Helen Burns
Founders · Relate Church, Vancouver Canada

Gary and Marilyn are two of the most humble, authentic, generous people we've ever known. We are, along with so many others, standing on their great shoulders as they've pioneered a movement to rescue and raise children, build a transformational church and empower women to become leaders within their community. It's been a 40 year journey to date and there is so much more in store. We can't wait to see all that God continues to do as a result of their faith-filled surrender!

Earl and Oneka McClellan
Shoreline City Church, Dallas, TX USA

The work of Pastor Gary Skinner and Watoto Church, to which he has dedicated his life, is a moral challenge to an indifferent world. Watoto is an admonition to those who defy Christ's rallying call to let our light shine.

Thanks to Watoto there are many points of light in some of the darkest spots in one of Africa's most volatile regions. The inspiration and passion Gary brings to his ministry is the live wire connecting those points of light. The story of Watoto is a powerful testimony of the power of love without measure. It is worth telling and retelling! I know because I'm a witness to the transformational work of Watoto in binding the wounds of war torn northern Uganda.

Norbert Mao
Minister of Justice, Uganda

~

garyandmarilyn.com

~ Biography ~

Gary and Marilyn Skinner are the visionary and passionate Founders of Watoto Church. In 1984, during a time of civil war, they planted this local church in Kampala, Uganda to speak hope and life to the nation. Today Watoto Church is a cell-based, community church with more than 38,000 people gathering in-person and online every week to celebrate the value and purpose they've found in Jesus Christ.

They passionately believe that it is the responsibility of the local church to solve community problems. Watoto Church cares for community holistically through over 2,700 small groups that meet weekly.

In 1994, they founded Watoto Child Care Ministries in response to the cry of millions of children who had been orphaned or left vulnerable as a result of war, poverty and disease. Since starting, they've placed thousands of orphans in families, empowered thousands of vulnerable women to reach their own families and communities, rescued babies and former child soldiers, kept over 30,000 girls in school, and sent more than 100 children's choirs across six continents.

As Watoto continues to work alongside the most vulnerable in their nation, they aim to rescue individuals, raise each one as a leader in his or her sphere of influence so that, in turn, they will rebuild the nation.

In over 40 years, the challenges facing Uganda and Africa have changed, but their vision remains the same. In all of this, Watoto remains a local church, committed to celebrating Christ and caring for community.

In February 2023 Gary and Marilyn handed over the leadership of Watoto to their successors, Julius and Vernita Rwotlonyo. Their desire now is to serve the Church at large. Gary and Marilyn are the proud parents of three children and grandparents to seven.

~

WHERE FAITH LIT THE WAY

A memoir of courage over fear ...

GARY SKINNER

Copyright © 2024 by Gary Skinner
Published by Gary M. Skinner
1405 Pentecostal Road, Cobourg, Ontario, Canada K9A 4J8

Printed in the United States of America

All rights reserved. No part of this publication may be reproduced, stored in a retrieval system or transmitted in any form or by any means - for example, electronic, photocopy, recording – without the prior written permission of the publisher. The only exception is brief quotations in printed reviews.

Library of Congress Cataloging-in-Publication Data
Names: Skinner, Gary, author.
Title: Where Faith Lit the Way / Gary Skinner.
ISBN 979-8-3507-2879-8

Scripture quotations marked (NIV) are taken from the Holy Bible, New International Version®, NIV®. Copyright © 1973, 1978, 1984, 2011 by Biblica, Inc.™ Used by permission of Zondervan. All rights reserved worldwide. www.zondervan.com The "NIV" and "New International Version" are trademarks registered in the United States Patent and Trademark Office by Biblica, Inc.™

Scripture quotations marked (AMPCE) are taken from the Amplified Bible, Copyright © 1954, 1958, 1962, 1964, 1965, 1987 by The Lockman Foundation. Used by permission.

Scripture quotations marked MSG are taken from The Message, copyright © 1993, 2002, 2018 by Eugene H. Peterson. Used by permission of NavPress. All rights reserved. Represented by Tyndale House Publishers.

Scripture quotations marked (NLT) are taken from the Holy Bible, New Living Translation, copyright ©1996, 2004, 2015 by Tyndale House Foundation. Used by permission of Tyndale House Publishers, Carol Stream, Illinois 60188. All rights reserved.

Scripture quotations marked TPT are from The Passion Translation®. Copyright © 2017, 2018, 2020 by Passion & Fire Ministries, Inc. Used by permission. All rights reserved. ThePassionTranslation.com.

Cover Design by Tim Skinner

~ Dedications ~

*In reflecting on forty years of life and service
for the Kingdom of God in Uganda and South Sudan,
I am grateful.*

*May all honour, glory and praise be to
God our Father.
Christ my Saviour.
And the Holy Spirit, an ever-present Guide.*

~

*I dedicate this work of love
to my children, Tim, Rachel, and James.
You sacrificed so much.*

*And above all,
to the person I love most,
without whom this would not have been possible,
a woman of immense courage,
my wife Marilyn.*

~ Contents ~

	Acknowledgements	13
	Foreword	17
	Preamble Hymn	19
	Introduction	21
01.	The Blind Corner at Namagunga	27
02.	From Dreams To Destiny	41
03.	Divine Assignment	55
04.	The Pearl of Africa	75
05.	Into the Heart of Darkness	91
06.	The Crystal Suite	105
07.	The Start of Something New	123
08.	Angels in the Night	137
09.	Struggle in the Shadows	153
10.	Trailblazers	169
11.	Beyond Belief	181
12.	No Easy Answers	191
13.	Reel To Real	207
14.	A Courageous Stand	219
15.	Silent Epidemic	231

16.	In the Line of Fire	241
17.	A Place Called Home	255
18.	The Songs of Children	265
19.	Pressing On	281
20.	Doing Life Together	295
21.	Strategic Alliances	311
22.	Some Good Things	323
23.	Celebrating Christ, Caring for Community	333
24.	Project Gulu	343
25.	Epilogue	363

~ Acknowledgements ~

~ The Nation of Uganda ~

To the people of Uganda, thank you for welcoming us and making us part of this great land we each call home.

The names and faces of each person connected to this memoir in any way, whether great or small, are too many to recall. I appreciate each one of you.

~ The Watoto Church Family ~

To the wonderful family we call Watoto Church, a very special thank you. Each and every one of you, no matter how long you have made Watoto Church your home, is a precious and vital part of this story. Your faithfulness to Jesus and His Church brings us great joy. You are in our hearts always.

There is not enough space in this book to highlight the sacrifice of so many, who over the years have fashioned Watoto into what it is today. From members of the choir who stood service after service to lead God's people in worship, to caretakers who washed the floors so that our place of worship was a welcoming place, we say thank you. To the Elders and Deacons, your wisdom, encouragement and love has provided the structure for who we are as a church. To those who have served in cell ministry and those who have carried out acts of love and selflessness without being seen by others, thank you. Together, we have given of ourselves to bring honour to King Jesus.

~ The Pastoral Team ~

To the wonderful men and women who have served on our team of pastors, thank you for working as shepherds to tend the flock of God. Your partnership in the gospel has been a joy and a delight. We love you and are extremely proud of who you are.

~ The Watoto Family of Friends ~

To all who serve the vulnerable in our community through Watoto Childcare Ministries, thank you. In Country Offices around the world, on boards and behind desks, your contribution to the dream is making a significant difference.

To the mothers who have risen every day for decades making sacrifices for the children, whether it was making them breakfast, being there when it mattered most, or the many other important things along the way, thank you.

I honour the teams of administrators, pastors, teachers, caretakers, and all others who have worked tirelessly to ensure the smooth operation of this transformative work.

To the volunteers and teams who invested time, talent and treasure to visit Uganda and build the infrastructure of the Watoto Villages and homes, your generosity and labour of love is not forgotten. To the sponsors, churches and individuals who have come alongside to provide the financial support necessary to care for the vulnerable women and children of Uganda, thank you.

~ Watoto International Board of Advisors ~

A monumental thank you to the men and women who served so faithfully and capably on the Watoto International Board of Advisors. Your wisdom, advice, counsel, and encouragement to me personally has been a rock of security and protection. Thank you.

To each and every one of you who have joined hands with us in this noble venture of missionary enterprise, I express my deepest gratitude. We could never have accomplished what God called us to do without you. Together we have written another paragraph of Church history.

~ My Parents and Siblings ~

Our parents gave Marilyn and me a rich Christian ministry heritage for which we are grateful. You were with us, especially in those very difficult early days, sending practical and material support when we needed it most. Thank you.

~ My Children ~

Timothy, Rachel and James, my precious children. Thank you. You are heaven's gift to us. The price you paid as we lived to fulfill the call of God on our lives is inestimable.

~ My Beautiful Wife ~

To Marilyn, my love, life-partner and companion, the most supportive wife a man could ever hope for, there are not enough ways to say thank you. Together, we are better. Time has proven that to be true. You are my treasure of love and loyalty that cannot be measured.

~ King Jesus ~

To the One I adore most of all, my Lord, saviour and friend, King Jesus, I bow and acknowledge that you are the first and the last, the source and sustenance of life. Without you, there is nothing and it is all meaningless. With you, anything is possible and life is truly worth living. In light of what you have done, no sacrifice is too great. All the glory, honour and praise is yours, and yours alone.

~

~ Foreword ~

Bob Hoskins
~ Founder · One Hope ~

Gary and Marilyn Skinner's life of ministry to the people of Uganda is nothing short of extraordinary and one of the most inspiring works of God. It is with awe that I have had the privilege to witness the Skinner's dynamic Gospel ministry flourish and transform countless lives for many years now. After reading *Where Faith Litced the Way*, an evocative narrative of their journey – the tests, trials, setbacks, and victories – I have a whole new level of admiration for their steadfast resolve to remain faithful to the Lord's call on their life.

Gary and Marilyn's love for the people of Africa, especially the younger generation in the "Pearl of Africa," is evident in this passionate and poignant recounting of their four decades of ministry in Uganda. Their love, without a doubt, reflects the heart of the Father to the lost, abandoned, and broken in Uganda, and I believe your heart will be filled and compelled as you read their story.

The Skinners incredible ministry journey began with establishing a church in the Ugandan capital, but eventually would include ministries to orphans, widows, and those affected by AIDS. In spite of the great challenges that they faced as the vision increased and the work expanded, the Skinners faithfully put their trust in the God of the impossible. As a result, there are countless testimonies of God's miraculous works that the reader gets to relive through their detailed narratives. Gary, Marilyn, and their children faced extreme circumstances and near-death experiences, but having counted the costs and having stood firm on the word of the Lord to them, they remained faithful to the God-given vision and trusted that HE would show His faithfulness to them.

The Skinners ministry in Kampala is not one confined to a single generation or to their lifetime, but they have devoted themselves to mentor and train leaders to carry on the work. Therefore, the great ministry that they began will transcend generations. Humbly, the Skinners have passed the baton on to those young leaders that they mentored, always making themselves available when needed, and trusting that the God who led them for 40 years has also called and equipped the next generation to spread the Gospel of Christ.

Watoto Church is one of the most impactful and fruitful Christian ministries on a continent that is at the center of worldwide church growth. By 2037, half of all Christians in the world will live in sub-Saharan Africa. Africa also boasts the youngest population on the planet. By the year 2050, fifty percent of all under eighteen-year-olds in the world will live in Africa. The 21st-century is the African century! Because Watoto Church has consistently and effectively proven to value and invest in the next generation, it serves as a model and catalyzer for transformation not just for Africa, but for the world. As the founder of OneHope, I know for certain that the Skinners and Watoto Church have contributed significantly to our vision of reaching all the children of the world with God's Word!

I am confident that as you read this incredible account of God's mighty works through Gary and Marilyn Skinner, hope and resolve will be sparked in your own life. Whatever God has called you to, He can be trusted to lead you and bring victory through every difficulty and challenge!

∼

God be in my head
And in my understanding;
God be in mine eyes
And in my looking;
God be in my mouth
And in my speaking;
God be in my heart
And in my thinking;
God be at mine end
And in my departing.

~ *A Hymn by H. Walford Davies* ~

(1869 – 1941)

LISTEN TO THE HYMN · PERFORMED BY
THE WATOTO CHURCH CHOIR

"The church is not confined to a building;
it's the people, empowered by the Holy Spirit,
making a difference wherever they go."

Unknown

"The church is the voice of hope, the hands of compassion, and the feet of action in the community."

Unknown

~ Introduction ~

~ A Radical Invitation ~

THE STORY OF AN ORDINARY COUPLE
FOLLOWING GOD'S EXTRAORDINARY CALL
· GARY & MARILYN SKINNER ·

Jesus said that he would build his Church and that nothing hell could throw at it would stop its advance. History has proven that to be true. The most successful institution on the planet, bar none, is the Church of the Lord Jesus Christ. It has stood the test of time. It has impacted and changed, for the better, the lives of more people than any other movement ever. It has survived brutal persecution. No internal factions, infighting or denominational division has held back its steady advance. It is alive and thriving in almost every nation and people group.

And the overriding hero of it all is none other than Jesus, who is worshipped and adored every day, all around the world, by more people than can be counted. That worship takes place in churches that meet in magnificent cathedrals or under sprawling trees in the most remote villages. The very best social and humanitarian work ever done is by the Church. The most blessed nations the planet has ever witnessed were built on the ethos, the culture and the character of Christ and His Church.

And here is the great thing about how God builds the Church! God uses ordinary people to accomplish extraordinary things.

Marilyn and I are ordinary people. We have many extraordinary stories, but the remarkable and miraculous things in the following pages have little to do with our ability, courage or strength. We have been privileged to play a part in God's remarkable work. That work is a movement, and it's called the Church. The part we play intertwines with so many other faithful people in

Uganda and around the world. This dynamic, life-changing movement, the Church, spans many generations and will continue until Jesus returns, and well after the two of us are gone.

This is our story. But it is more than that. It records what Jesus can do through people who choose obedience. It is the story of what an all-powerful, all-loving God can do in and through each of us when we say "Yes!" to Him. Yes, to his radical and life-altering invitation, not just to believe but to walk in His footsteps and to follow him far beyond the comfort and complacency that has become all too common in the modern Church.

That is the heart of this book and our story. We want to share and celebrate the marvellous things God has done in calling us to Uganda and encourage, challenge and inspire those who read it. We pray that you will discover God's radical calling for your life. He is inviting you, just as he invited us, to follow him on the adventure of a lifetime and to bring about transformation in this world through the powerful working of His Spirit who lives in you.

Hudson Taylor, the missionary to China in the 18th century, who, after immense trial, confidently wrote, "All our difficulties are only platforms for His grace and love manifestations."

We have had a front-row seat to many wonderful and miraculous works of God. Tens of thousands have believed the good news about Jesus, have received Him as Saviour and Lord, and fellowship together in one of the campuses that make up this local church. Thousands of orphaned and abandoned children have been given a family and a future. Uganda's most vulnerable and ostracised women are being cared for, restored, and empowered so that they can build better lives for themselves and their children. The bitter wounds of child soldiers abducted from houses and homes, their innocent youth ripped away from them at the point of a gun, have been healed, the chains of their brokenness have snapped, and new life has been breathed into those who once were enslaved by injustice. A counter-cultural, next generation of young servant-hearted Christians has been raised and is poised and ready to lead Uganda and Africa into a bright future and bold new day.

And it all started with the tiniest of seeds that God planted in our hearts. He prepared the soil, watered and fertilised the ground, reinforced the trunk, pruned the branches, and transformed that tiny seed into something we could have never imagined. He has set up a family of changed people committed to bringing healing to their communities, people who have come to understand that God's work is not what one man does behind the pulpit on Sunday but what everyone does in the community every day. We have witnessed the birth, growth, and maturity of a multi-generational church that is committed to raising young leaders who embrace this simple but powerful truth: all of life is a sacred gift of God, and all of life is a sacred act of worship.

This book is not about what we have done but what Jesus has done in and through us. If you walk away with anything from this book, know that He is the true hero of this story.

We could not have fully fathomed in 1984 when we planted what is now known as Watoto Church, the vibrant, servant-hearted, transformational community that exists today. We could not have seen all that God had in store for us and our little family. We've been through so many difficult, painful, and terrifying situations. We have had to sacrifice a great deal. We have laid our lives on the line for the call that God put on our hearts. But Jesus has never failed us. Not once has he let us down. We have not only seen the tough side of life but have witnessed miracles of provision and protection, God's goodness and unfailing grace. We have lived the fullest of lives as we denied self, taken up our crosses and followed Jesus. (Matthew 16:24)

When we first came to Uganda, God gave us a promise from Isaiah 58. The Psalm is about true fasting and service to God.

> *"If you are generous with the hungry and start giving yourselves to the down-and-out, Your lives will begin to glow in the darkness, your shadowed lives will be bathed in sunlight.*
>
> *I will always show you where to go. I'll give you a full life in the emptiest of places - firm muscles, strong bones. You'll be like a well-watered garden, a gurgling spring that never runs dry.*
>
> *You'll use the old rubble of past lives to build anew, rebuild the foundations from out of your past. You'll be known as those who can fix anything, restore old ruins, rebuild and renovate,*
>
> *make the community livable again."*
>
> *Isaiah 58:9-12 MSG*

Through it all, Jesus was, and still is, faithful, strengthening us for each new step, surrounding us with the right people at the right time, and bringing us through seasons of intense difficulty and trial. We followed him out of our comfort zone, away from the safety nets, far beyond a life of security and control. He places this radical invitation before you today. He invites you to discover life you can live to the full, not by playing it safe, watching from the sidelines, or living for yourself. We have discovered that the life worth living for is the life worth dying for.

~ A Little About This Book ~

We've tried to write this book many times but have stopped short of completing it. Part of the problem is being unsure of what not to leave out. There are so many stories that have come out of the Watoto Church community, accounts of restoration and new birth, stories that tell of the compassion and mercy of God for His people, stories of His love powerfully transforming the hearts and lives of so many. Each of these memories is valuable and powerful, and Jesus is the hero of them all. We cannot share them all here.

Instead, we want to tell our story, our perspective, and parts of the account of a few others, specifically where they intertwine with our own. In this, we honour our church family and share a broad overview of the Watoto story through the lens of our experiences. If you are a part of the Watoto story, know that, though you may not be included by name in these pages, your journey matters and is valuable to us. God watches and monitors your faithfulness.

This account is written from my perspective, but it is just as much Marilyn's story as mine. She is my God-given partner and co-worker. We chose to write from my perspective for readability and simplicity. We write this book to tell our story, just as we have lived a fruitful life of service side by side, hand in hand, together.

Lastly, though this book may sometimes be read as a memoir or autobiography, we pray that through it, Jesus will draw you closer to Himself and inspire you to be His committed follower and disciple.

We've provided questions at the end of each chapter for you to reflect on what God may be saying to you. Perhaps you could consider them with a trusted friend or group.

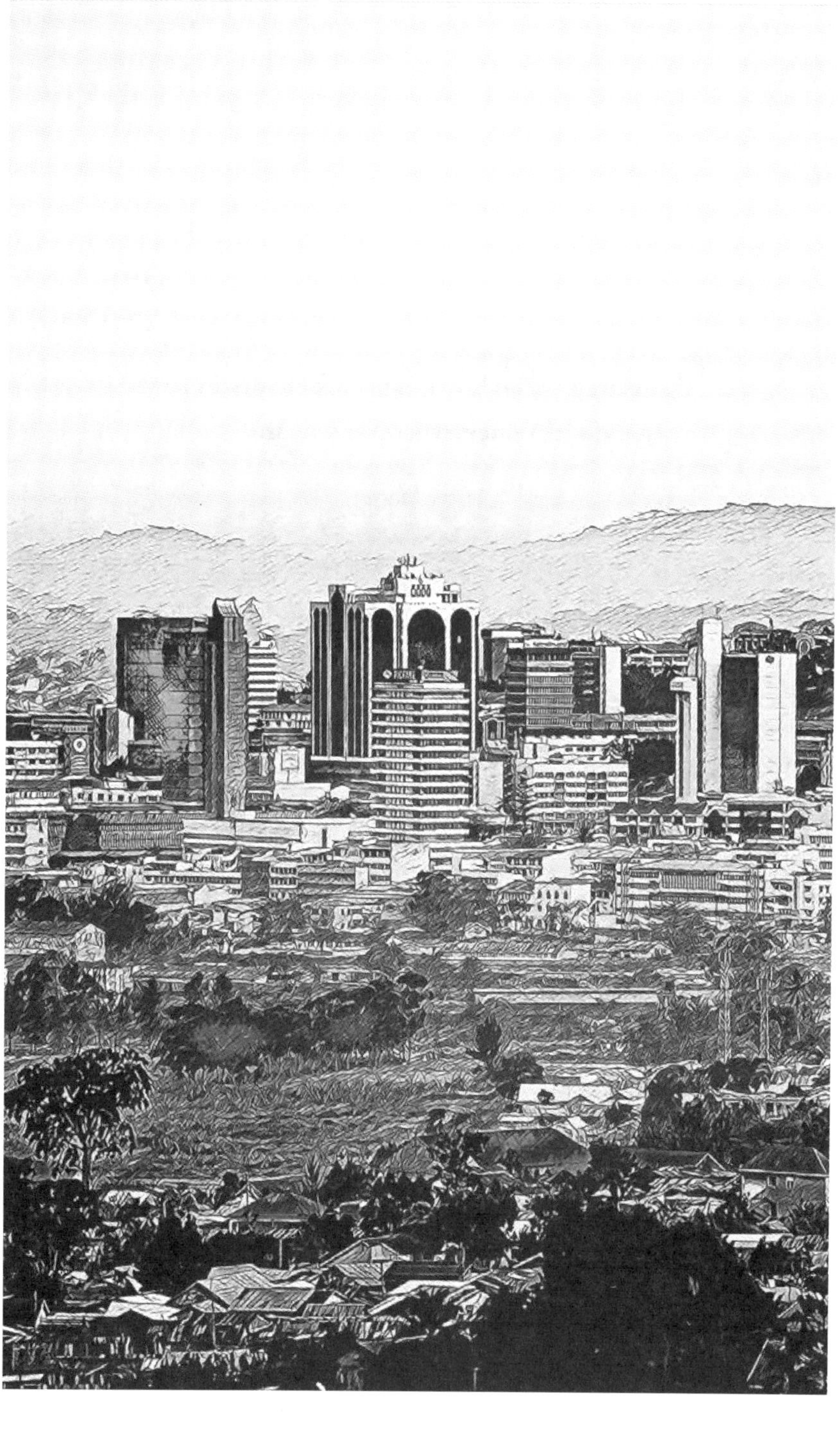

"If you are ever inclined to pray for a missionary,
do it at once, wherever you are."

Mary Slessor

"I believe it will only be known on the last day
how much has been accomplished in overseas missions
by the prayers of earnest believers at home."

James O. Fraser

"To get generations back on their feet,
we must first get down on our knees."

Billy Graham

01

~ The Blind Corner ~
at Namagunga

Travelling at almost 60 miles an hour and with just meters separating us from a head-on collision, I had less than a second to react. Yanking the steering wheel to the left, I pulled the Peugeot 504 sedan off the road and onto the rough shoulder. With a vicious growl, the truck flew by, missing us by inches, and continued on. I tried to control the skidding car, but the wheels caught on the jagged edge of the pavement and set us wobbling violently from side to side. The car shot back across the road and hurled itself into the ditch, hitting the dirt embankment.

The front end made impact first with a crunch of crushed metal. Time seemed to stand still. I heard every scrape and sound with intense clarity. Gravity propelled the back end of the car forward and into the air. There were a few moments of surreal quietness as it lifted off the ground and then came down onto its roof. I was thrown out of the front windshield. With a calm and strange comprehension of all that was happening, I was floating above the vehicle, watching the entire scene as it unfolded below. Each detail crawled past in slow motion. A sense of amazement and wonder surged through me, and then I had a very clear thought, "I wonder if this is the moment that I die!"

A thousand other thoughts flashed through my mind in those silent moments as I was flying though the air, the spinning car below me. "Will I feel the pain that kills me?" "I wonder if Marilyn and James will also die?" "I guess I won't get to start that church in Kampala."

Then, snapping me out of my thoughts, I felt the blow to the back of my head as I collided with the road. I waited for darkness to envelop me and then for the blinding white light I had heard described by those with near-death experiences. Gravel, dirt, and glass shredded my shirt and tore into my flesh as I slid down the road on my back. I came to a stop, rolled over, leaned up on my elbows and watched the car slide down the road upside down. The grating screech of metal against asphalt filled my ears as I watched sparks shoot out from under the crushed roof. It came to a grinding halt, the wheels still spinning.

"Well," I thought, "I guess I'm not dead!"

We were returning from a short road trip into Kenya to pick up the final supplies we needed to start the church. The launch date was only three weeks away. We thought the trip would be simple and uneventful, now it was turning out to be anything but!

Nairobi was bustling with life. The city had never been through the kind of civil conflict that Kampala was going through, and supplies were much more available. We bought the items and printed materials we needed for the start of the church. We were in Nairobi for only three days, just enough time to get what we needed. Timothy and Rachel stayed back with missionary friends in Kampala. James, not yet in school, came along with us on the ten-hour road trip to the Kenyan capital. Since we were still waiting for our new vehicle to arrive from France, we used a small, cream-coloured Peugeot 405 sedan. It belonged to Canadian missionary Wilbur Morrison and was a very popular car in East Africa at the time. The trip had gone without a hitch until we were almost back home.

After crossing the border back into Uganda, we reached a place called Namagunga, just 40 kilometres from Kampala. The road curves its way between the hills outside the town of Lugazi. I remember, ever so vividly, the scenes and events that took place next. On our right were small rural houses surrounded by gardens of vegetables, bananas and fruit trees. On our left was a tea plantation covering the slopes of the gently rolling hills. Giant Mvule trees, 30 meters tall, stood between the wide patches of lush, green tea fields. It was as if the mighty trees were sentries guarding the crop, their thick trunks growing straight up until, at about two-thirds of their height, huge boughs split off, creating a canopy that cast heavy shade onto the fields below.

As we took in the scene, we approached a corner, the road bending sharply to the right and disappearing from view. Two oncoming vehicles emerged around the corner. An old, dilapidated bus came down the highway on the proper side of the road at an awkward angle, the rear and front axles out of alignment. On our side of the road, overtaking the bus, was a green army truck with soldiers clinging to the railings of the open bed. It came at us with astonishing speed and with no obvious intent of making way. Marilyn threw her face into her lap to protect herself from what was happening. I can still see the giant chrome letters of the truck's Indian manufacturer, T-A-T-A, emblazoned on the grill as it barreled down towards us.

It was about three in the afternoon on another wonderful sunny day in Uganda when Satan tried to kill us and abort the dream God had placed in us to plant the church in Kampala. The forces of hell wanted to terminate God's plan before it had the chance to be born. As I lay on my stomach watching the wheels on the wrecked car still slowly spinning, I realised something good. I wasn't dead! Satan had failed. God's plan was not going to be thwarted!

I stood up and, propelled by adrenaline and instinct, stumbled down the road after the car. I noticed that one of my shoes was missing and my glasses were no longer on my nose. Blood trickled down my face and into the corner of my mouth, the salty, metallic taste reminding me that I really was still alive. I staggered forward, wondering if my beautiful wife and little boy were also still alive.

As I got to the car, I heard the familiar sound of James crying. What a thrill to hear that cry. I found him lying on his back, his arms and legs sprawled across the pavement behind the car, tears running down his cheeks, the ground around him covered with glass and blood. There was a gash in the centre of his forehead and, from it, a trickle of blood flowing onto his face. I scooped his little body up into my arms.

"James, it's going to be alright."

His eyes opened, and he looked straight into my face. As he lifted his head, the blood trickled down and fell in large drops from the tip of his nose. I felt my chest twist and tighten at the sight of my precious little boy like this.

"James! Jesus is looking after us!"

By now, a small crowd was gathering. A short, stocky, European nun stepped out and walked up towards me.

"Give me the boy," she said in a thick Irish brogue.

I held James closer.

"Give me the boy," she repeated calmly. "It's going to be alright. I am a nurse from Mount Saint Mary's College just up there."

With a gentle toss of her head and a pursing of her lips, in a typical Ugandan gesture, she indicated a collection of buildings about two hundred meters up a small dirt road.

"We'll take care of him, and I will send back some help."

Looking into her eyes, I recognised compassion and genuine concern. I leaned towards her. Gently, placing one arm under James' neck and the other under his legs, she lifted him from my grasp. She turned and walked up the hill. James' tiny blond head bounced like a rag doll on one side. She disappeared onto the school grounds with my son in her arms.

I heard Marilyn's voice.

"Gary," she said searchingly. "Gary, get me out of here."

I scrambled around to the other side of the car and looked into the mangled wreck. Marilyn hung upside down, her seatbelt holding her firmly in the passenger seat. Her window had been smashed in, and there were shards of glass strewn everywhere. I pulled at the door handle, but it was jammed shut because of the caved-in roof. The only way to get her out was to pull her through what was left of the side window. I reached through, careful not to cut myself on the sharp edges of the metal and shattered window. With one arm, I began to lift Marilyn's body so that I could get her into a position that would help her escape.

"Can you reach out and touch the floor?" I asked.

"I think so."

She reached forward with her arms, wincing in pain. I looked at her left shoulder and saw a gash of mangled flesh and blood.

"I can do it," she said.

"On three I'm going to undo your seatbelt. Then I'll lift you out. Are you ready?"

She nodded. Taking a deep breath, she flattened her palms on the metal roof below her, preparing to push down with all her strength.

"Okay, here we go. One... two... three."

I wrapped one hand around her waist and, with the other, unfastened her seatbelt. I felt the weight of her body in my arms and, as gently as I could, pulled her through the window, guiding her carefully through the web of broken glass. She crawled out and stood up. She looked up into my eyes and buried her face in my chest. I held her close! We were all alive. Jesus was looking after us.

Another Irish nun pushed her way through the crowd.

"Thank God you can all walk," she said. "We must get you to the hospital,"

I heard the crowd behind me begin to rock the vehicle back and forward in order to get it right side up again. Their momentum slowly grew until it rolled over with a loud grating sound back onto the wheels.

As soon as the car was upright, a man stepped forward and, reaching into the trunk, grabbed the first thing he saw and fled with it into the tea fields below. Immediately, the crowd descended upon the vehicle and began to loot anything they could. For a moment, I stood watching in disbelief. I had heard that this was often the case. If someone had been killed in an accident, some of the crowd would descend upon the body and strip it of anything of value. Shoes, belts, and watches were removed, pockets emptied, and any cash taken. Sometimes, the unfortunate victim wasn't yet dead, still gasping for life, only to be robbed as they lay dying.

A silent rage boiled up inside me.

"Stop! Now!" I shouted with surprising authority.

Everybody stood, looked at me, then at each other, then again at me.

"I am missing one shoe and my glasses. Can I have them back, please?"

THE BLIND CORNER AT NAMAGUNGA

Amazingly, the crowd turned their attention away from their pilfering and began scouring the roadside for the missing items. In less than two minutes, my glasses, scuffed but intact, were back on my face, and the shoe was on my foot.

I looked at the mangled car. The front end was a crumpled mess of tangled metal; the roof caved in just several inches from the gear lever. How had we survived that? We had just come through an horrific crash but experienced a wonderful miracle. As I looked at the wreckage, I knew that Satan and death had waited for us on that blind corner at Namagunga but that Jesus had sent His angels to protect and deliver us. God had plans for something bigger and better. He had work for us to do.

The Irish sister reappeared.

"Don't worry about the car or your things. I have someone here who will look after everything. Come with me up to the school."

She led Marilyn and me up the road to the school on the side of the small hill and then into the dispensary where James was being attended to. He was lying on a small table where a nurse was tending to his wounds. Marilyn leaned over and kissed him on the cheek, reassuring him with a few gentle, motherly words. I put my hand on his blond hair, and he looked up into my eyes again.

"Daddy! Pray for me!" he asked, his little voice quivering.

I felt a lump form in my throat. To see my boy like this broke my heart. We put our hands gently on his tiny body and prayed for comfort, healing, and strength. We thanked God that he had spared and protected us from death. After the nurses had cleaned our cuts and gashes as best as they could, they drove us in a school van to Saint Francis Hospital at Nsambya in Kampala.

The medical staff at the hospital attended to our needs. Marilyn had whiplash and needed stitches for the wound in her upper arm. James was burnt on the left side of his body and needed stitches to repair the gash on his forehead. I had broken ribs and lacerations down my back. It took the nurse almost an hour to remove the stones and broken glass from the congealed bloody mess of debris and tattered shirt.

That evening, Tim and Rachel came to visit us in the hospital. It was reassuring to be together again as a family, and we were all thankful to have come through the ordeal. Jesus had been right there, with us, through it all.

A sombre silence settled on the room that evening as I lay in bed and relived the events of the day. It was just three weeks to the scheduled launch of the church. Were we going to heal in time? Would we have to postpone the launch? Had we wasted our money on the television ads? What was God's purpose in all this?

In those moments of reflection, I was reminded again of the words Jesus had spoken so clearly to me.

"In this place, you will shed blood, sweat, and tears, but if you are faithful to me, I will be faithful to you."

God did have a plan. His agenda was much bigger than us, but we were going to play a part in it. I also realised that his purpose was subject to attack from the evil forces of darkness and Satan, who did not want to see God's kingdom flourish and blossom, and bring healing to this broken city.

As 1 Peter 5:8-9 reminds us:

> *"Be alert and of sober mind. Your enemy, the devil, prowls around like a roaring lion, looking for someone to devour. Resist him, standing firm in the faith, because you know that the family of believers throughout the world is undergoing the same kind of sufferings."*
>
> *1 Peter 5:8-9 (NIV)*

A few broken bones and painful wounds were minor when compared to what others had endured in their obedience to the call of God. Over nearly two millennia, faithful emissaries of the Kingdom of God had gone to the far corners of the world motivated and inspired by their passion and devotion to the Lord and their love for their neighbour. They endured incredible trials and difficulties, some laying down their lives, many burying their loved ones because of disease, war, and persecution. Could I honestly baulk at what we had been through?

I knew that "in all things God works for the good of those who love him, who have been called according to his purpose." (Romans 8:28, NIV)

THE BLIND CORNER AT NAMAGUNGA

God's ways are always better than ours, and if the Easter launch and our planning needed to be adjusted, I was confident that He would work out what was best. We committed ourselves to walking through this situation with joy and confidence.

The next day, we were discharged from the hospital and able to return home. That afternoon, Gerald Morrison, our missions director drove all the way from Nairobi to be with us and make sure we were okay.

He sat on a chair beside my bed, reached down and picked up his briefcase.

"I have something I want to show you," he said.

Placing the briefcase on his lap, he opened the lid, pulled out the Pentecostal Assemblies of Canada missionary prayer calendar and handed it to me.

For many years, the Missions Department had printed an annual prayer calendar. Each day of the month highlighted the name, photo and ministry of one of the missionaries that the denomination had sent out. The calendar helped Canadian Christians focus their prayer for that specific missionary and their needs on that day.

"Take a look at yesterday's date," Gerald said.

I opened the calendar and flipped through to April 1984, running my finger across the page until I arrived on Thursday, April 4th, 1984. My heart skipped a beat. I checked again just to make sure I wasn't mistaken.

In the square marking the day of our crash was a photo. The inscription below it read. "Gary and Marilyn Skinner, Church Planting, Kampala, Uganda." My heart skipped a beat!

"On the very day of the accident," Gerald said, "thousands of people all over Canada and around the world were praying with special intent for you and your family."

Tears filled my eyes. This was no coincidence! Jesus was demonstrating His sovereign love, grace, faithfulness and protection. We were now even more resolute to surrender to all that he wanted to do in and through us.

Word of our accident spread quickly. Letters of encouragement from family and friends and people all around the world, people we had never met, filled our mailbox. They told of how they had been interceding for us. At the exact moment that I was flying above the flipping vehicle, James was being thrown out of the window, and Marilyn was hanging upside down in the wreckage; they had been on their knees or sitting at a breakfast table, praying. And they were praying for us!

Several months later I heard about Peter, a young man attending Eastern Pentecostal Bible College, the same school I had graduated from in Peterborough, Ontario, Canada. On the day of the accident, while sitting in the daily chapel service of the college, surrounded by several hundred students, Peter felt an irrepressible urge to pray for us. He stood up and, as only Peter could do, boldly interrupted the preacher in the middle of his sermon.

"Please excuse me but we need to pray," he said, loud and confident.

The students and faculty gawked at him open-mouthed.

"We need to pray for the Skinners in Uganda," he said firmly, "and we need to do it right now."

He began to pray out loud, and others quietly joined him. Soon, the entire hall was united in prayer for our family, who were at that very moment flying through the air as the car was hurled into the ditch on the side of the road in Uganda.

And the stories didn't stop there.

We heard from a women's gathering at Evangel Temple, a church in downtown Montreal who had devoted their morning session of prayer for the Skinner family, the missionary on the prayer calendar for that day.

I learned that on the evening before the accident, my grandfather, who was an associate pastor at the Agincourt Pentecostal Church in Toronto, was leading the evening bible study. The scheduled guest speaker failed to show up, so they turned the service into an evening of prayer. Those who had gathered included in their prayer the missionary family who was on the prayer calendar for the next day. To my grandfather's delight, the missionary on the calendar was his grandson. Little did they know how important their prayers were, as they called for the Lord to protect and go before us.

We were dramatically reminded of God's great love and care for us, His promise to be with us, never to leave or forsake us and his desire to see us do our part in His work here in Kampala. I remember weeping again and again as we heard of these accounts of faith-filled prayer. All of this was nothing short of God's miraculous intervention in the lives of His children.

On the first anniversary of the day of the crash, I was travelling to Jinja for a meeting. On the trip back to Kampala, when I reached the blind corner at Namagunga, I pulled the car off the road at the very spot where the crash had happened. I turned off the engine, opened the door and got out of the car. I stepped onto the edge of the highway, and, pointing my finger deep into the bowels of the earth, I shouted with ferocious zeal.

"Satan, you liar! You thief! You came to destroy me and my family at this place. You tried to stop us from starting the church in Kampala, but we're still here. We started the church. It's doing great, and you are never, ever going to stop what Jesus is doing. Never!"

A group of bystanders, perhaps some who had been in the crowd on the day of the accident, stopped and stared as I lifted my voice to shout at the devil. Maybe they were wondering who this crazy white man was, pointing at the ground, jumping up and down, shouting at Satan.

I'll tell you who I am! I'm a child of God, chosen and anointed, picked and appointed as an ambassador of Heaven, to plant a church in the heart of Kampala, announcing the good news of Jesus to the broken, bringing healing and hope to those in need.

When I was done, I got back into the car and drove home.

Ahead of us was an adventure of faith waiting to be unveiled!

What a great God we get to serve.

~ Reflect and Discuss ~

As you reflect on your own story and engage in discussion with others, consider the following:

1. Facing Difficult Situations With Faith:

    • What stands out to you most about the story of the car crash?

    • What do you learn about God's protection and provision?

    • Contemplate what specific incidents in your life have come as an unexpected challenge and yet demonstrate that God was at work.

    • How did these incidents shape and build your faith?

2. Praying for God's Workers:

    • Reflect on the importance of praying for those who are involved in Christian ministry and missionary work.

    • What specific issues should you pray for when praying for missionaries and other workers in the ministry?

    • How can you make prayer for those in Christian ministry a part of your regular small group or family routine?

During your discussion, offer encouragement, support, and prayer for one another. Share personal insights, experiences, and aspirations as you seek to discern God's leading and participate in His redemptive work. By aligning with God's purposes, and trusting in His faithfulness, you can experience His transformative power and be a beacon of hope in the world.

∼

41

"If God can work through me,
he can work through anyone."

St. Francis of Assisi

02

From Dreams
~ to Destiny ~

"Finding purpose in partnership."

Joy filled our hearts as we looked out at the sea of faces in the auditorium. Each one shone like a star, a reflection of the bright and beautiful people we had been honoured to serve. Friend and mentor Bob Hoskins joined us on the platform. The church's leadership team surrounded us, laying hands prayerfully on our shoulders. They blessed us and thanked Jesus for the work he had done in Uganda over the past forty years.

The transition service that night provided Marilyn and me an opportunity to bless and commission those who would serve as the Watoto Church team leaders as we fulfilled our mandate. It was also a chance for us to remind the church family of something true. It's not about Marilyn and me. We are an ordinary couple, called into God's extraordinary plan. It is about what God will do through fully consecrated lives.

~ Gary ~

My heritage is richly rooted in faith, specifically the Pentecostal tradition. My great-grandfather, John McAlister, was a circuit-riding holiness preacher. He travelled between small rural Canadian towns, preaching and planting churches. A fresh boldness and zeal he experienced during the birth of the Pentecostal movement at the turn of the twentieth century, transformed his life and ministry. He planted what became some of the largest and most successful churches in Canada. The fire of the Pentecostal revival spread across Canada, and around the world in what is arguably one of the most significant spiritual awakenings in history.

His daughter, my grandmother Lila, saw first-hand the power and influence of the Holy Spirit on her father's ministry. When James Skinner fell in love with her and wanted to begin a relationship, she turned him down. They were both teaching at the same school in Parkside, Saskatchewan. Lila had a deep faith and love for Jesus and wanted to serve in ministry. James was a flirtatious, self-conscious young man who had been one of Canada's fastest sprinters. He had qualified to represent Canada at the Olympics, but didn't meet the age requirement. He didn't have a relationship with Jesus. Church wasn't on his agenda, and he certainly had no interest in church ministry. He was, however, interested in Lila. With persistence, he followed her to church, heard the gospel message and saw God's life-changing power and love in the followers of Jesus. He decided to surrender his life to Christ. Lila eventually reciprocated his love, and they were married.

In 1936, my grandparents responded to the call of God for missionary work and were appointed to Kenya, in East Africa. James and Lila Skinner spent their most fruitful years serving the people of Africa in Kenya and then Southern Rhodesia, now Zimbabwe, starting schools, teaching in bible college, and planting new churches.

My mother was an only child, born in London a few years before the start of the Second World War. Her parents were disillusioned with life in post-war England and seeing little prospect for a happy future in the United Kingdom, moved with their daughter, Doris, to Africa. They settled in the same quaint little town as my dad's parents, Umtali, Southern Rhodesia, what is now Mutare, Zimbabwe.

Mom and Dad met in High School, fell in love, and married after graduating. Dad worked in a printing press. Charles Austin Chawner, who ran a very successful missions printing press in South Africa, was killed in a car accident. Dad was invited to take over the press. We moved to Nelspruit, a farming community in the Eastern Transvaal in South Africa. That's where I spent most of my boyhood.

I have always loved Africa. I have always felt uniquely blessed to be born and raised in Africa. Africa shaped me. The natural beauty of the continent, it's unique animals, and the friendly nature of its people, held a special place in my heart. I thrive in the tropical heat, and I withered during the few painful Canadian winters I had to endure. There is a strange longing and love for Africa inside me. Throughout my childhood, I never dreamed of leaving Africa.

I graduated from High School with a burning desire to be a game warden in the Kruger National Park, which was just a few miles to the northeast of the town we were living in. We would visit the game reserve regularly. As I grew up, I couldn't imagine doing anything other than caring for, preserving, and walking with the wild animals that Africa is famous for. I dreamed of starry African nights around a blazing campfire, listening to the mournful howl of hyenas and the grunt of a leopard in the dark. As a teenager, I memorised the Latin names of birds and animals. I knew how to identify them by the sounds they made. I knew their gestation periods and learned their peculiar habits and habitats. I was sure that when my opportunity to serve Africa finally came, it would be by caring for the animals of the African bush. My favourite book was "Jock of the Bushveld." It's the story of a young dog and his unique and adventurous life serving his master as they hauled goods on ox wagons through the heart of the African bush country from the coast into South Africa. That was the life I wanted. A life in the bush working with animals.

Shortly after graduating from High School, I landed an interview at the local botanical garden. Getting a job there would be the first step toward serving in a game reserve. When they learned that I was a Canadian, they turned me down. I was devastated!

Several things happened that shaped the course my life would take.

The first was that a friend was killed in a motorcycle crash. He and some buddies were racing down a steep, winding road just out of town. He missed a corner, went over a steep, rocky, precipice and his life was over. I realised from his death that life could be wasted or wisely invested. What would I do with my life that would add meaning and value?

The second life-changing moment was on an evening when I came home late from a Friday night party with friends. As I sneaked quietly into the house, I heard my parents praying for me. I stood with my hand on the doorknob, listening to them speaking to God about their son. Again, I wondered what

I should be doing with the life God had entrusted me with.

The third was a conversation with Jesus.

God still speaks to us. He spoke to Moses from a burning bush and to Noah to build an ark. Hearing from God is not mystical or strange but is developed out of a relationship that we have with Him. He will speak in different ways to different people, but God is not silent. He may speak through His Word, or through a strong impression or through other people, but He does let us know what he desires for us and from us. For me it seems to come in an almost conversational way and while I don't hear the words from Him audibly, they are as clear to me as if they were. That's just the way it works for me and has been demonstrated as genuine through what I have been blessed to witness in my life and ministry.

One day, during a quiet time, he said, "Gary! I want you to look after people, not animals."

I didn't like what I was hearing!

"But Jesus!" I replied. "I don't like people. I like animals. When people give you a hard time, you have to love them. If animals give you a hard time, you just shoot them."

Deep down in my heart, I knew he was asking me to serve and love him by serving and loving the people He loved rather than the animals I loved.

Dad suggested that I should study at Eastern Pentecostal Bible College in Canada. I reluctantly applied and was accepted for the autumn semester beginning in September 1970. A few months later, I packed my few belongings into a single small suitcase and waved goodbye to my parents from the deck of an ocean liner, sailing from the port city of Durban in South Africa. That ship carried me away from my beloved Africa. I was seventeen years old. I had embarked on a journey into adulthood, into a lifelong adventure of faith. It would lead me to the people, education, and experiences that would prepare me for what God had ultimately made me for. I didn't know it then, but I do now! He was getting me ready for Uganda.

My time at Bible College was not only a time of learning but also a time of growth and maturity. God was working on my heart, shifting my priorities, changing me. One experience changed the outlook of my life. I went out one afternoon to a coffee shop near campus to have a chocolate doughnut and a coffee. As I sat, minding my own business, I noticed a man of about forty at the table next to me. He was very drunk but handling it quite well. He sat there chewing and blinking his droopy eyes very slowly.

I tried to watch him inconspicuously. And then something unexpected happened. My heart broke for the man. I knew that we are all sinners in need of the love of Jesus. I was no exception and had experienced so much from Jesus. The tears welled up in my eyes and I began to cry softly. I tried to keep it gentle, but the sobs from deep down inside me intensified, and I started to shake. The tears dropped off my cheeks onto the table. I got up, the chair scraping against the floor, and leaving my coffee behind walked back to campus. I was a different person. Something had happened to me. It was something supernatural. The Holy Spirit had baptised me with compassion for people. I realise now, how important that moment was. He was giving me His heart. It is utterly impossible to do God's work without His compassion.

I continued my education, but have never excelled at school. The desire or the discipline to get top marks wasn't in me. The studies in theology were enlightening and inspirational, but time in class was something I had to endure rather than enjoy. I did love to lead worship with my guitar and travelled with some of the professors when they visited nearby churches. There was a sense of destiny in me. I knew that somehow, sometime, I would end up back in Africa, not as a game ranger but as a pastor, caring for people.

~ Marilyn ~

Marilyn grew up in a loving family that moved from community to community in rural Ontario. She would tell you that she is the daughter of "simple Canadian pastors." I would say she was born into a legacy of great faith. She arrived two months premature and had to spend the first weeks of her life in an incubator, connected by tubes to keep her alive. Marilyn doesn't remember a time when she didn't love Jesus or want to serve him.

Her grandparents were pioneer pastors in Canada during the Pentecostal revivals of the 1920s. She was an infant when her grandfather died. Her grandmother, only 55, moved in with Marilyn's family. On the day she came home from the hospital, Grandma Rosetta Mable cradled her first grandchild in her arms and whispered into her ear.

"All the love I would have given to your grandfather, Art, I am going to give to you."

It had a profound impact on Marilyn's faith and development. Rosetta Mable was a consistent figure of love throughout Marilyn's childhood. She remembers waking many nights and hearing her grandmother praying for her. Marilyn grew up in the home of a pastor who loved Jesus and his family more than anything. Her dad, Harold Dawson, never led a congregation of more than 250 people, but you could not find a more faithful and loving man.

When she was eight, Marilyn began to develop headaches that led to a loss of hearing in one of her ears. She was diagnosed with an ear disease that, if left unresolved, would eventually end her life. Marilyn was scheduled for surgery that would save her life, but leave her deaf in one ear. Her father called her before the congregation at church the day before the surgery, laid his hands on her head, and prayed a simple prayer of healing.

"Father God, I ask that you supernaturally intervene and heal my daughter Marilyn. When the doctors prepare to operate tomorrow, may they find her well."

The nurses wheeled Marilyn into the operating theatre the following morning. Her parents waited quietly for news of their little girl. Half an hour later, the doctor came out to inform them that they could take Marilyn home. He smiled.

"When we looked into your daughter's ear, we found only scar tissue where the disease had been. Your daughter is perfectly well."

Marilyn gave her life to Christ at six years of age. She recalls passionately loving Jesus and being willing to do anything for him. At nine, she started to play the piano at the church services. She vividly remembers sitting one day at the piano and praying.

"Lord! Whatever I do in this life, may I be useful to you."

At fifteen, she responded to the call from Jesus to become his disciple. She had come to understand, at youth camp, that those who choose to follow Jesus must take the things nearest and dearest to their hearts, whether plans or people, and kiss them goodbye for the sake of God's Kingdom. Marilyn knew instinctively that this invitation was for her.

She knelt before Jesus at the altar that night.

"I'm yours, Lord. Do with me whatever you want."

Not long after, Dave Johnston, a travelling evangelist and friend of her father, was putting together a Christian rock band to tour across Canada and the United States for the summer. Marilyn, only sixteen, knew what she wanted to do. She wanted to join up. The band, "Surging Revival," would sing and preach to young people in parks, schools, street corners, and beaches. God was preparing Marilyn for the life he had chosen for her.

She didn't know it yet, but the band would include a young guitar player from Africa. I had been invited to be part of the team, to play the acoustic guitar and sing. That's how Marilyn and I met. We were in a rock and roll band together. We've been making beautiful music together ever since. Thousands of young people came to Christ while touring those three months. She was the petite, quiet, young pianist who would one day be my wife, the love of my life, my partner in ministry, and my best friend.

The band went full-time the following year. I was invited to be a member when I graduated from Bible College and gladly agreed. David asked Harold if Marilyn could join the team as well. Marilyn's Dad turned down Dave's request feeling it important that Marilyn finish her last two years of High School. Marilyn was distraught. She had her heart set on travelling with the band and did all she could to convince her father to let her go. She wanted to be in ministry.

"That's great! I'm so glad God has called you into ministry! Bring me a high school diploma, and then you can go." Her father was firm.

Knowing she would never go against her father, Marilyn went back to Jesus.

"Lord, I know you want me to go on this tour, but how will I get a high school diploma? I still have two years left in High School!"

She remembered the certificates she had earned by studying classical piano at the University of Toronto. She took them to her guidance counsellor at school and explained that she needed to graduate that year. She was hoping the certificates could be credited to her High School diploma. The counsellor agreed to send them off to the Ministry of Education. They were approved, and a month later, she presented her High School Diploma to her astonished parents, who agreed that she could join the band. That's the Marilyn I know. She never gives up on a God-given dream. She's as tiny as a mouse but as tenacious as a bulldog.

After graduating from Bible College, Marilyn and I became part of the evangelistic team touring and ministering across Canada and the States. We would sing in high schools, doing assemblies during the day and inviting kids back to an evangelistic service that night. We saw young people jump out of their seats and run to the front of gyms and auditoriums to receive Jesus during altar calls. Thousands of teenagers gave their hearts to Christ, and we were baptised with fresh compassion over and over again, our call to ministry growing ever stronger.

~ Falling in Love ~

One day, as we were performing, I looked back from where I sang. Marilyn was doing her thing on the keyboard. She winked at me. To this day, she denies it ever happened, but I know what I saw. It took my breath away.

The band was getting ready to take a short break. Before we went our separate ways, I knew what I had to do. We had pizza, and as we got up to leave, I asked Marilyn to stay for a moment. I looked across the table into her eyes and told her I loved her.

Her response was to the point!

"Get behind me, Satan."

It wasn't what I was expecting. She was serious about her call and didn't want me to distract her from it. But from a twinkle in her eye, I knew I should gently pursue.

"I'm serious, Marilyn," I said. "Would you pray about you and me together?"

We both committed to do so.

On my knees one morning, as I asked Jesus about Marilyn and what He thought about our possible relationship, I had another one of those life-changing moments. His powerful but gentle, sweet presence flooded the room. He didn't say a thing but lingered for a little while and then left. I waited, trembling at the intensity of the moment. I thanked him for what I knew was a yes.

I was eager to see Marilyn when we returned after the break. She smiled and said it was a "yes," too. It wasn't long before I asked the inevitable question: "What do you think about being a missionary to Africa?"

In her sweet, wonderful way, she smiled and assured me that whatever God had for us, she would do; wherever God wanted us to go, she would go. She was committed and wanted to share life with a man who loved her, loved Jesus and felt the same. She willingly agreed that we should marry and that I should ask her father for permission while we were on Christmas break.

I had never met her Dad. I was the first man she was bringing home. She was still a teenager. This was the first time I had done this. How would it go?

I remember standing nervously before her kind, but confident father. I asked for his daughter's hand in marriage. I think he knew the question was coming. He smiled.

"When were you planning this event?" he asked warmly.

I swallowed. "June." Pause. "Sir!"

"You mean June next year?" He asked.

"No, sir. June this year. Like six months from now."

His answer was clear and decisive. "No, that can't happen this year."

Marilyn and I were both disheartened. We were also determined to honour her father and submit to his decision. We knew that the Lord had brought us together, and He would work it all out.

A few weeks later, we were heading off on tour again. We stopped at a conference Marilyn's Dad was attending to say goodbye. After eating together, Marilyn's father pulled out his day calendar.

"I think June 1st would be a good day for a wedding." He looked up at me and then over to Marilyn.

"June 1st, next year?" I asked.

"No, this year!"

"What changed your mind, Dad?" Marilyn asked.

"I couldn't sleep a couple of nights ago, and the Lord spoke to me. 'Let her marry him. He's a good man.'"

Six months later, we were married. We embarked on an adventure of a lifetime together, far surpassing any dreams we might have had. The Lord brought about a good in our lives that we cannot put into words. Together, we are much better than each is alone. We are partners in life and ministry. If we have accomplished anything for God, it has been because he stood by us and gave us each other. We complement each other perfectly. I am so thankful to the Lord for such an incredible, faith-filled helper and friend. Her love and loyalty to God, and to me, are amazing.

Through the twists and turns in life, through the possibilities and opportunities that come our way, there is only one way to choose. His way! He leads and guides. He oversees and directs. His way is perfect. We are imperfect, but the Lord puts His hand on us as we surrender to Him. He chooses to work through us, to use ordinary people to do extraordinary things.

Looking back, after all these years, Marilyn and I have become more and more confident of this one thing: God is working all things "for the good of those who love him, who have been called according to his purpose." (Romans 8:28, NIV)

When we choose to live a life of love, surrender to God, listen for his voice, and take the steps of faith he calls us to, it is remarkable where he will take us and what he will do in us and through us.

~ Reflect and Discuss ~

As you take time to reflect on your own narrative and engage in conversation with others, consider the following questions.

1. Hearing God's Voice:

   • Consider how God speaks to us? How do we know what God wants us to do?

   • Think about a time when God wanted you to do something. How did you hear and know it was God's voice?

2. Pivotal Moments and God's Guidance:

   • Think about significant moments in your life where God's presence or intervention changed the course of your journey. Reflect on how these experiences have shaped your character, relationships, and spiritual growth.

   • Share examples of how you've witnessed God's ability to use these pivotal moments for good, even in the face of challenges or uncertainty. Discuss how these experiences have deepened your trust in God's faithfulness and sovereignty.

3. Challenges in Perceiving God's Presence:

   • Identify areas of your story where it's challenging to perceive God's presence or understand His intentions. This might include seasons of doubt, suffering, or unanswered prayers.

   • Explore how God might intend to uplift and reassure your heart in these moments. Consider the ways He may be speaking to you through His Word, the encouragement of others, or the inner prompting of His Spirit.

4. God's Guidance and Invitations to Trust:

• Reflect on how God is currently guiding your journey and leading you forward. Pay attention to His promptings, whether through Scripture, prayer, circumstances or friends.

• Discuss areas of your life where God may be inviting you to step out in greater trust and dependence on Him. This could involve surrendering control, embracing uncertainty, or taking bold steps of faith.

These questions are designed to provoke deep personal reflection and foster meaningful group discussions, encouraging participants to apply the lessons and insights from the chapter into their own lives and communities.

∼

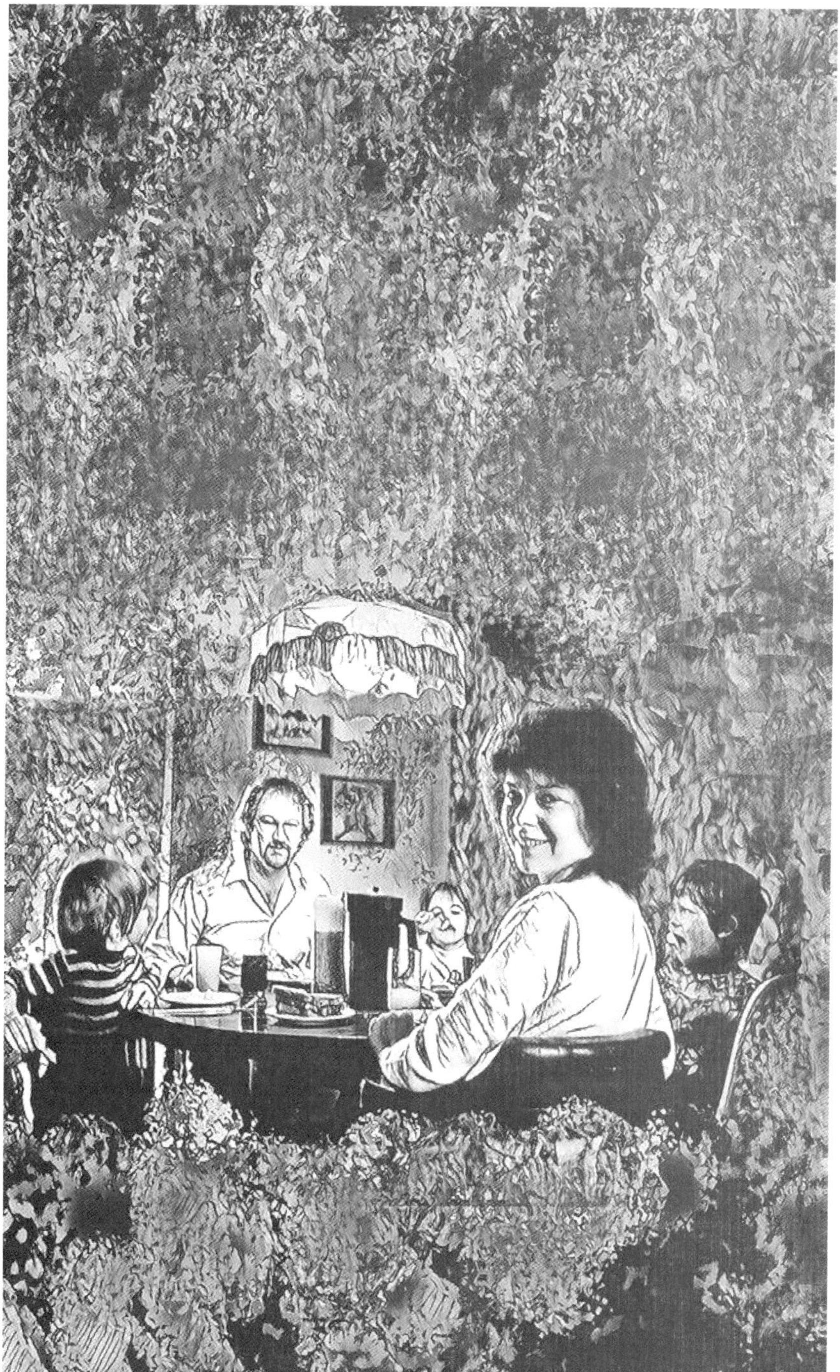

"God is more interested in your availability than your ability."

Brother Andrew

03
~ Divine Assignment ~

"Visionaries in the service of hope."

The first year of our marriage, Marilyn and I travelled across Canada and the USA, doing musical street evangelism. We slept on the floor in churches that hosted us, ate enough tomato sandwiches to last a lifetime and rode in the back of a huge truck, sometimes for days on end. Hey! We were young, in love, and making memories. We were also learning a whole lot about life and ministry, about things that would stand the test of the years that lay ahead of us. It came to an end with a gentle nudge from Jesus to move on.

Two very different local churches offered Marilyn and me positions to serve as their youth pastors. One was in sunny Fort Lauderdale, Florida. The invitation came with a good salary, a new car, and even a house with a swimming pool. The other was from a small church in Brockville, Ontario, Canada, a community that few people knew of. The church could hardly pay us, let alone offer us a car or a beautiful house. The decision was an easy one.

But, we felt God speaking to us again, "I want you to go to Brockville." So, that's what we did.

Serving as a youth pastor with little income in a small town was tough. Marilyn was pregnant at the time. For the first three months, we slept on the floor of a Sunday school classroom because we couldn't afford rent. Though difficult, our time in Brockville was special. The lead pastors, Vern and Marj O'Brien, were father and mother figures to us, and Timothy, our first child, was born while we served there. There were days that we would wonder how we were going to feed our new baby, and we'd wake up to find a bag of groceries on our doorstep stocked with baby formula. Another time, Marilyn, needing a new pair of winter boots, found a shiny black pair in her exact size sitting on the doorstep. We had told no one of our need. God had provided! We learned invaluable lessons in faith and what it meant to really trust God. We learned that He cared about the small details of our lives.

After just two years in Brockville, we felt God prompting us to make ourselves available as senior pastors to a small congregation in another rural town, Listowel, in Western Ontario. We drove the six hours one Sunday to "preach for the call" as it was known. Essentially, it was a tryout. I would preach, and the congregation would vote on whether they thought we should be their pastors. Still young, Marilyn nineteen and me twenty-two, we pulled up to the quaint little church feeling excited and hopeful. Later, we would find out that the congregation's first impression was to wonder what these "kids" were doing here. But when Marilyn sat down to play the piano, and we led the congregation in worship, and even before I had preached, they had made up their minds. If she could play the piano like that, who cares how he preaches? After the service, they invited us to serve as their pastors.

At the time, we owned nothing, except for our hippie van. It was banana yellow with striped, green, orange and brown carpeting covering the floor and walls inside. It was perfect for cool youth pastors. Marilyn had decided we needed about $2500 for some new furniture, and had been asking God to provide it. Each day, she would look in the mailbox to see if a miracle cheque had arrived. It became a bit of a joke. When she would come in from collecting the mail, I would ask her if her $2500 cheque had come. When the church offered to pay for our moving expenses, I politely declined, explaining that everything we owned could fit into the back of the van. The chairman of the church board told us that they had decided to reallocate the moving expenses to help us pay for furniture when we moved into the church manse. The cheque they gave us was for $2500!

Throughout our lives and ministry, God has never let us down. His vision comes with His provision. That's the way He works. He is good, gracious, faithful and generous. Always!

We moved to Listowel to care for the congregation of about one hundred wonderful people. They were mostly farmers, and we often found ourselves out on pastoral visits to their homes. I remember arriving at a farm one morning and hearing the farmer call to me from inside the barn. He said that he wasn't able to come out to welcome me. I wondered why and strolled into the barn to find him up to his armpit inside the rear end of a cow whose calf, about to be born, needed turning.

We would care for those wonderful people, and they would care for us. Slowly but surely, that tiny rural congregation became our family. They were so good to us, treating us with such kindness and generosity. We saw God move in that little church. People were saved, backsliders restored, and others filled with the Holy Spirit. One of our greatest joys while there was the birth of Rachel, our beautiful daughter. We look back on our time there with such fondness.

In both Brockville and Listowel, we developed friendships and memories that have lasted throughout our lives. However, God was preparing us for something that, at that point, we couldn't even imagine. He was strengthening and training us to trust in him, so that He could do something extraordinary. Deep in our hearts, we knew that, ultimately, we would end up in Africa.

Africa defined me. Way back in 1936, my grandfather, James William Skinner, travelled by slow boat to Kenya with his wife Lila and my father, their three-year-old son Bob. They traded the Canadian Prairies of Saskatchewan for the forested hills of the Nyangori Mission Station on the north shore of Lake Victoria, near Kisumu in western Kenya. My grandparents began an association between the Skinner family and the continent of Africa, which continues to this day.

I was born in Africa. The year was 1952, and I went on to spend my entire childhood in southern Africa. When I was two, my father, mother, my younger brother Dean, and I moved to Nelspruit in the Transvaal province of north-eastern South Africa. It was during these years that I developed a deep love for Africa. I retained my father's Canadian citizenship, but my entire worldview was shaped by my experiences of life in Africa. My first breath was African. My first awkward and tentative steps as a child were on the same African soil that soaked up my first tears. Africa sustained and nurtured me, and as I grew older, I never contemplated living anywhere else. There is a certain phenomenon that prevails in those of us who might be called foreigners in Africa, but were born into a place where our heritage, our lineage, is relatively short. At times, we feel the need to justify our identity. In a place like Africa, contrasts can be stark, and history has so often found the occasion to divide people. However, at a very early age, I knew myself only as African.

~ Zambia ~

After only two years in Listowel, we spoke with the Overseas Missions Department of the Pentecostal Assemblies of Canada, the denomination our families had been a part of for four generations. We shared with them the longing God had put in our hearts for Africa, and that we felt ready to serve if needed. We were assigned to Zambia, a landlocked country just north of Zimbabwe. It wasn't long before we found ourselves packing up to move to Africa. We were tasked with the responsibility of caring for the English-speaking congregation in Kitwe, the second-largest city in the nation. We inherited the pastoral duties from Winston and Gloria Broomes, a missionary family from the West Indies. They had done well, and the church was full of lively people.

It was all very new to Marilyn and the children as it was their first time living in Africa. Life adjustments were required! Not only was the culture and comfort level very different, but there was a huge problem with petty theft in Kitwe at the time. Our home was broken into more times than we can remember. Fortunately, it was never violent, but there is something unsettling and violating that made those experiences difficult for us. It was a huge learning experience for all of us. Zambia was trying, arduous, and stretching. God was, again, pulling us out of our comfort zone, teaching us to trust in him above the circumstances, and teaching us the necessity of surrender and sacrifice to a life lived for him. We had yet to learn how those events would pale in comparison to what was to come.

The congregation in Kitwe taught us more about pastoring a church in Africa than we taught them. They were gracious, kind and responsive. James, our youngest child, was born while we served in Kitwe.

After two years, we were asked to transfer to Northmead Assembly in Lusaka, Zambia's capital city. The church was larger and in a very healthy condition as a result of the ministry of Vern and Belva Tisdale. Leading that thriving community of 500, we saw God mature us as pastors. Much of what we have become as missionary pastors, we credit to the two years we spent at Northmead Assembly. The people were warm, friendly and helpful. I began to feel more confident in my leadership, who I was in God, and what He was calling us to do. I was to lead a great church in Africa.

One evening, while sharing a meal with some friends, the subject of the atrocities going on in Uganda, over two thousand kilometres to the north, came up.

In 1971, the notorious dictator Idi Amin took control of Uganda's government through force, staging a military coup with the backing of the British government. He seized power from Uganda's first president, Milton Obote, who was a corrupt despot in his own right. Under both leaders, the Ugandan people suffered greatly, with Amin going down as one of the most evil men of the twentieth century. During his nine-year rule, an estimated 300,000 people were killed in the political and ethnic conflict.

As clearly as anything I've ever heard from God, Jesus whispered to me.

"Gary, I want you to move to Uganda and plant an English-speaking church downtown Kampala, Uganda's capital city. Through the church, I will touch the city, and I will touch the nation."

The words I heard from Jesus that day embedded themselves indelibly into my spirit. That's the way God works. He chooses people for tasks in His Kingdom. He is the Lord of the harvest. He speaks specifically and intentionally to those He calls into service. He has assignments for them and commissions them to "Go." And He goes with them. He provides the resources and strength to accomplish what he calls them to do. In fact, in the most dire and difficult circumstances of fulfilling that call, when everything seems to be working against us in obeying God's directive, it is the absolute certainty of that clarion call from God that strengthens us and sees us through any situation, any seeming impossibility. If He asks us to do it, then He will give us whatever we need to see it through to completion. He will never abandon or forsake us. He will take us into the middle of situations where we seem sure to fail, but there, He will come through and demonstrate His greatness. Just as he calls us, he grants the miracles we need to see us to the finish line. Joseph found this true in Egypt. David experienced this when he stood before Goliath. Peter was provided with taxes out of the mouth of a fish. Paul survived a shipwreck and snake bites. God cannot and will not fail us when He calls us.

We must hear from God. Every generation needs a word from God, a specific call to accomplish tasks in their day and then act. Everything that has occurred since the call I heard at a dining room table in Zambia demonstrates the faithfulness and veracity of the call He burned into our hearts.

It is never an easy thing to simply uproot yourself from the safe and familiar, and venture out into unknown territory where you are thrust into circumstances that require radical faith that will test you to the core. You can see the obstacles, or you can see the opportunities. Faith never accomplishes where it is not first tried. God never uses someone whom He doesn't first call, then test and as sure as the sun comes up, He finally comes through for them. The greater the battle, the greater the victory. If God asks us to do something that seems way too difficult, then look up: God is about to do something magnificent for His glory.

I had never been to Uganda, let alone thought of planting a church in a country that was an active war zone. Yet, there was that deep and unrelenting conviction that grabbed a hold of me and wrapped me up with such force that I simply could not escape it. God's word and His call that evening was as crystal clear to me as anything I'd ever heard from Him. I received it as a revelation from God, as His purpose for our lives and ministry. We were to go to Kampala. The question then simply became, when?

As we began to pray about the details of such a move, the situation in Uganda continued to deteriorate. My knowledge of Uganda was limited to the common understanding that it was a nation that had gone through incredibly difficult circumstances. The country was suffering from decades of misrule, insecurity, dictatorship and war. For twenty years, as many as a million people died as a result of internal civil conflict. The very name Uganda conjured up imaginations of fear, horror and political lunacy. Chaos, disorder and mayhem were the order of the day. To think of Uganda was to think of death.

Milton Obote, the first post-independence President, had been forced into exile, first in Kenya and then in Tanzania. He continued to work to regain power, which he eventually did in 1979, with the help of Tanzanian armed forces. In 1980, with the belief that the highly unpopular Obote had rigged the election for his second presidency, rebel forces, under the leadership of Yoweri Museveni, opposed the reinstated president and his military through an active campaign of guerrilla warfare. This civil war, known as the Ugandan Bush War, would last seven years and claim hundreds of thousands of lives.

It was in the middle of this conflict that we were getting ready to move to Uganda. Marilyn had a difficult time with this. The ongoing violence in the country was being extensively reported in the press around the world. Women and children were bearing the brunt of the nation's instability, war and violence. If we were to go to Uganda, God would need to convince Marilyn, too. She had some hard conversations with Him about what he was asking us to do.

"God, I'm going to be raped or killed and my children won't be safe there. If it be your will, Lord, let this cup pass from us," she prayed.

During this time of waiting on God for direction, we hosted a missionary meeting where we led worship. As Marilyn sat at the piano, the Lord gently and compassionately reminded her of the commitment she had made years earlier. She saw the image of her nine-year-old self sitting at the piano, praying.

"Jesus, you have been so good to me. Whatever I do in this life, I want to be useful to you, no matter the cost."

As the memory filled her mind, she began to softly weep as we sang the chorus "Jesus Use Me." The lyrics were especially impactful:

> *Jesus, use me; oh Lord, don't refuse me.*
>
> *Surely there's a work that I can do.*
>
> *Even though it's humble*
>
> *Lord, help my will to crumble.*
>
> *Though the cost be great, I'll work for you.*

That day, Marilyn reaffirmed her commitment to Jesus.

"Lord, I take the things nearest and dearest to my heart, and I kiss them goodbye, all for the sake of your Kingdom."

And in that moment, Marilyn knew what we would do. The call of God for us to serve in Kampala was now firmly embedded in our hearts. But we had still never been to Uganda.

~ My First Visit to Uganda ~

In 1982, we were returning from Zambia to Canada for a year of furlough. On the way, we stopped in Nairobi, Kenya, where we had been invited to lead worship at the World Pentecostal Conference. While there, I decided to make the short journey into Uganda to see for myself what it was like and what it would mean for us to move there. My father, who was living in Kenya at the time and running the Evangel Publishing House on the grounds of Pan Africa University, drove me to the border. Paul and Gloria Willoughby, Canadian missionaries who were already living in Mbale in eastern Uganda, met us at the border post. As I stepped into Uganda for the first time, I felt a sense of destiny.

On Sunday morning, we went to a small church in Kumi, a rural peasant community near the Kenya border. The rustic little church building, with mud walls and a shiny tin roof, was down in a fertile valley surrounded by plantations of maize, bananas, sweet potatoes and beans. Nearby was a row of low-lying hills covered with massive rocks and boulders. We were going to have church in the hills.

The pastor told us of how the church was persecuted when Idi Amin was the President of Uganda. During his infamous rule, the mad dictator banned many churches, including the Pentecostal Assemblies of God, the church denomination planted by the Pentecostal Assemblies of Canada in the early days of the 1940s. At that time my grandfather, James Skinner, was teaching school just across the border in Kenya. He was among the first Canadian missionaries to respond to a call from Christians in Uganda to come over and help the fledgling Pentecostal Church. Hundreds and eventually thousands of churches were planted across the breadth and width of eastern and northern Uganda. When President Amin, a Muslim, led Uganda, he chose to banish and crush the Church. Thousands of Christians were brutally slaughtered just for worshipping Jesus. The General Superintendent of the fellowship of churches that we belonged to, the Pentecostal Assemblies of God (Uganda), was killed after preaching in one of the local churches.

The pastor of this little church told of how government soldiers would attack and kill congregations as they met. In order to continue worshipping, the Christians would, instead, hold the service in the hills among the huge rocks and under the shade of the massive fig trees that grew up among the boulders. From this vantage point, they would post church members as sentries who watched for approaching soldiers as the little congregation sang vibrant songs and worshipped Jesus. When soldiers were seen, the sentries would let out an alarm to signal that danger was imminent. The people would quickly but quietly disperse among the hills, melting into the countryside and fields to avoid being caught. Once the danger had passed, they would reassemble to continue where they had left off. I was moved by the determination and tenacity of these Christians, who had such a deep commitment to practice their faith despite the many dangers they faced.

Idi Amin was gone by now. He had been driven into exile by soldiers from Tanzania, who backed the incoming military forces of Obote's Ugandan army. We weren't in any danger that day as we met in the same beautiful natural amphitheater of rocks and trees on the hilltop near the little church building.

It was one of the most amazing times of worship and celebration I have ever experienced. People were seated on the rocks under the shade of the fig trees. One of the huge boulders was the pulpit from which I preached my first sermon in Uganda. The singing and dancing was electrifying. The people danced and jumped and trilled to the sound of the drums and local musical instruments. As they clapped and swayed to the rhythm and beat, in typical African style, a song leader would sing the lead line of a song, and the congregation would all answer back. Sometimes, it was the women who led, and the men would answer back. All of this was out in the open, under the trees, with a gentle breeze rustling in the canopy of leaves, through which flitted some of the most strikingly beautiful birds. It was a little bit of heaven on earth, and it was the first of so many wonderful times of worship, praise, preaching and fellowship that we would experience in Uganda.

I desperately wanted to travel to Kampala to see the capital city for myself, but I was persuaded that the trip was much too risky. Kampala was still a dangerous city, and yet, even as we journeyed back through the border into Kenya, I felt the pull of it on my heart. By now, God had burned three words into my consciousness, "Kampala...Downtown...English." I had yet to visit the city, but with each passing day, the import of those words grew in their gravity and resonance. They were specific directions, a starting point for me to understand with profound clarity what we were supposed to do in the heart of Africa.

We returned to Canada for a year of furlough to pray and prepare for what was ahead. The Lord continued to show us how faithful he was and would always be. A member of the congregation we had served in Listowel met us at the airport in Toronto with his brand-new car for us to use for the year. Another gave us a credit card to pay for the fuel. We knew that God was with us and for us and began to look forward, with anticipation, to what was ahead of us in Uganda.

The denomination, on the other hand, still needed some convincing. We had made known to the Overseas Mission Department the call God had placed on our hearts for Kampala, but they were apprehensive. The civil war in Uganda showed no sign of coming to an end, and the danger was very real. The missions committee rejected our dream to plant a church in Kampala. We were informed that they did not support the planting of a city centre church in Kampala at this time.

It was a significant and real disappointment, and presented a dilemma. As much as anything I have ever known, I knew, absolutely knew, that Jesus was leading and calling us to Kampala, but my leaders were telling me something else. Marilyn and I continued to pray as those three words weighed down upon my heart.

I found myself at one of the great crossroads of my life's journey. Do I submit myself to those in authority over me, or do I remain faithful to the profound call of God on my life? Are the two mutually exclusive? Is it possible for them somehow to harmonise? How can I tell? What should I do?

My initial reaction was to prepare to go to Uganda independently, to release myself from the constraints of being sent by the missions department of a church denomination. In my heart, I knew with certainty that we were to go to Kampala. Why should a committee of men on another continent determine our destiny and call? Surely, they could hear from God, too. And yet, the more I headed down a path of what seemed to be liberty and independence, the realisation dawned on me that I was isolating myself. I was a fourth-generation Pentecostal Assemblies of Canada minister and a third-generation missionary with the same church body. I was as much a part of the denomination as anyone else, maybe more. And yet, the call to Kampala was as crystal clear as anything I had ever heard. In my heart, I knew that submission to authority was the right choice. It was what I knew was the biblical thing to do. I needed to submit, even if it meant surrendering a God-birthed dream. It was a tough decision.

And then there was a lingering sense inside my spirit that I was being tested. Marilyn and I both knew that God never rewards rebellion, just implicit, childlike, simple faith and obedience. David, though called and anointed to be Israel's king, submitted to King Saul because Saul, at that time, was God's appointed leader.

I knew that God had plans for Kampala. He had placed them deeply in my heart, but as I considered the situation, I knew that I should not allow ambition of any kind to derail me from doing what He wanted us to do. God would fulfil His plan for Kampala with or without me. If He wanted us to be a part of those plans, He would arrange it.

So, I did one of the most difficult and heart-wrenching things I have ever done. I buried the Kampala dream. I let the dream die. I surrendered it totally to God. I submitted to those who were in authority over my life. And it hurt. Really hurt! I determined to love and surrender to a sovereign God who could make anything possible.

We were informed that we had been reassigned to serve a second term in Zambia. We put our Ugandan dream aside and began to prepare for a return to the church we had left in Zambia. It came as a wonderful surprise when, two weeks later, the Missions Department called to let us know that they had overturned their decision and our transfer to Kampala had been accepted.

I have since learned that as we walk with God, He will test us. If you want to go to the next level, you must first pass a test. That's the way it is in school, and it seems that's the way it is in life. That's how Jesus works with us. He wants to take us to a higher level of ministry or business and success, so He puts us through a test. And here is the crux of the matter! Are we living for the dream He placed in our hearts, or are we living for Him? He will sometimes take away the very dream that he has given to you. You have to trust God and let it die. He is faithful and will always do what is right. When we show him that He is first, that He is central and that He is our priority, He is our love and life, and that we will not compromise integrity even for a God-given dream, then He gives the dream back again. That's how he did it for us, and the dream He initially put in our hearts for Kampala became a reality and has flourished into a full-grown tree bearing rich fruit.

Now knowing that we were going to Uganda, I resolved to take a trip to Kampala to see for myself what we were getting into. What exactly was God taking us into? I also wanted some confirmation, some sign, that this dream that had been planted in my heart was a God dream.

It was still impossible to fly into Uganda's main airport at Entebbe, which is only 35 kilometres from Kampala. The country was still in chaos, so I had to fly into Nairobi, Kenya and make the last leg of the journey into Uganda by car. To do this meant braving the derelict and hazardous roads of East Africa. The trip from Nairobi to Kampala was split into a two-day adventure.

The first day, Gerald Morrison, the field director for the Missions Department in East Africa, drove me to the Uganda/Kenya border post at Malaba, where Paul Willoughby, a Canadian missionary, met me, and we drove on to their home in the picturesque little colonial town of Mbale. Canadian missionaries from the Pentecostal Assemblies of Canada had been stationed here for more than half a century, among the foothills of Mount Elgon, Africa's second-highest mountain.

In the 1940s, several young Ugandan men went to Kenya to find work and were employed at the mission station where my grandfather, James Skinner, his wife Lila and their son Bob, my father, had been living since coming to Kenya in 1936. The Ugandan men found jobs but also heard the gospel message about Jesus for the first time and surrendered their lives to the Lordship of Jesus. Their lives were changed by what they had experienced, and they knew that this message needed to be heard by the people living in their mountain villages back in Uganda. With the blessing of the missionaries in Kenya, they decided to return and spread the good news. Sometime later, the missionaries, who had heard that the men had planted a church in their home village, decided to go to Uganda to visit the new church.

They found the young men and their new church worshipping Jesus way up in one of the mountain villages and encouraged them to plant another church down in the valley, as it was too difficult for the people in the valley to go up the mountain to worship. So, a second church was planted in the valley, and then a third one in the closest community, the town of Mbale, where we had just arrived on our long journey from Kenya.

Mbale became the hub for the subsequent revival that swept through the eastern and northern parts of Uganda. Over the next couple of decades, many more churches were planted. God blessed the preaching and teaching of the new work with incredible miracles of healing, deliverance and transformation. A Bible College was started in Mbale to train pastors to care for the hundreds of young churches that were springing up. New missionaries from Canada arrived and spread the message south to Tororo and then west to the town of Jinja, where the headwaters of the Nile River cascade out of Lake Victoria. But, for some unknown reason, their efforts to plant churches in Kampala and further on into the south and west of the country strangely failed.

We had an evening of reminiscing about the past but also looking forward to the future. The following morning, we made the nerve-wracking, bone-rattling, six-hour journey to Kampala. The roads were in terrible shape. You would spend as much time driving on the sides of the road as on them. Over time, the rains, in gushing torrents, had washed away chunks of the asphalt and soil.

We encountered army checkpoints every ten or twenty kilometres along the battered road seeing first-hand the devastation and terror of the war. The government's soldiers, most of them just teenagers, imposed themselves harshly on the terrified civilians with a thuggish arrogance. When speaking with these boys at the checkpoints, they absentmindedly fidgeted with their automatic weapons. The air in the nation was thick with tension.

As we finally drove into Kampala, I was overwhelmed by the devastation and ruin. There were few traces of what had once been a famously beautiful garden city of East Africa. The streets had been lined with majestic Mvule,

Musisi, and African Tulip trees as they led to the immaculately manicured gardens of the colonial and local residences on the green forested hills of Kololo, Nakasero and Mengo. The air was freshened by the gentle wind blowing in off the waters of Lake Victoria, and the city was regularly watered by the rains that collected over the massive expanse of lake water just beyond the other residential hills of Muyenga and Buziga.

But that city was long gone. The city I was looking at now was a skeleton. Most of the stately trees had been chopped down for firewood. The streets, gutted by years of neglect, were, in some places, nearly impassable. Aged buildings, tired and crumbling, lined the roadside. Walls that hadn't been gutted by fire or destroyed by bombs were decorated with bullet holes and layers of dust. Windows were barricaded with planks of battered wood. Mounds of garbage were heaped up in the traffic circles. Stray dogs and ragged children waged battle on them for the choice pickings. On the lampposts, above them, vultures hovered menacingly. I was appalled at what we were looking at.

Driving through the derelict city, I watched a magnificent thunderstorm forming on the horizon. Dark and ominous, the afternoon storm brewed over the green hills surrounding the city, a skyward reflection of a place both beautiful but broken. A sadness for the city and its inhabitants surged through me. But, at the same moment, I felt a sense of hope spark to life in me. As the raindrops began to spatter on the windshield, I knew that I was in the right place, at the right time. God wanted to do something here. He wanted us to settle and serve here, war-torn, poverty-stricken, battered, broken Kampala, Uganda.

We finally arrived at the Anglican guest house near Namirembe Cathedral, Kampala's oldest place of Christian worship. Namirembe means "hill of peace." The Cathedral was perched on the top of one of the seven hills of the city. It was built with bricks that were hand-carried from all the distant corners of Uganda to stand on the highest hill, overlooking the capital city as a monument to the glory of God.

As we looked out across the shabby buildings and broken streets, and as a blanket of smoke from a thousand cooking fires settled over the scene, I saw a city run down by years of war and neglect. The natural beauty of the hills and swamps along the shores of Lake Victoria stood in stark contrast to the dilapidated skyline, punctuated by an ugly minaret at one of Idi Amin's mosques, leaning precariously to one side.

"How could any place come to be like this?" I wondered.

I watched the swirling thunderstorm, the rain falling heavily on the streets below. The afternoon sun slipped beneath the clouds, bathing the hill on which I stood in a golden glow. The orange sunlight cut across the storm, catching the drops of water as they fell from the heavy clouds. That's when I saw the rainbow, its arc stretching across the entire city.

"This is a promise," I thought. "God has a promise for this city, and beneath this rainbow lies a treasure waiting to be unearthed."

I turned the promise that God had given to me over in my head again.

A church! Kampala! Downtown! English speaking!

I knew now more than ever that this was what God had called us to do. Our little family would willingly obey this call. We would move to Kampala and plant God's church.

When God speaks, things happen. The same voice that spoke the universe, the heavens, the earth and every living thing into existence, speaks to us. We do not need to force God's will into being through our own strength or schemes. If we had allowed ourselves to circumvent the authority God had placed over us and who, in reality, had our best interests at heart, we would have ultimately been living in pride and sin all in the name of obedience. The Lord was teaching us that when following Jesus, it is not only that we obey, but how we obey, that matters.

~ Reflect and Discuss ~

As you reflect on your own story and engage in discussion with others, consider the following:

1. Listening to Jesus' Voice and Responding:

    • Recall a specific moment when you felt Jesus speaking to you or guiding you. Reflect on how you knew that it was His voice in the confusion of the noise of life.

    • Share how you responded to Jesus in that moment. Did you follow His leading with obedience, or did you hesitate or resist?

    • Discuss the impact Jesus' voice had on you and your life during that time. How did His guidance shape your decisions, attitudes, and relationships?

2. Making Difficult Choices:

    • Consider a time when you felt called to do something that would require sacrifice and commitment.

    • Discuss any internal conflicts or challenges you faced in responding to what you were being called to do.

    • What factors should we consider when making difficult choices that require sacrificing personal comfort for a higher calling or greater good?

    • Discuss how faith can support and influence us in making difficult choices.

    • Share an example from your own life where faith helped you make a sacrificial decision and the outcomes that followed.

3. Facing a Test:

- God tests those he wants to use. We see this in this chapter and in the lives of Bible characters like Joseph, David and Peter.

- What signs or feelings might indicate that a challenge you are facing is a test of your faith or character.

- Recall a time when you were faced with a test of your faith or character. How were you able to navigate the challenge of being tested?

These questions are designed to provoke deep personal reflection and foster meaningful group discussions, encouraging participants to apply the lessons and insights from the chapter in their own lives and communities.

During your discussion, offer support and encouragement to one another as you navigate the complexities of following Jesus. Share insights, challenges, and aspirations, and commit to praying for each other.

By seeking to follow Jesus faithfully, you can experience His transformative power and contribute to His kingdom work in the world.

∼

75

"The kingdom of Uganda is a fairy-tale. You climb up ... and at the end there is a wonderful new world. The scenery is different, the vegetation is different, the climate is different, and, most of all, the people are different from anything elsewhere to be seen in the whole range of Africa ... I say: 'Concentrate on Uganda'. For magnificence, for variety of form and colour, for profusion of brilliant life – bird, insect, reptile, beast – for vast scale — Uganda is truly the pearl of Africa."

Winston Churchill

04
~ The Pearl of Africa ~

"A journey through Africa's heart."

Africa! The mere name conjures up images of wildness and exploration. From arid deserts to thick, steamy tropical jungles, from high craggy mountains to deep lush valleys, from long winding rivers with magnificent waterfalls and freshwater lakes to the wide-open plains dotted with animals found nowhere else on the planet. Africa is vast, it's varied, and it's beautiful. It's a continent of hugely untapped resources. The agricultural potential is astounding. Moderate weather and good rainfall bless much of the continent. But the undiscovered wealth of massive mineral deposits and oil that lie buried deep in the soil of Africa, waiting to be discovered, unearthed and used, pales into insignificance beside Africa's greatest resource, its people, especially its youth. The future of Africa belongs to the youth.

Uganda is the youngest nation in the world, with 50% of the population being under the age of fifteen. When we came to Uganda, the average Ugandan woman gave birth to 7.4 children. By 2021, that number had dropped to only, hold your breath, five per woman. Uganda has an overwhelmingly dependent population. The life expectancy of a Ugandan was only 50 years when we came to Uganda, but as a result of AIDS and war, it dropped to 42 in 1995 but rose back up to 54 years in 2021. 75% of the population is under the age of thirty. Only 2% of the population is over the age of 65. Grey-haired seniors are an obvious minority. Uganda is a nation full of young people and, as a result, full of potential.

Uganda is a fertile plateau of tropical plains and jungle, 3256 feet above sea level. It lies in the Great East African Rift Valley between a mountainous spine that runs down the eastern side of Africa, dominated by Mount

Elgon on the east and the snow-capped Ruwenzori mountains on Uganda's western border. Beyond the mountains is the chaos they call the Congo. The Ruwenzori Range is volcanic and the site of the fabled "Mountains of the Moon." The world's largest gorilla population lives on the slopes and in the forests surrounding the mountains. It's also home to the Pygmy people, the shortest people on earth.

Uganda is a bird watchers' paradise, boasting more species of birds in the Queen Elizabeth National Park on its western border than all of North America. Visiting migrant flocks pass through Uganda, down the Rift Valley on their way to a winter African home or back up to their European summer homes. Resident bird life teems in the treetops and along the coasts of the lake and the wide-open plains. The melodious songs of the birds greet each morning. Their vibrant colour and the variety of their song is overwhelming. Tiny little birds skip through the undergrowth or flit from tree to tree. Fish eagles cry along the lake shore, and the national bird, the impressively beautiful Crested Crane, is found throughout the country. The African grey parrot or lilac-breasted rollers swoop through the sky to roost and rest in the treetops. Uganda is alive with bird life.

The National Parks are bouncing back to their once well-stocked variety of game animals. Elephants, antelope, lions, leopards and herds of buffalo are roaming the plains and forests again. The Rothschild giraffe, unique to Uganda, a magnificent russet colour with unusual skin rosettes, is a sight to behold as they lean up into the highest tree and flick out an eighteen-inch-long tongue to strip off the tiny acacia leaves.

Uganda sits astride the equator, which runs across the northern part of Lake Victoria, the earth's second-largest freshwater lake. The Nile River, the longest and greatest river on the planet, spills out of the north side of the lake through the Bujagali Falls, beginning its 4132-mile journey (6650 Km) from the highlands of East Africa to the Egyptian port city of Alexandria on the Mediterranean coast. It winds its way across the plains of Uganda, into Lake Kyoga, and then turns left for several hundred miles, passing through Murchison Falls National Park. The falls are only twenty-five feet wide, where the river rushes through a huge gash of rocks. Below the falls, the river levels out and is populated with schools of grunting hippos and enormous, one-ton Nile Crocodiles basking along the shore in the tropical sun. It was here that Sir Samuel Baker, the early British explorer, capsized his boat but made it safely to the shores, his wife Mary swimming beside him while dodging the crocodiles. It was here that Ernest Hemingway crashed his aeroplane and came up with the concept of one of his legendary books, "The Green Hills of Africa."

The river flows into Lake Albert, named after Queen Victoria's consort. It then empties out of the lake, passing through the Lado enclave, once the home of the world's biggest elephants. It crosses the border into South Sudan, eventually entering the huge Swamp of the Sudan. Here, it's called the Blue Nile, but at Khartoum, in Sudan, it merges with the White Nile, which flows from its headwaters in the mountains of Ethiopia. Finally, it passes through the Sahara in Egypt, the largest desert on the planet, where it passes through Cairo and into the Mediterranean Sea. The sun evaporates the water and sends it back as rain to fall on the mountains of Central Africa and start the journey all over again.

The lush equatorial climate of Uganda, with moderate temperatures, supports an abundance of agricultural wealth. Fruit and vegetables grow all year long. They grow large and sweet. Uganda can proudly claim to have the finest pineapples and bananas found anywhere. It's the true banana republic. Crops grow easily and support a mostly rural agricultural population with grain, fruit and livestock. An adage about Uganda is, "You tickle the earth with a hoe, and it laughs with a harvest."

The Ugandan menu is varied and unique in each part of the country. In the north, the staple is a millet porridge or bread accompanied by spinach greens and stewed meat or chicken. In the south, a green banana, called Matoke, is steamed in banana leaves over a wood fire and garnished with a red peanut sauce. Greens with meat, chicken or fish, also steamed in a wrapped-up banana leaf, complement the bananas. Despite the ravages of war, food production has not been a problem. The people are hospitable and welcoming to visitors, sharing their meals as a matter of social interaction.

Market stalls are radiantly colourful with fruit, vegetables and meat products gaily arrayed in heaps on the ground, wooden shelves or hanging from makeshift trellises. It's noisy, buzzing and alive with activity and children. Each week, a clothing market emerges out of nowhere on a busy street corner or empty lot. Crowds mill through the lines of used items, plastic shoes from China, with belts, jeans and shirts hanging on makeshift wooden racks. Women sit on the ground with their feet gathered up under them as they serve and barter with their customers.

~ A Little Background ~

Uganda is home to fifty-four different tribal groups who speak more than thirty languages. The largest and most dominant tribe are the Baganda.

Early missionaries and administrators told of finding in Buganda the most developed form of government in Africa. It was a feudal system ruled by the Kabaka, an autocratic and ruthless king. He governed through a system of chiefs with top officials like the Katikiro, the Prime Minister, the Mujasi, the chief executioner, the Gabunga, the Admiral of the fleet of canoes and so on down to the ordinary people clothed in flowing robes of cinnamon coloured bark cloth beaten from the bark of a local fig tree.

Bishop Alfred Tucker in his book "Eighteen Years in Uganda" tells of the early days of missionary work. Lubaale or spirit worship, a form of witchcraft characterised by a blend of vile and bloodthirsty practices, was the religion of the land. It dominated all of communal life. Human sacrifice was common. Slave raiding was a way of life and a mainstay of the economy. The king of Buganda kept an army of 6000 soldiers just to raid the surrounding tribes to bring home slaves. Whole tribes were decimated by war, and the victims were taken and sold into slavery. Large tracts of land were empty of people because of the inter-tribal conflict and slaughter. Pioneer missionary Alexander Mackay wrote to The Times newspaper in 1889 and reported that tens of thousands of men, women and children were sold to Arab slave traders out of Uganda every year. Three out of every four slaves from East Africa died of hunger en route to the slave markets of Zanzibar and the Middle East.

The early pioneer days of European expansionism saw an antagonistic and sometimes violent contest between the English Protestants, the French Catholics and the Arab Muslims for the favour of the king. Several bloody wars ensued, with British Protestant Christianity finally gaining the upper hand. Today, as a consequence, English is the official language of the nation. English was adopted because it was the language of the colonial power that had governed it for seventy years, but primarily as a unifying force in a land of diverse cultures and languages. No one tribe could dominate the other if English were the official language of the nation.

What's more, English is the language of international business, aviation and education. It opens up huge possibilities for future generations to think globally and not just locally. English releases the youth from the cultural restraints and biases of local culture to think differently about the possibilities in life in a rapidly changing world.

As we planted an English-speaking church in the heart of the capital city, we saw the youth flock to experience a style of worship and liturgy that was fresh, new, vibrant and life-giving. It opened the door to a contemporary style of communication, worship and interaction that young people were eager for. It wasn't Western or Canadian. It was an emerging, new African expression of the Church.

For centuries, Africa was known as the Dark Continent, perhaps because so little was known about her. Perhaps, too, it was because the people lived in the darkness of superstition and witchcraft, the light of the good news of Christ having never reached them. The mysteries of the land and the people lay hidden deep in the interior of Africa. The population of the ancient world and then of Europe and America had been puzzled and filled with wonder and not a little speculation by the thought of venturing into and discovering the unknown depths and secrets of Africa. And then she was opened up! The primary quest was to find the source of the great River Nile. At first, it was the British explorers Burton and Speke and then the missionary explorers such as the Scotsman, David Livingston. He spent years and incredible energy to open up Africa. He walked the full width and length of south and central Africa several times. He was out of contact for such a long time that it was rumoured that he was dead. In 1871, The New York Herald commissioned the correspondent Henry Morton Stanley to find him. They finally met in the small village of Ujiji in what is now Tanzania. As Stanley shook the famous missionary's hand, looking deeply into his tired old eyes, he uttered, in classic understatement, those famous words, "Dr. Livingstone, I presume."

Stanley's time with the missionary statesman changed him, and he went on to become one of the greatest explorers of Africa. In 1875, Stanley was hosted at the court of the Kabaka, the king of the Baganda. He was deeply impressed by what he saw in Buganda, its people, culture, her aspirations and in her king. He realised that Uganda presented a massive opportunity for both the redemptive message and culture of Christianity, and the developmental influence of Great Britain. He wrote a letter to the people of England and sent it with a French soldier to deliver to the Daily Telegraph newspaper in London. The soldier was killed on the way, and a year later, the letter was found in the boot of his decomposing body and finally forwarded on.

Stanley's impression was that "Nowhere is there in all the pagan world a more promising field for a mission than Uganda?"

The response to the letter was immediate and overwhelming. Dozens of young men came forward, ready to do missionary work and plant the Church in the heart of Central Africa on the shores of the newly discovered Great Lake. Eight young men were chosen and commissioned to the work.

Alexander Mackay, the youngest, was last to speak at the commissioning service in 1876.

"Yes; is it at all likely that eight Englishmen should start for Central Africa and all be alive six months after? One of us, at least, will surely fall before that. But what I want to say is this: when that news comes, do not be downcast but send someone immediately to take the vacant place."

Within three years, seven of the eight had died, or been invalidated back to England. Two died of malarial fever, hostile tribesmen killed two, and three returned home for health reasons. The first two Bishops sent from England to oversee the fledgling church died en route before setting foot in Uganda. Bishop Hannington was speared to death days after arriving at the Nile River on the edge of Buganda. Bishop Walker, his replacement, died of fever on the south end of the Lake just before making the final push into Uganda.

MacKay served for 18 years with other missionaries without significant results before dying at the age of 40. The radically committed young missionaries experienced not only the opposition of the Arab Muslim slave traders and the witchdoctors of Lubare, the national and traditional religion, but also the antagonism of the Catholic priests who arrived in Uganda shortly after them. The king, Mteesa, played each group against the other to receive their favour and gifts. In 1884, Mteesa died. Mwanga, one of his many sons, succeeded him. The insecure young king acted out of frustration, fear and pure evil. In that volatile political atmosphere, persecution of the new faith of Christianity provoked the martyrdom of hundreds of new converts who were mutilated and burned to death. Some of the missionaries were exiled, while others were allowed to remain. Their persistence, patience and tenacious faith eventually saw the planting, growth and building of one of the greatest missionary enterprises in history. The Church of Jesus had been planted in Uganda. It went on to completely transform Uganda.

Hunters and businessmen who dreamed of adventure and wealth followed in the footsteps of the missionaries. And then came the administrative structures of the colonial powers of England, Portugal, France and Germany.

The people of Africa were being governed by rulers who were despotic and cruel. Child sacrifice, ritual murder and slavery were a way of life. Human sacrifice at the whim of the king was normal. People were grabbed by the king's soldiers and sacrificed. On one day, as many as two thousand were slaughtered. Whole tribes were decimated by war, and the victims were taken and sold into slavery. Large tracts of land were empty of people because of the inter-tribal conflict and slaughter. But as Africa opened up to Western Christendom, the culture of Christianity brought civilisation and order. Nothing and no one has done more to dignify the continent of Africa than Jesus through His Church. For the first time, Africans heard about a God of love, grace, mercy and kindness, a concept unheard of in the evil morass of witchcraft, animism, superstition and despotism. Law, order and development replaced the old African way. Churches were planted across the breadth and width of Uganda. A magnificent Anglican Cathedral was built on one of Kampala's seven hills.

Yes! Africa was carved up into nation-states led by the colonial powers of Europe. It was a decision that would have dire consequences when Africa would later gain independence from colonial rule. Traditionally, hostile and warring people groups were included in the new Colonial nation-states. Order remained while governed by Colonial masters, but it was a recipe for the mistrust, suspicion and infighting that would plague an independent post-colonial Africa. Three of East Africa's nations, Rwanda, Burundi and Uganda, are perfect examples of post-colonial genocide and warfare.

The Church, led by the missionary enterprise, was at the forefront of education, medicine and progress. The Church founded the best schools and hospitals in Africa. Selfless, hard-working, generous and committed missionaries pioneered God-centred institutions that changed the course of African history. Alongside the Colonial government, the Church established a new way of thinking, a new culture and lifestyle based on the worldview of Western Christendom, undergirded by the Biblical moral code and the teaching and character of Jesus. Agriculture and business boomed. Footpaths were turned into modern highways. The East African Railway wound its way from Mombasa on the coast of the Indian Ocean through the Kenyan highlands, past snow-capped mountains that sat astride the equator. It terminated on the shore of a huge inland lake that was home to the Bantu tribes of Central East Africa. The land's natural resource was exported to Europe, where it was manufactured into goods and services that saw Africa begin to develop.

While it must be said that, as under any political or social system, especially in nations under Colonial Catholic rule, some inequities and injustices did much harm, the horrors of the Belgian Congo are a perfect example of this, but, as a whole, the quality of life and the standard of living got so much better for the African people. For the duration of Protestant Colonial rule, war, disorder, chaos, injustice and inept rule were held at bay.

Then came a wave of national independence from the perceived constraints of the colonial empires of the West. India led the way, and then, one by one, the nations of Africa experienced self-rule. The Colonial order was replaced by a crop of new African leaders who proved themselves to be as corrupt, inept and brutal as their ancient tribal ancestors. Life didn't get better for the people of Africa. It got worse. A lot worse! Despair, hopelessness and fear took hold of Africa. Again! Incompetent, self-serving and inadequate government ruined the economies of most of Africa's newly independent nations. Poverty became endemic. The necessities of life were difficult or impossible to procure. The poorest and most regressive countries in the world were now on the continent of Africa. Governments changed hand by the bullet rather than the ballot. Violent regime change, a string of military coups and the slaughter of millions of innocent civilians left the people of Africa confused and uncertain, dashing miserably their hopes of a bright and prosperous future.

That certainly was true of Uganda when we first arrived in November of

1983. The country was in disarray. All infrastructure had broken down. Water, electricity and telephone communication was, at best, erratic, more often non-existent. It took nineteen months of negotiating to get our first telephone installed. There were no supermarkets or organised shopping. Meat and vegetables were purchased from ramshackle wooden stalls and open marketplaces on the side of the road. The flies were waved off the newly butchered goat, bull or pig so you could make your selection, which was then hacked off with a panga, producing a spray of blood and bone chips. The roads were in a state of complete disrepair. There was often more pothole than road. We used to joke that if children were swimming in the pothole, it was probably too deep for the car to go through. And, after all, you didn't want to disturb the children who were having too much fun cooling off! Garbage was piled in the streets, often several meters high and crowned with dogs, storks or cattle looking for something to eat. A great number of the people were barefoot and dressed in ragged old clothing.

Every mile or two sported a "roadblock," providing the policemen or soldiers with an opportunity to get something "to eat" from the few drivers or pedestrians who passed by. "To eat" means getting money from someone. Gun-toting soldiers looted and pillaged at will. How else were they going to be paid? The nation was bankrupt and mismanaged by politicians who kept power and garnered personal wealth by the strength of brute force. Fear was the order of the day. Everyone hurried to be home by dark to avoid being beaten, robbed or killed. Each day, as we drove out of the gate on the way to town, we honestly wondered if we would return with the car or have it taken from us at the point of a gun. It wasn't a matter of *if* the car would be stolen. It was a matter of *when*. Sure enough, the first two cars we drove in Uganda were robbed from us by armed thieves. No one slept soundly at night. Every little noise was a potential threat to personal safety and security. It might be just a rat scurrying along the rafters overhead, but it could just as well be a lone thief or a gang of thieves breaking in through a window or door. We heard the rat-a-tat of gunfire every night. Not most nights! Every night! We retired to bed each evening, honestly wondering if it would be our last night on earth.

And yet, there was this quiet confidence that came with the call of God. This was where we belonged! God loved Africa! No matter what she had been through, He wasn't finished with her yet!

During the fifty years of Uganda's colonial heritage, the church had prospered. The Anglicans and Catholics built schools, hospitals and churches across the country. In the 1940s, the Pentecostal Church began to make tremendous inroads into the nation. Classical Pentecostal Church movements, including the Pentecostal Assemblies of Canada, planted thousands of churches primarily in rural communities. There were no English-speaking churches. Worship was conducted in the local languages and dialects. Anglican and Catholic worship was expressed through conservative forms of liturgy that young people found boring and unappetising. A strong paternal dominance of leadership and family dominated the youth and held back their aspirations. Church politics and leadership wrangles spawned a plethora of independent Pentecostal split-off congregations. Church services would often last four or five hours. Several sermons were preached. Giving and an emphasis on prosperity led to abuse and manipulation. The youth were not attracted to that kind of church either.

It was into this political, social and spiritual atmosphere that God called us to plant an English-speaking church downtown in the heart of Kampala, Uganda's capital city. His words were very clear to me.

"Through this church, I will touch the city; I will touch the nation."

One of the clear words I heard from Jesus as we contemplated the responsibility, He placed upon us was, "Gary, in this place, you will shed blood, sweat and tears, but if you are faithful to me, I will be faithful to you!"

Nothing of great value from God comes without great cost. Our faith rests on the foundation of a sacrifice so great that it cost Christ the Messiah, the Son of God, the Lord of life, his precious blood. The sacrificial gift of himself, on a Roman cross, for the sin of the world, is at the core of the gospel. It is the perfect example of how those of us who follow him are to live our lives. We, too, are called to lay down our lives, our hopes, our ambitions and plans, and we are to do it for Him. We are called to take up our cross and live sacrificial lives in order to extend His Kingdom on the earth. That certainly is the story of so many pioneer missionary ventures which have taken place all around the world, just as it was through the missionaries who went, many years ago, into the heart of Africa, into Uganda. And so, it must be for this generation as God calls and commissions us to build His church.

Have we lost the wonder and awe of the celebration, \ eminence of the Saviour and Lord, the Christ? Celebrat of Christ is not a church service or form of liturgy. It is a way of living that is grounded in the character and culture of Christ and established on the Word of God. Have we substituted comfort and convenience for obedience and radical faith? Have we replaced His inestimable majesty and glory for a vain pursuit of the cheap and fading trinkets of life? Have the eternal truths been pushed aside by the passing fads of the day? Have we so run after prosperity, comfort and ease that we have forgotten what it means to care for others by the sacrificial, committed and consistent gift of ourselves and our resources to reach the lost, the lonely and the poor? Have we turned away in our rush for the accumulation of stuff that we no longer remember the call of the Lord of the Harvest to go and to preach the good news to all the world and to make disciples of the nations?

Have we begun to cower, in a state of fear, on the sidelines of life when confronted by the barrage of violent and pervasive opposition and ridicule from a hostile secular, Hindu or Islamic world? Have we forgotten what it means to speak up on behalf of God? Are we silent in the face of the obvious and blatant malicious lies, insinuations and accusations against the Church and our faith in God? Is there no more ground to be gained? Are there no more battles to be fought and won? Is the best behind us or before us? Where is the spirit of adventure and audacity that consumed the heroes of the biblical record and the valiant missionary efforts of the past? Are we content to concede and throw in the towel in the contest for the souls of the men, women and children who have not heard of Christ? Are we willing to surrender the nations to the domination of failing, man-made political institutions or to the sovereignty of Christ? Will we bow at the shrine of secularism and worship mammon?

Or will we bend the knee to Christ and offer ourselves in loving, selfless service for that which will not and can never fade or pass away? Others have gone before us and changed the course of human history by their going. This is not the time to pull back, hold back or wait while the forces of evil sweep through the nations that, in truth, belong to no one but the creator, Jesus.

David Livingstone, perhaps the most influential missionary in history, said, place no value on anything I have or may possess, except in relation to the kingdom of Christ. If anything will advance the interests of the kingdom, it shall be given away or kept, only as by giving or keeping it I shall promote the glory of Him to whom I owe all my hopes in time and eternity."

We need a new generation of faith-filled followers of Christ to get up and go!

~ Reflect and Discuss ~

As you reflect on your own story and engage in discussion with others, consider the following:

1. Willingness to live a life of courage and sacrificial service.

    • What are the areas of comfort and security in your life that you take for granted or may feel entitled to, but that you may need to surrender to Christ in order to enter into a deeper realization of mission, purpose and cause.

    • Think about the cost of discipleship. What does Jesus mean when he asks for those who follow him to carry their cross. (Matthew 16:24-25)

    • Reflect on the matter of courage as an essential tool in order to overcome the obstacle of a difficult challenge.

2. Resisting the pressure of secularization.

    • Discuss the pervasive influence of the secular worldview on your way of life.

    • Consider the pressure and demands secularization makes as you consider ministry and mission work among the poor of the world and in other nations.

    • Reflect on things you can practice as a means of lovingly countering the influence of secularism.

These questions are designed to provoke personal reflection and foster meaningful group discussion, encouraging participants to apply the lessons and insights from the chapter into their lives and communities.

During your discussion, encourage one another by sharing stories of God's faithfulness and provision in your lives. Take time to pray for each other, asking God for wisdom, strength, and boldness to live out His Kingdom purposes. By engaging in open dialogue and mutual encouragement, you can deepen your understanding of these concepts and grow together in faith.

~

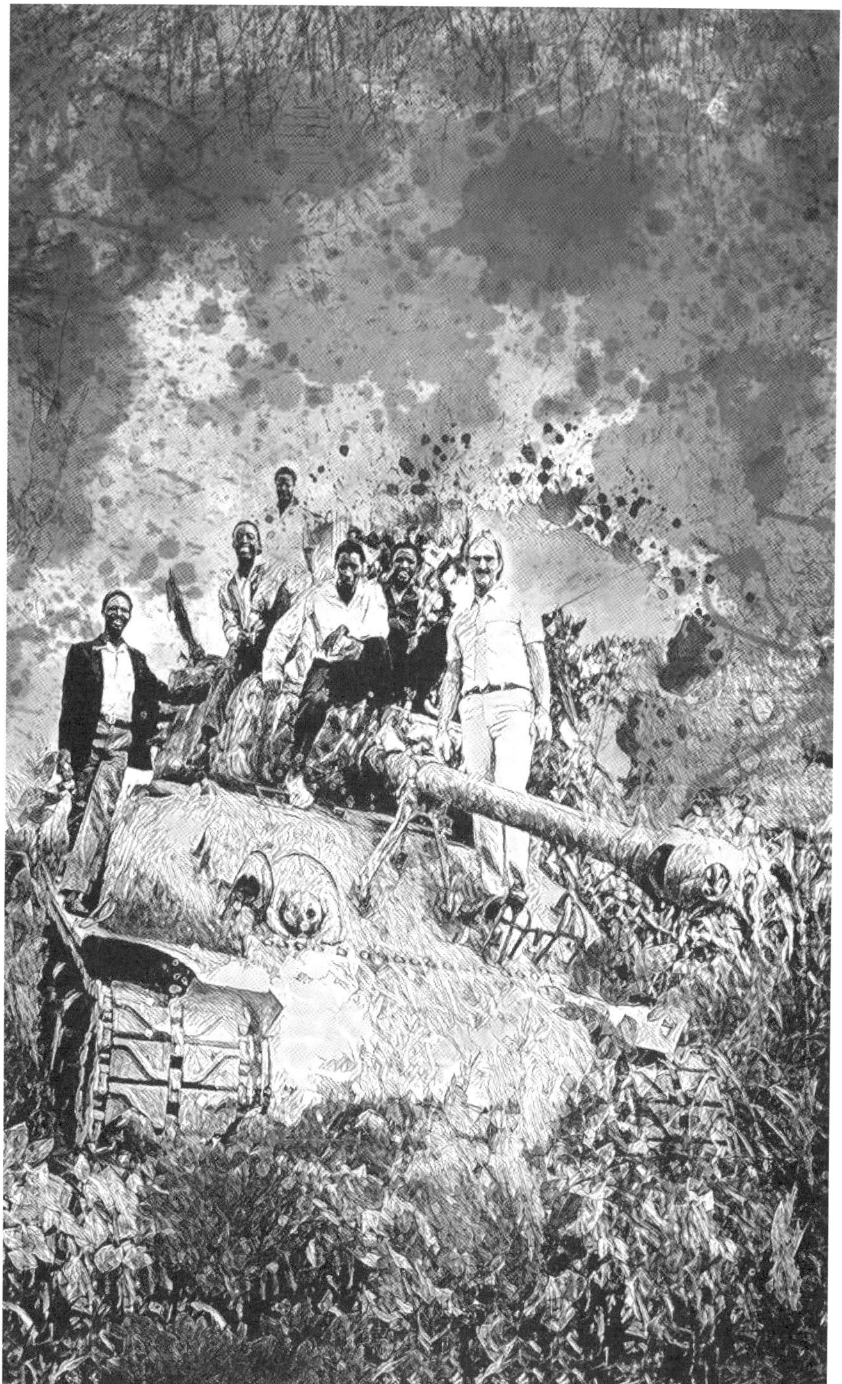

> "When Christ calls a man,
> he bids him come and die."
>
> *Dietrich Bonhoeffer*

05

~ Into the Heart of Darkness ~

"Arrival in war-torn Uganda."

We arrived in Uganda on November 5th, 1983. Marilyn, our three children, a new German Shepherd pup and I came by road across the Kenya-Uganda border at Malaba. No planes were flying into Uganda at the time. The airport into the country was closed to all air traffic. The International Airport at Entebbe sits on an outcrop of land on the edge of Lake Victoria. It became infamous when, on the 27th of June 1976, Idi Amin, the President of Uganda, welcomed a plane load of passengers highjacked by the Palestine Liberation Organization. It included ninety-four Israelis on board Air France Flight 139 from Tel Aviv to Paris.

In a daring rescue plot, one week later, the Israeli Air Force skimmed in low, over the lake, by-passing the radar and dropping down on the dishevelled airport, rescuing all the hostages except for three Israeli citizens who were killed in the raid and seventy-four-year-old Dora Block, who had fallen ill and had been taken into hospital in Kampala. She was later removed and killed, and her body dumped in a sugar cane field just outside the city. The only Israeli military casualty of the audacious raid was Yoni Netanyahu, the brother of Israel's Prime Minister Benjamin Netanyahu.

Even though Amin had fled the country by the time we arrived and was now living in exile in Saudi Arabia, Uganda was still in an ongoing civil war. It was too dangerous for airlines to land at Entebbe, so we would have to drive the 650 kilometres from Nairobi to Kampala in an old, white four-by-four, the vehicle we would use until our new Peugeot 504 station wagon arrived from France. The new car was being sent by Wing the Word, a ministry funded by the youth of the Pentecostal Assemblies of Canada. It supplied missionaries with the vehicles they would need on the field.

On the way to Kampala, we stopped to spend our first night in Uganda at Mbale. The Pentecostal Assemblies of Canada had its Ugandan headquarters in the quaint little border town. Paul and Gloria Willoughby, who had done so much to prepare for our arrival, welcomed us into their home. I remember lying in bed that first night and listening to the sounds of the African night. There seemed to be a million frogs in the little valley behind the house, all in raucous chorus, accompanied by the occasional barking dog or passing motorcycle. Excitement bubbled up in our hearts, and we were filled with wonder and anticipation at the adventure that lay ahead.

The next day, we continued to Kampala, leaving behind our new friends and the gentle slope of the volcanic Mount Elgon. The caldera of this giant volcano marks the border between Kenya and Uganda. I watched the mountain slowly fade into a misty haze in the rearview mirror, along with any prospects of a normal life.

As we drove along the battered highway, an eerie presence filled the atmosphere. There was a heaviness, an evident oppression that seemed to rest on the people. Most were barefoot and unkempt, as they trundled along the roadside. Something was not quite right about this place.

The route was interrupted by frequent military roadblocks. A soldier, often just a teenager, would saunter up to the car with a submachine gun slung loosely over his shoulder. The soldiers were friendly enough, but there was a palpable tension in the air. After the usual questions as to who we were and where we were going, we would be waved on.

We pushed on westward through the rice paddies at Kibimba. The early morning mist still hovered gently over the wetland patches as flocks of birds glided overhead. Smoke emerged from huts and houses beyond the thicket. The smell of burning charcoal and roasting corn was carried on the morning air and swept in through the open windows of the car. The kids were asleep in the back, and Marilyn sat in the passenger seat beside me. She looked out and surveyed the land, searching with hope for something to fall in love with – a smell, a colour, a certain warmth. All she found was uncertainty.

When we pulled into the town of Jinja, 80 kilometers from Kampala, I woke the children because I wanted them to see where the Nile begins its long journey from Lake Victoria to the Mediterranean. In 1952, the British colonial government built a hydroelectric dam at Owen Falls. The bridge spanning the river here is the only route into Kampala from the eastern side of the country. Guarding the bridge, on both sides, were heavily armed soldiers, men and boys carrying Kalashnikovs and bazookas. They wore rounds of brass-coloured ammunition wrapped around their bodies like jewellery. They were uneasy and stern because of the dam's great importance. Not only was it the country's only route into Kampala from the eastern side of the country, but the dam provided Uganda with its only source of electricity.

We passed slowly over the bridge. The lake lay to our left. Directly beneath us, the massive wall held back and channelled the flow of the river, forcing it to spin the huge turbines that generated the country's power grid. To our right, the water spat out ferociously, shooting out from the wall in massive arches and marking the start of the Nile River below. In the mirror, I saw the children staring with open-mouthed wonder, clamouring over each other to get the best view of the powerful scene.

With access to cheap electricity, Jinja had been Uganda's industrial capital. After the expulsion of the Indian community by President Idi Amin in 1972, most of the Asian-run factories were abandoned or given to Amin's political allies, who neglected and mismanaged them. The town had fallen into a state of decay that was typical throughout Uganda. There was a factory in the town that still produced mattresses. Needing some, we stopped, bought a couple and strapped them onto the roof before going on. Kampala was now less than two hours ahead of us.

Before long, we entered the majestic Mabira Forest. The car was enveloped by a tunnel of trees of all sizes, many covered with low-hanging, creeping vines. The growth of thick jungle was so dense and wild that you couldn't see much beyond the edge of the road. The air was heavy with the scent of foliage, bark, and moisture unique to tropical forests. Occasional bursts of bright blue sky punctured the tangle of branches and leaves in the canopy above. There was an awesome natural beauty, a calm tranquillity, as monkeys frolicked in the trees and giant hornbills fluttered between the tree limbs above.

But danger lurked in the forest. Mabira was home to rogue bandits known for waylaying passing vehicles, robbing the occupants, and, at very best, leaving them stranded on the side of the road. The military checkpoints were now a reassuring sight as we continued through the thick canopy of trees. We all seemed to breathe a sigh of relief when we finally broke through the western edge of the forest. The blazing equatorial sun was nearing its mid-day point in a brilliant blue sky.

Next, we passed through the sugarcane and tea fields of Lugazi, the rolling hills manicured and a deep, lush green. Just ahead was our destination and new home.

As we drove into Kampala, the state of disrepair was blatantly evident. The city looked forlorn. I had always thought that my upbringing as a child of missionaries had prepared me for any hardship I would encounter, but what I was looking at was more than just neglect. It was a total breakdown.

At Lugogo, the first suburb, we passed an old cricket oval. The road, pockmarked with ragged potholes, widened out into a divided boulevard with two lanes in each direction, but there were almost no cars or bicycles in sight. Tired industrial buildings lined the highway opposite a rundown and abandoned cemetery. The headstones and crosses were faded and crumbling, some lying at perverse angles. Small trees and shrubs had taken root between the rows of graves. Telephone poles, with broken lines hanging down, leaned precariously as if ready to collapse. Marabou storks stood to attention on some of them. The few streams we crossed were clogged with refuse and sewage that poured down from the shacks and shanty towns crammed onto the sides of the city's hills. Even in the roughest areas of Kitwe and Lusaka in Zambia, where we had lived for four years, I had never seen such deplorable conditions.

In silent amazement, we followed the directions we had been given to the house we would be living in. I thought that we must be passing through a slum or makeshift settlement and that we would soon arrive at a neat neighbourhood laid out with some kind of plan and order. Instead, we travelled around corners, over hills, and through swamps, encountering mile after mile of shacks and run-down houses.

At one spot, we crossed a railway line, now obviously unused. Traders had set up wooden stalls down the abandoned tracks and were displaying a few meagre wares alongside the cabbages and tomatoes. Empty market stalls and wild overgrowth were reclaiming what I later learned had been one of Africa's most beautiful cities. It had once been called the Garden City of East Africa in a country that Winston Churchill, who had visited in 1908, had called the Pearl of Africa. Now, the once magnificent city in the heart of Africa was in shambles.

I looked over at Marilyn. Her face reflected the same dazed shock.

"How are we going to survive this?" she asked herself silently. "How can we live here? We're surrounded by death and decay. How can our children grow and learn and develop in this mess? What are we doing here?"

She breathed in heavily, maintaining her composure.

The house the mission had rented for us was in Kansanga, a residential neighbourhood eight kilometres south of the city centre. As we got closer, we noticed that many of the houses were enclosed with high walls, embedded with shards of glass and broken bottles to deter intruders from getting onto the property. Pulling up to the house, we saw that a rusty chain link fence and a patchy evergreen hedge defended it. It was built on the side of a gently sloping hill. At the top of the property, next to a broken gate, there was a big mango tree, its branches heavy with ripening fruit. Next door was a dilapidated mud house with a rusty corrugated roof.

I could feel Marilyn tense.

I drove the car down the short, steep driveway, parking in front of the garage. There was a large open space in front of the house that may have been a vegetable garden in the past but was now full of weeds, tall grass and overgrown shrubs. The children, restless from the long trip and eager to explore their new home, threw open the car doors, only to have the little pup hop from the car and disappear into the overgrown yard. The kids ran after the dog, overcome with excitement. Marilyn and I watched from the car, able to make out only the top of Timothy's head as he ran wildly through the long grass. Rachel, James and the dog simply vanished into the bush. A few seconds later, they re-emerged, delighted at the prospects of the adventure and discovery that lay, literally, on their doorstep.

Marilyn stepped out of the car, but I paused a moment, letting the dust settle around the car. I turned the engine off and sat quietly. Taking a handkerchief from my pocket, I wiped the sweat from my forehead, got out of the car and joined the family, trying to make sense of the surroundings.

A dusty haze hung low over the city, settling like a fog in the low-lying valleys. Billowing cumulus clouds drifted across the scene, and then, as if on cue, just as had happened on my prior trip to Kampala, a rainbow appeared. It spread from one side of the city to the other. I exhaled deeply, releasing any tension from the journey. Staring at the vibrant colours, I felt God's promise of blessing fill me with fresh hope. The trauma of the nation's past was coming to an end. Ahead lay the opportunity for something new. Healing for the city and the nation seemed to spread out before us and was the reason why we were here. Despite the devastation and the brokenness, there was a good future before us. I felt a promise, an assurance, and a rest from God settle over me. I knew there was hope for the city, the nation, and the continent of Africa.

We had arrived home!

After unpacking our few belongings, I took a walk to the nearby market to buy something for lunch. I strolled through the gate, feeling the exhilaration of God's bright promise, that fresh hope growing inside me with each step.

Marilyn, on the other hand, was having a completely difference experience.

She stood in the empty house, all alone, the kids and dog playing in the jungle-like yard outside. There was no furniture, no table, and no chairs. The mattresses laid out on the floor were to be our beds. Looking around at the simple house with our few things scattered around in boxes, anxiety and despair bubbled up into tears and ran down her cheeks. Her tears grew into a steady sob. She dropped down to the floor on her knees, and with a flood of despair, she wept.

Trying to pull herself together, she wiped aside the tears, got up and went into the kitchen to wash her face at the sink. She turned the tap on, and a filthy brown liquid spat from the faucet. A sick feeling filled her stomach. Even her worst expectations had not prepared her for this.

"Lord," she said out loud, "when I told you I would go anywhere you asked me to, I didn't think you were going to send me to hell."

Her heart was racing.

"Why have you condemned us to this? Why here, God? Why me?"

And then Jesus nudged gently at her spirit, reminding her of a small gift that a friend had pushed into her hand at the airport in Toronto on the day we left Canada. She closed the sputtering tap and went back into the living room. Finding her suitcase, she pulled out the neatly wrapped gift and sat on the floor to open it. Setting the wrapping aside, she read the short inscription carved into the surface of a small wooden plaque.

"The will of God will never lead you where the grace of God cannot keep you."

The simple words pierced her heart. It was the tender but appropriate message from the heart of God to His precious daughter as she faced a new, uncertain, and daunting future.

Steadying her breathing, Marilyn spoke firmly to herself.

"Get up. Pick yourself up and open your eyes to the opportunity that lies in front of you."

Looking down, she noticed the geometric patterns of the wooden flooring. She smiled. It was small, but it was something. The house was exactly what we had prayed for when we sat at our kitchen table in Canada just a few weeks earlier.

She lifted her head and made for the hallway. There were three bedrooms on one side of the house, which were serviced by two bathrooms. The central living area was connected to an office space at the opposite end of the house, and the floors were covered in attractive strips of parquet. It would require considerable effort to make the place livable, but Marilyn took heart, aware that God had invited her into something bigger than herself. He would not abandon her now.

Still shaky from what she was going through, afraid and somewhat overwhelmed, she began to focus on one small task at a time.

While I was at the market buying some food, she began arranging a place for us to eat. She created a makeshift table on the front porch, propping a piece of plywood on the window ledge and the other on the trunks we had used to carry our clothes and groceries. She dressed up the table as best she could, with plates and napkins and silverware. She took a step back to admire her work. It would do just fine she thought, and kept working on other little tasks while she waited for me to get back with lunch.

I wasn't gone very long, but my shopping trip wasn't hugely successful. Even the most basic supplies were unavailable. Soap, milk, sugar, and toilet paper, anything manufactured had to be brought in from Kenya. As far as food went, all I could come up with was a cabbage, some onions, and a few tomatoes. Marilyn and I took a deep breath and smiled at each other with all the optimism we could muster.

We boiled some water on a Coleman camper stove we had brought with us, adding the cabbage, tomatoes, onions, and the little bit of salt we had also brought from Kenya. It wasn't going to earn a Michelin star, but it was food. We each had a full bowl of the simple soup. I looked around at my young family, trying to keep a brave face. Here we were, in war-torn Uganda, with three young children, sitting on the porch of an empty house surrounded by debris, decay, and overgrowth, and with little more than the clothes on our backs. We had our work cut out for us.

That night, Marilyn and I lay down on the mattress on the floor and listened to the sound of the Kampala night. A cacophony of frogs and crickets pierced the blackness, their song interrupted by the occasional sound of gunfire. A pack of dogs howled, and somewhere in the distance, I was sure I heard someone scream. I leaned over to kiss Marilyn. She was wide awake, staring vacantly into the darkness.

"Well, Sweetie," I said, "I wonder if we're going to live to see the light of day."

I was only half joking, but strange as it may seem, those words became a nightly ritual for us, an intentional recognition and constant reminder of how much we were completely dependent on the grace and protection of God, and how clueless, hapless, helpless and incapable we were of forging a future in this place without Him. Jesus' words to his disciples in John 15 were taking on a whole new life for us.

"I am the vine; you are the branches. If you remain in me and

I in you, you will bear much fruit; apart from me, you can do nothing."

John 15:5 (NIV)

If we were going to make it through this, He would need to be our rock, our source of security and success. He had called us here. Nothing else could have persuaded us to do what we were doing. Every instinct cried out for us to take stock of reality, open our eyes and understand that this was a fool's errand. Had we believed that it was up to us, we would have baulked, cut our losses and headed back to Canada.

But that's the thing about the call of God. It's not hard to imagine that He would call us to something we are fully equipped for, something within ourselves we are capable of overcoming. But faith in Jesus, obedience to His will no matter what the circumstances are, is something we needed to learn by being thrust into what seemed an impossible situation. We had to come to a place of confidence that He, as the Lord of the Harvest, would lead us out of our comfort zone, beyond the boundaries of our capabilities, and into situations where, without Him, we would fail and then prove Himself faithful and good. As Paul, who faced imprisonment, persecution, and ultimately death for the Gospel, writes to his dearly loved spiritual son, Timothy,

> *"We can only keep on going, after all, by the power of God, who first saved us and then called us to this holy work. We had nothing to do with it. It was all his idea, a gift prepared for us in Jesus long before we knew anything about it. But we know it now. Since the appearance of our Savior, nothing could be plainer: death defeated, life vindicated in a steady blaze of light, all through the work of Jesus."*
>
> *2 Timothy 1:9-10 MSG*

To venture into a Kingdom calling is to join Jesus in His work and to rely on the strength of His Spirit inside of us. As we follow him with loving surrender, we will see our sovereign Lord do remarkable and inexplicable things which we get to participate in and play a part in bringing him glory. And, in this process, we will find our faith and character develop and mature in ways we could never have imagined.

As we stared up into the darkness of the African night, I felt my spirit fill up with an irrational happiness that was entirely out of place. A voice I knew so well and loved so deeply whispered into the ears of my heart.

"If you are faithful to Me, I will be faithful to you."

I sighed deeply, fully aware that the road ahead would be anything but easy or smooth.

Marilyn lay in silence for a few moments, letting my strangely morbid comment from a little earlier hang in the air.

"I don't know that I can do this," she said flatly.

I nodded, staring into the dark. "I know. Me neither."

And then, we drifted off to sleep for our first night in Kampala.

~ Reflect and Discuss ~

As you reflect on your own journey and engage in conversation with others, consider the following:

1. Experiencing Moments of Despair:

   Recall a time in your life when you felt overwhelmed by despair or hopelessness, similar to Marilyn's experience on her first day in Kampala. Reflect on the emotions and challenges you faced during that time.

   Share how you handled that situation. Did you turn to God for strength and guidance, or did you rely solely on your own abilities and resources?

   Consider how God may have been present for you in that moment, offering comfort, reassurance, or unexpected help. Reflect on any signs of His presence or interventions that provided hope amidst despair.

2. Temptation to Rely on Our Own Strength:

   Reflect on instances where you've been tempted to rely on your own strength rather than trusting in God's provision and guidance. Explore the reasons behind this temptation, such as pride, fear, or a desire for control.

   Discuss the challenges inherent in trusting in Jesus' strength instead of our own. Consider how our limited perspective and human frailty often lead us to doubt God's ability to intervene and provide.

3. Stepping Outside of Comfort Zones:

Reflect on the idea that God can use our weaknesses as instruments in His hands. Share personal experiences where you've seen God work through your weaknesses or limitations.

Explore practical ways you can cultivate trust in God's strength and guidance, such as through prayer, seeking wise counsel, and taking intentional risks.

During your discussion, offer encouragement and support to one another as you navigate the challenges of trusting in God's strength and stepping outside of your comfort zones. Share insights, struggles, and victories, and commit to praying for each other's faith and obedience to God's leading. By leaning on God's strength and wisdom, you can find courage to embrace new opportunities and fulfill His calling on your life.

~

105

"The church is Christ's body, in which he speaks and acts, by which he fills everything with his presence."

The Apostle Paul - Ephesians 1:23 MSG

06

~ The Crystal Suite ~

"Exploring new beginnings."

We celebrated my thirty-first birthday just a few days after arriving in Kampala. I carried a raw, youthful optimism and a willingness to work hard. So did Marilyn, but she still wrestled with our new reality. Her deep connection to Jesus and trust in His plan kept her going in those early days. Her unswerving faith would continue to be vital to our perseverance for decades. What lay ahead would be far more difficult than we could ever have imagined, and our trust in God's goodness and love would become our lifeline in the following years.

We needed to figure out what we had to do next and come up with a plan. At the top of the list was where to have church, and when to start. We also needed to learn how to survive and thrive in Uganda. We started with the things we knew were true.

We knew that Jesus had brought us to Uganda as a family. We were in this together! God had plans for all of us. This shared awareness of calling and purpose was important. It wasn't just about what I had to do. We were all participating in this venture. We knew we were to live in Kampala, connected to the day-to-day lives of the Ugandan people we were here to serve. We also needed to understand the Ugandan culture we were living in.

We enrolled Timothy and Rachel at the Lincoln International School. It was a small school, with the entire student body no more than two dozen children and a couple of teachers. Each morning, we would drive them to the school, which was held in an old colonial house on Buganda Road close to the city centre.

With the children settled into school, we began to establish order in our day-to-day living. We focused on making the house a home. It was important that it be a place of rest in the tumultuous city. Organising, decorating, and adding furnishing was the first step. On my earlier exploratory trip to Uganda, I realised that it would make a big difference if we brought along things that would make home as comfortable and convenient as possible. So, just a month after we arrived, the 20-foot shipping container that we had packed and prepared in Canada arrived.

It had almost everything I thought we might need, graciously provided for us by the kindness of those who supported us in those early years. There were bunk beds for the boys and two waterbeds, one for Rachel and another for us. There was kitchenware, furniture, office supplies, bedding, a washing machine, a dryer, a fridge, a stove, garden hoses, a lawnmower, tools, jerry cans, three bikes for the kids, a motorbike for me, and four years of clothes in different sizes for the kids to grow into. There was a sound system, a guitar, and an electronic keyboard for worship at church.

And then there was the food. There was macaroni and cheese, dried spices, powdered milk, every kind of canned soup you could imagine, laundry detergent, toothpaste, deodorant, soap, and, most important of all, two dozen glass bottles of Heinz Ketchup. Marilyn has always loved ketchup, the real kind made by the H.J. Heinz Company.

The kids were beside themselves with excitement, and Marilyn was encouraged to have these things available. She knew that material possessions were meaningless. But something as insignificant as ketchup or having a nice plate to serve meals on can help you feel at home in a new place.

We had spent four years in Zambia and understood that we could provide some simple things to make life in difficult circumstances better. If I wanted Marilyn to stand beside me in a very challenging assignment, then the least I could do was provide some basic items to show my love and appreciation for her willingness. It encouraged her to realise that she had items that would make life easier in Uganda. We felt our Father God's blessing and generosity towards us in this.

Those pioneer missionaries in the early days of missions went to places where they could carry only the basic necessities. And there they lived alongside the people they were reaching. That close association with the community opened the doors for the message of the gospel to be declared. The missionary displayed and modelled the difference the Gospel makes in one's life. Christianity works! It is effective in the life of the believer, even in time of suffering and difficulty. This proved to be attractive to the pagan mind. As people believed the message and surrendered to the Lordship of Christ, the community was transformed.

Uganda is a perfect example of this. The missionary community's consistency and commitment to go through the challenges the community faced, be it war, opposition, disease or other things, demonstrated their love and loyalty to God and to the community being reached. Missionaries frequently died of disease or the brutality of conflict in the service they were providing to the community. They suffered significant loss in demonstrating their commitment to Christ, their unswerving dedication to the establishment of the Church and their total immersion into the community they were reaching.

And this is what we did when we moved to Kampala in the early 1980s. We moved into a community that was dangerous and living with ongoing, brutal conflict. We faced, daily, the potential of imminent death alongside those we were reaching. We fully identified with them in their suffering. At the same time, we demonstrated a life that was to be desired, not by the possession or use of material things but by the possession of a balanced life and the potential that all could enjoy the same full life in a society governed by peace, obedience and order under Christ.

Let me assure you that we did not go to Uganda to just survive in a state of disorder. We were not there to submit to a culture that was evil and oppressive. We went to see the transformation of individuals and community through the power and demonstration of the gospel of Christ and the establishment of a biblical order and the culture of Christ. A washing machine and clothes dryer were just conveniences we didn't have to live without to show our love and loyalty to Christ and to the people we were reaching. We wanted the lives we lived and the Christian ethos we fully embraced to demonstrate the transformation they, too, could experience. What has transpired over the forty years we have served in Uganda has proven this to be true.

As our new home started to come together, I wanted to grasp an understanding of the city, the culture, the people and the way things worked. Kampala was a melting pot of local cultures, languages, tribes, and people, and, despite the ongoing civil war, the city served as the country's economic and political hub. Half to three-quarters of a million people lived in the city, and several million more in the surrounding areas. The infrastructure was a tangle of broken asphalt, makeshift dirt roads, and disintegrating highways. The electrical, water, and telephone supplies were erratic or unavailable in most of the city. It took us 18 months to have a telephone installed at the house. We would have to stand, sometimes for several hours, in what was considered a line at the post office to make a call. There were no supermarkets. Shopping for food was all done in the local markets, in a tangle of colourful vegetables, fruit and meat stalls. Figuring out our way around would take time and patience.

We had never planted a church before, and I had no idea how, where, or when to start. Finding a first footing from which to launch would be a challenge. It was easy to feel discouraged. I began to look for the positive around us, encouraging things that would build on the promise we carried inside. I found it in the people themselves. As we met and befriended those around us, we realised that, despite the countless challenges Ugandans faced, the life within the people was irrepressible. In so many, we sensed a spark just waiting to burst into full flame. I noticed it in the children who ran alongside our kids and playfully sang to them, "How are you, Muzungu? How are you, Muzungu?" (Muzungu means White Person.) I noticed it in the brief morning exchanges when greeting those we met. The joy, warmth and hospitality were infectious and encouraging.

I remember how, after a particularly nerve-wracking night of gunfire and explosions, those I encountered would smile and respond to my greeting with, "Well survived!" At first, I was perplexed by this interaction. It seemed a bit of a joke with Kampala's residents, which I found somewhat morbid. But as we became more involved in the lives of those around us, those who had lived in the presence of constant danger, and a high potential of immanent and violent death, I began to appreciate the unique humour and quiet determination that enabled them to endure their unbelievable struggles with quiet dignity and grace. I realised that I could only understand them if I was willing to see things from their perspective, to try to understand their history and unique story as a people and to be willing and cheerful in going through it with them.

The strange phrase, "Well survived," became a typical greeting during those bad years, and our new friends were teaching us to collectively laugh in the face of danger rather than cower in the silence of defeat. Contrary to my first impressions, people had not given up hope. I began to look at the country with a fresh perspective and noticed that these sparks of life and joy were everywhere.

Uganda was like a fertile but neglected garden. Kampala, despite the slums and filth, was also a swathe of overgrown and wild vegetation. I noticed trees growing defiantly from beds of boulders and hard rock. Strangler figs wormed their way out of the cracks in the pavement or up the sides of a neglected wall. The relentless equatorial sun and the abundant rain that falls throughout the year sparked the wonder of creation. I am still amazed at the speed at which a tiny, discarded seed grows into a tree that can overwhelm and dominate an entire garden.

In a way, this was a parable for the vibrant life I saw in the Ugandan people themselves. They had every reason to despair, every excuse to give up on hope and joy and kindness. The soil they were living in was rocky and rough, a city wrecked by war. And yet God planted in the people a genuine joy for life, an authentic hope that things could be better. I latched onto this glimmer of light and sensed something to build on here, something God wanted to tend and prune.

At the same time, I set out to tame the jungle that was my backyard. I wanted to harness the power of the fertile soil and grow something beautiful right here on our doorstep, something we could enjoy, something that shouted out that things could be better. On a trip to Nairobi, I bought some books on gardening and seeds to get started. I analysed the yard's layout and decided that, because of the slope on the property, the best thing to do was to create three flat terraces, each separated by flowerbeds and pathways that led from one level to the next. I hired a bulldozer parked on the road near our gate and had the driver reshape the earth in front of the house.

On the upper level, near the gate, there was a fig tree from which I hung a swing for the kids to play on. Also, at the top of the property, there was a mango tree, which the kids loved to climb and bore fruit twice a year in June and December. Rachel especially loved that tree. One day, she took a book and a blanket and fell asleep in it. We heard her crying when she fell from the branches and landed with a heavy thud. Luckily, she escaped with only a few minor bruises.

I planted bougainvillea shrubs on the barrier that separated the top and middle terraces and created a walkway that connected the two levels. The middle terrace was flattened out to make a lawn about the size of a tennis court. Here, the kids played football and raced each other around the yard. Lining the lawn, I planted a hedge and trimmed it to waist height. It separated the open grassy terrace from the third level below, where I planted a garden and grew cabbages, carrots, peppers, beans, cauliflowers and other vegetables.

We enjoyed the beauty of the tropical flowers and ate the fruit and vegetables produced by the soil and sun. We were amazed at how quickly and how big everything grew. The cabbages were the size of steering wheels. As I watched the garden grow, I began to feel an emerging connection to the place God had brought us to live in.

I thought of how the work God had called us to in Uganda could be understood through the work of a gardener. Kampala was neglected, chaotic, and wild. The people were desperate for change, for opportunity, for hope, and for new chances. They were tired of the oppression, fear and death they had faced daily. Instead of suffering unspeakable hardship, constant harassment, a chronic lack of necessities and ongoing uncertainty, they wanted what we all want, to live long, rich, happy, full lives. And I knew that was what God wanted for them, too.

He had called us here to plant a seed, knowing that something beautiful and fruitful would grow. We had to plant it, nurture it, and prune it like the roses I'd planted in the garden. The social landscape was like the fertile soil of Kampala's rolling hills. It was ready to yield an abundance that would amaze us all. After all, we were joining God in His work, which he had set up long before we arrived. Just as He had done in the life of Joseph, God was in the process of taking what was intended for evil and bringing about what He meant for good. (See Genesis 50:20)

I am also reminded of what the Apostle Paul says about himself and another early church leader, Apollos when he writes,

> *"I planted the seed, Apollos watered it, but God has been making it grow. So neither the one who plants nor the one who waters is*

anything, but only God, who makes things grow. The one who plants and the one who waters have one purpose, and they will each be rewarded according to their own labour. For we are co-workers in God's service; you are God's field, God's building."

1 Corinthians 3:6-9 (NIV)

We were joining a work of God already in progress, which will continue long after we are gone. Although difficult to see then, we trusted that, like our garden, the bountiful harvest would one day leave us stunned and in awe of a God of growth, healing, and renewal.

I'm not sure, I could have communicated all that back then. I was a young man, just thirty-one years old, with an unwavering faith in God's calling and a willingness to do whatever it took to see the task through. What kept me going was not just a beautiful image of hope in God but a relentless stubbornness and unconquerable conviction that we were where God wanted us and at precisely the right time. Looking back on those early days reminds me that if God could use us, He surely can use anyone.

As imperfect as my perspective was, it was useful in accepting neither defeat nor fearing failure. Some mornings, I would wake up, glad to be alive and thinking that this was crazy. What are we doing here? But I continued, blundering on through those early months as God continued to impress three words on my heart: "Kampala. Downtown. English."

Those words and the conviction that we were doing the right thing at the right time carried me forward despite the craziness or the unpredictable hurdle I would face that day. We were not called here for some vague, undefined purpose, some general goodness. Our calling was specific and precise. Plant an English-speaking church downtown in the heart of the city! It was this identifiable task that gave us a direction to start moving in.

We started by simply talking to anybody willing to give us the time of day. Generally, our Ugandan hosts were friendly and eager to learn more about us. Most people were baffled that we had traded Canada for Kampala, and this curiosity provided an entry point for us to start building relationships. At times, I was bewildered at the contradictions that these relationships exposed about Ugandan society. The Ugandans we met were warm, loving, and generous people, and yet their daily lives were ruled by chaos. There was something mysterious and deeply beautiful about this confrontation, and I don't know if I have ever fully understood it. I am just so thankful for the friendships we made in those pioneer days.

On Sundays, we visited different church communities and familiarised ourselves with the culture of Ugandan churches. Often, we were invited to introduce ourselves and were always warmly received. We let the local pastors know that we were not there to draw away their people. We urged church members to remain faithful to their pastors and not join us in the church plant. Soon, we began to understand the character of the local evangelical and Pentecostal fellowship.

Invariably, churches fell into one of two categories. The traditional Anglican system had heavily influenced some churches. In these services, there was little celebration of the faith. The services were stiff, conservative, and ritualistic. The young people, who made up such a large percentage of Uganda's population, were bored with this kind of church.

Other churches took the complete opposite approach. They were disorganised and unpredictable affairs. They usually started considerably late and lasted an insufferable duration, sometimes five or six hours. We would attend these wild, out-of-control services, and just as we thought the thing was ending, we would realise the pastor had not even begun his sermon. Many of these churches did not relay any consistent redemptive message; instead, they served as theatres for charismatic pastors to prance across the stage and work the crowd into a frenzy.

As we continued to attend different churches, Jesus whispered a word into my heart that would become pivotal for the community we would start.

"Gary, I want the church to be alive but not wild, conservative but not dead."

Jesus, the Lord of the Harvest, was giving us a prescription for the style of church service and liturgy the youth of the city would be drawn to. We have done our very best to do exactly this. Church is to be a place that is exciting to be at, but also a place of security and stability.

Another key thing was that many of the churches in Kampala, at that time, were conducted in Luganda, the language of the Baganda, the largest tribal group in Uganda. Other churches were conducted in one of the other languages spoken in the country. English had become the official and commercial language of the nation and was widely spoken by many in Kampala, particularly the young people. God was calling us to plant an English-speaking church to reach, train and empower the youth and to demonstrate unity for all Ugandans.

I also became convinced in my heart as to the message we were to declare and announce. God deeply loved Uganda and had a specific and magnificent plan for the nation. He is the God of the nations. That's who He is! The nations belong to Him. He raises up and tears down. The world is not just spinning in space, out of control. He has a plan and a purpose, not just for individuals but for the nations.

I love what Paul says to the church he planted in Ephesus, the second-largest city in the world at the time,

> *"God raised him (Jesus) from death and set him on a throne in deep heaven, in charge of running the universe, everything from galaxies to governments, no name and no power exempt from his rule. And not just for the time being but forever. He is in charge of it all, has the final word on everything. At the centre of all this, Christ rules the church. The church, you see, is not peripheral to the world; the world is peripheral to the church. The church is Christ's body, in which he speaks and acts, by which he fills everything with his presence."*
>
> *Ephesians 1:20-23 MSG*

Jesus is seated on His majestic heavenly throne, in charge of everything. The Church is central and critical to God's plans and objectives for the health of the nations. The Church is to model how life should be lived. The Church is to establish, as a culture for the community, the biblical values that undergird society. The Church is the only hope for the desperate healing needed in society. The Church is Christ's body, present and active in shaping a healthy and whole culture based on biblical truth and the righteous character of Jesus. We were to announce this message of redemption, restoration, transformation and hope to a broken city and nation, something not overtly presented by the churches we attended.

I must say here that my intention is not to be critical of the Ugandan church at that time. It was wonderful to see how the church had survived, even thrived through the dark, difficult years of war, civil conflict, and political chaos. The Church of Uganda, which is the equivalent of the Anglican Church, had remained true to God and to the message of the gospel. Faithful church leaders such as Anglican Archbishop Janani Luwum and Gideon Okakale, the General Superintendent of the Pentecostal Assemblies of God had both been murdered at the command of Idi Amin for their consistent faith and practice. The church was emerging from decades of incredible difficulty. It was strong, but God wanted the Church to step into something fresh, something new, and I'm convinced Jesus brought us to Uganda at just the right time.

We were the ones He chose to do this work as a continuation of the ongoing plan and purpose of God for the nation. Without the faithfulness of God's people who came before us, our work would not have been possible. We were standing on the shoulders of giants, the faithful men and women of God from Uganda's past and present who had planted and built the Church in Uganda. God wanted to launch the church forward with something new and fresh.

As we moved ahead in obedience, God began to sharpen the edges of our calling. He birthed within me a clear vision of why we were here and what He wanted to accomplish in the nation. We started to become aware that we were to focus our attention and ministry on the huge population of young people in Kampala, to lay out a moral foundation for them, to nurture and empower them. I sensed that God wanted to raise a generation of young Christian leaders through whom he could rebuild Ugandan society and culture. The church would be English speaking, alive in the Holy Spirit, passionate about Jesus, fully committed to the Father and attractive to young people who would become disciples of Jesus, carrying the culture and character of Christ into the core of Uganda's communal life.

God emphatically tells us in Jeremiah 29:11-14a,

> *"For I know the plans I have for you," declares the LORD, "plans to prosper you and not to harm you, plans to give you hope and a future. Then you will call on me and come and pray to me, and I will listen to you. You will seek me and find me when you seek me with all your heart. I will be found by you," declares the LORD,*

"and will bring you back from captivity."

Jeremiah 29:11-14a (NIV)

This passage, prophesied over Israel while captive in Babylon, held within it a promise for the people of Uganda.

With God shaping and moulding this vision in our hearts, we searched for an appropriate facility to hold church meetings. We focused on finding something in the downtown city core, feeling very strongly that this was an essential part of what God wanted for us. Finding a suitable place was a real challenge. Kampala was in tatters. The city centre bore the brunt of the civil conflict and war that the country had endured since its independence in 1962. Our search took us into buildings that had been bombed out, shards of broken glass and fallen masonry still lying about from the impact of the conflict and fighting. Many had no electricity or running water, the stench of open sewerage assaulting our nostrils as soon as we walked through the door.

I remember walking with Marilyn into what is now an upscale restaurant in the Kampala Sheraton Hotel. What we saw was a damp and disgusting dungeon. The room was large enough to seat 300 people, but it was in complete shambles and unusable. Broken chairs were strewn haphazardly about, and many of the windows had been smashed in. The carpet had been ripped from the floor, leaving only some stubborn patches of faded rug and adhesive. Years of water damage left the walls and ceilings stained, a testament to the heavy torrents that would stream freely into the room whenever there was a downpour. Electrical fixtures dangled dangerously from the roof, and the sockets on the wall had long since disappeared. A grand piano lay sprawled upside down in the centre of the room, its legs hacked off and strewn nearby. The strings of the instrument were gone, probably being used for some menial task, to hang clothes on or mend a broken fence. The place felt entirely abandoned except for the piles of fresh and stale human excrement that littered the floor and was smeared in filthy brown streaks on the walls, the stench of it lingering in the damp room. I tried to hold back the reflex in my stomach that made me want to vomit. This hall was a potent symbol of the neglect that defined Kampala and had reduced it to a theatre of waste.

We walked out of the building, back into the sunshine and fresh air, needing a few minutes to overcome our shock. Despite this, I was reminded that behind every obstacle is a greater opportunity waiting to be discovered. I recalled the day when I had first visited Kampala to scout out the land. God had stretched a beautiful rainbow across the city. Beneath the storm clouds lay a promise for the city, and regardless of what I had seen with my eyes, I felt that same hope rise again. The treasure, the pot of gold, was here, buried beneath the rubble of the ruins, hidden deep within the hearts and minds of the people. Our job was to unearth it and release it to reach its full potential.

Clinging to this dream, we kept on searching, and five months after we had arrived in Kampala, God provided a place to start what was to become Kampala Pentecostal Church. It was a function room in the Grand Imperial Hotel called the Crystal Suite. The place was neither grand, imperial, crystal, nor sweet. The old Colonial-style hotel sat on the edge of a traffic circle at the junction of Nile Avenue and Speke Road in the city's centre. It was the best option only because everything else was worse.

A tattered red carpet, well worn by the decades of stilettos and shoes, covered a wooden floor. The walls, which hadn't seen a new coat of paint in a long while, were smudged with dirt and dust. The electrical sockets had been stolen sometime in the past, and the lighting was dull and patchy. The toilets stank and, with the lack of consistent water supply, were choked with human refuse and vomit from the Saturday evening discos and parties held in the room. There were no chairs or tables, just an empty, run-down space that could seat about 200 people. The best access to the room was through a decrepit and smelly drinking establishment called "The Copper Bar."

The hotel proprietor was happy to rent us the room on Sunday mornings, and we committed to fixing the place up to make it more presentable. Although not what we had in mind, we knew with some repairs, a new coat of paint, and a good scrub, the hall would serve as the meeting place for the church. It was time to get ready for the first service of Kampala Pentecostal Church.

We set the launch date for Easter Sunday, April 22, 1984, just six weeks away. The Uganda Television station was the only channel available in the country, so we put together a simple advert to play on the station. It ran immediately after the weekly program of the very popular American pastor and televangelist, Jimmy Swaggart. We flew in 200 grey steel and plastic chairs from a supplier in England and kept them chained to the water pipes in the hall during the week. We still have those old chairs, and they're in good condition even forty years later.

Our preparations were nearly complete. We just needed to fix up the Crystal Suite. So, three weeks before the Easter Sunday launch, Marilyn and I decided to make a quick trip to Nairobi to pick up some supplies. We thought the trip would be simple and uneventful. It was anything but!

THE CRYSTAL SUITE

~ Reflect and Discuss ~

As you reflect on these questions and engage in conversation with others, consider the following:

1. Community and Connection:

- Consider the importance of identifying and building meaningful relationships with the people of your local community. Jesus did this by becoming fully human and entering our community. We call this "incarnational ministry."

- Reflect on the role of the church as Christ's body, called to model His example. (Ephesians 1:20-23 The Message) How does this understanding impact your view of the church's mission and activities?

- Discuss ways you can connect more deeply with the people of your local community. What actions can you take to foster genuine relationships and serve the people of your community?

- Reflect on areas of struggle, brokenness, or uncertainty within your community where His light and presence can bring about redemption and transformation.

2. Gary's Garden as an Illustration of Following God's Call:

- Explore how Gary's garden in Kampala serves as a metaphor for following God's call. Reflect on the patience, diligence, and trust required to cultivate a garden and how these qualities parallel the journey of obedience to God.

- Meditate on 1 Corinthians 3:6-9 and its implications for your perspective on the work God has for you.

Consider how this passage challenges you to view yourself as a co-worker with God, participating in His redemptive work in the world.

- Contemplate what it means to join God in His work. Explore how you can align your actions, attitudes, and resources with His purposes, trusting in His power and guidance.

3. Greater Hope and Joining God's Good Work:

- Prayerfully consider where God might want to ignite greater hope in your life or surroundings. Reflect on areas of struggle, brokenness, or uncertainty where His light and presence can bring about transformation.

- Explore how God may be calling you to join Him as He brings about good in difficulty. Look for opportunities to extend compassion, offer support, and be a bearer of hope in your community and beyond.

These questions aim to provoke thoughtful reflection and meaningful discussion, inspiring faith, commitment, and generosity among the participants as they consider the chapter's content and its application to their lives.

During your discussion, offer mutual encouragement, support, and prayer for one another. Share personal insights, experiences, and challenges as you seek to discern God's leading and participate in His redemptive work. By leaning on God's faithfulness and joining Him in His work, you can experience His transformative power and be a source of hope and light in the world.

~

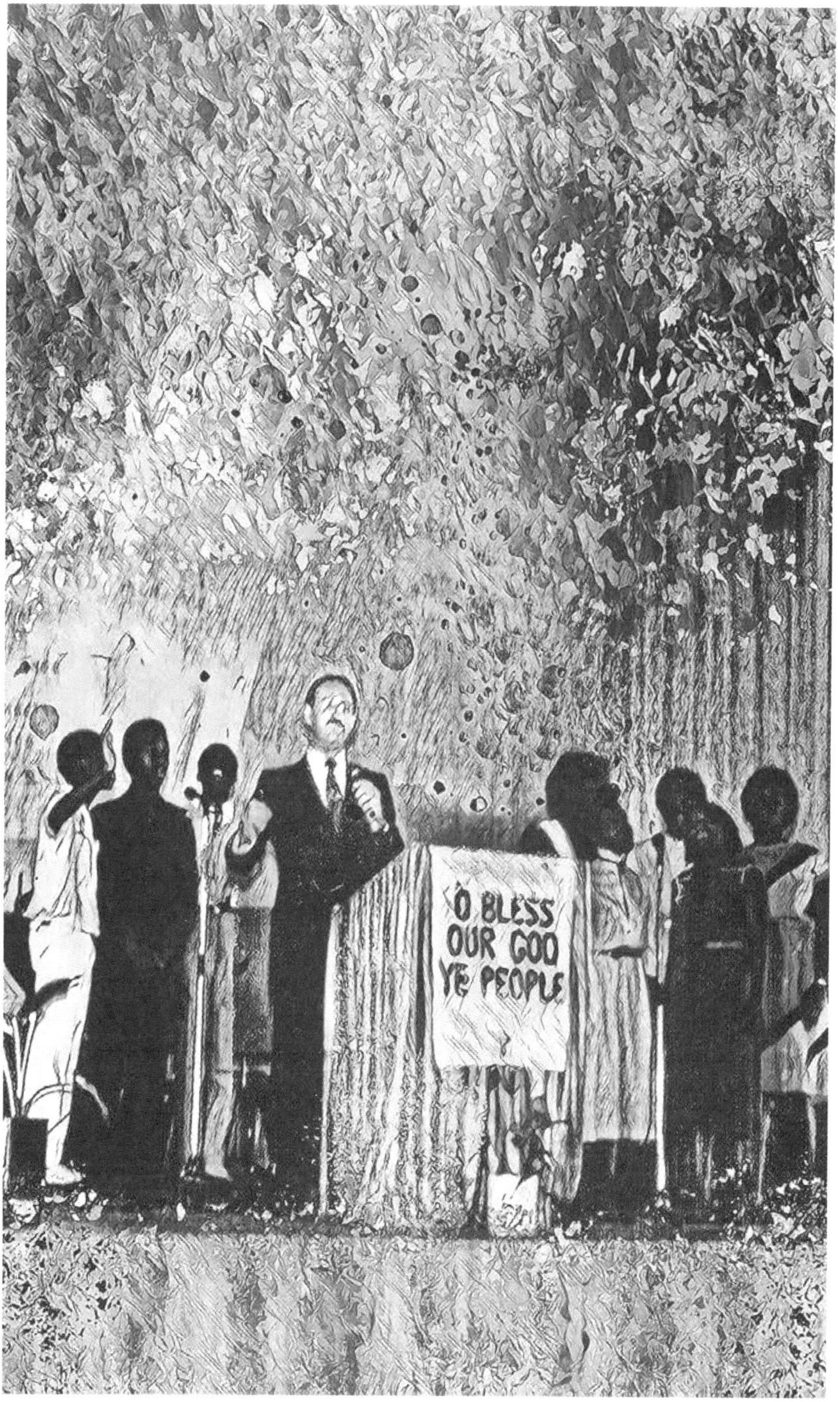
O BLESS
OUR GOD
YE PEOPLE

"Preach the Gospel at all times,
and when necessary, use words."

St. Francis of Assisi

07

The Start of Something New

"A new church in the heart of the city."

The trip to Nairobi in Kenya to pick up the supplies we needed to start the church had been anything but simple and uneventful. At the blind corner at Namugongo we had been confronted by Satan and death. The car had been completely wrecked but we were alive and recovering. We had experienced a miracle of protection from our Father God.

For the first weeks after the accident, we stayed home to recuperate. Each day passed with an improvement in our situation. As our recovery progressed, all thoughts of postponing the Easter Sunday launch were put out of mind. James had to borrow his sister Rachel's summer dresses for a week because his t-shirts and shorts irritated the burns on his little body. He wasn't excited about the idea, but he soon healed and was back to his normal self. He even began to wear the scars as a badge of pride.

I spent the time following the doctor's instructions to stay in bed so my broken ribs could heal properly. I spent hours alone reflecting on what we were going through, and I couldn't help but ask my self if we were out of our minds to be here? We had been in Kampala for less than six months. Daily life was a challenge. The city was in tatters, broken and disheveled. I thought about what we had been through in those few months and we hadn't even planted the church yet. Every night we went to sleep with the sound of gunfire in the background. The insecurity in the city was rampant, and the feeling of immanent danger and threat was palpable. Now we had been through an horrific car accident that had nearly taken our lives. Is this really where Jesus wanted us and where we were to be?

At every time of wonder and reflection about our situation, I came to the same conclusion. I had a call from God to plant an English-speaking church in the heart of the city. There was no way I could deny or escape the reality of that call. It burned inside me like a fire. This is what we were supposed to do and that's all there is to it. History is replete with examples of others who had been commissioned to a Kingdom task and had also endured great trial and difficulty. And then there is the simple truth that if you want to experience a miracle you need to find yourself in a place where, without God, you cannot make it. With God beside you, you can't fail. Yes, you might have setbacks and fall down but if you get up and persist in the fight, God will intervene, especially when you're doing what he's called you to do. Like David, you only see the giant fall when he's there, and you confront him in the name of the one who sent you.

So, on the morning of Easter Sunday, April 22nd, 1984, just weeks after the accident, we woke ready to answer what God had called us to do: plant an English-speaking church in the heart of Kampala, Uganda's capital city. It was a call we could not escape. He had been preparing us for this. We put on our Sunday best, which in those days meant suits and ties, and nice dresses, and packed the car with the things we would need for church. This included a full sound system with speakers, a mixer, microphones, cabling and a keyboard. I was a little particular about packing the car and pretty good at it, making sure everything fit into its proper prearranged slot. The kids used to give me a tough time about packing that car, teasing me that I could have fit a herd of hippos into that small station wagon.

Once the car was packed, the five members of our little family wriggled into it, squeezing into whatever space was left. It was a short drive from Kansanga to the hall in the city centre, and there was hardly room for any of us to breathe. I think I held my breath the entire way anyhow, anxious about what lay ahead. Would anyone join us for the service? Would all our hard work and the things we had gone through bear the fruit we were hoping for? I swallowed my concern and remembered the God who had saved our lives, the God who had walked faithfully with us up to this point. No matter what was ahead, he would not fail to bring about his good purposes.

We parked outside the Grand Imperial Hotel and unloaded the equipment into the hall. The smell of cigarettes and booze lingered in the air from the disco that had been hosted there the night before. Bottle-caps and empty beer bottles littered the room. Some had been knocked over and lay in pools of stale beer. In one corner, a pile of thickening vomit let off a foul stench. Combined with the other smells in the room, we wanted to gag. I don't want to tell you what the toilets were like! Marilyn brought out the cleaning supplies we had carried with us, and the entire family got to work. We spent the next hour cleaning and getting it ready to be a place of worship.

Once clean, the five of us put the sound system together. The electrical sockets had all been stolen, so we had to wire the sound system directly to the live wires. In those early days in Kampala, the electricity was most erratic, and would go off without warning. When that would happen, we would just carry on without a sound system. Happily, that was not an issue that Easter morning. We set out into neat rows the two hundred chairs we had flown in from England. Though modest for an Easter service, our efforts certainly helped to make the room look and feel the part. Now, it was just a matter of waiting for people to show up for the 10:00 am service.

Having never planted a church we were not sure what to expect and, no matter how many people turned up for the service, we were ready. At about 9:45, a few people began to arrive. Timothy and Rachel stood at the door and handed out printed copies of the order of service, smiling as they welcomed each one to the gathering. Marilyn and I moved around and introduced ourselves to those who had come.

At five minutes to ten, as people continued to drift in, Marilyn sat down at the keyboard and began to play. The beautiful melodies created an atmosphere of worship as people acquainted themselves with the space and with one another. My anxiety drained away as I looked around at those wonderful people God had brought in to witness what was happening in that room. At exactly 10 o'clock, with seventy-five of us in attendance, our hearts pumping with joy and anticipation at what God was about to do, Kampala Pentecostal Church was born.

It was a very simple service. We sang some popular hymns and worship songs, and joined hands to pray for those around us, for the city of Kampala, and for the nation of Uganda. I shared some vision for the future, preached a simple gospel message, and gave those who were there an opportunity to respond. There was no elaborate display of any kind. As those who had

THE START OF SOMETHING NEW

gathered worshipped and honoured Jesus, who was raised from death to life, He showed up. It's the presence of Jesus that makes all the difference. That same peace-filled, healing presence has graciously been with us all through the passing years.

As that first Sunday came to an end, we hugged and thanked those who had come to celebrate with us. Our hearts were filled with anticipation for what Jesus was going to do in the days and years ahead. We had only done, to the best of our ability, what God had called us to do. It was a small seed that we had planted and would grow into an English-speaking church in the heart of the city. Now, we simply had to remain faithful, tending to this small community that he was starting. And from that, just as He promised, Jesus would grow a great church, a loving, dedicated family of followers and disciples who would touch the city and touch the nation.

It was wonderful to watch the church family steadily grow after that inaugural service. Every Sunday, we welcomed first-time visitors. Most were young people, still in high school or university. Africa is a continent full of youth looking for a bright and beautiful future. The youth had very little, if any, influence in Ugandan society. We were determined to take them seriously, expressing our confidence in their God-given abilities and callings, not condescending or patronising them. Each week, they would join us, as a team of volunteers, early on Sunday morning to get the room ready for church.

From the start, we knew that the hope for healing in the city, in the nation, and on the continent was in raising a new generation of God-fearing, Jesus-loving, Bible-believing youth. Initially, they came because of the style of worship and preaching. The celebration services started and ended on time, something unusual for an African Pentecostal church. But I think they stayed because we treated them with respect and interest. We began to lay out a vision for a better future, for a transformed nation built on the authority of biblical values, and the sovereignty of Jesus over all of life. At Kampala Pentecostal Church, or KPC as it became known, this generation of young people found a place where their contribution was valued, and they had a purpose to live for. We taught them that with God's help, they were capable of changing their society for the better, and they began to embrace that message.

I began to feel a deep conviction from God that we were to mentor and raise up leaders. I knew that this goal was critical to who we were to be as a church. This was a concept that was new to me as the pastor of a local church. Leadership development was not to be informed by secular scholastic institutions that marginalised Jesus and His leadership principles, or considered the Church as irrelevant and outdated to modern social life and development. Rather, leadership development was to be taught and modelled by the Church. Over the next years, this approach to leadership development, growing out of a biblical understanding of life and society, grew stronger in me.

So, only a few months after the launch, we started the Timothy School, a discipleship and leadership course. The Apostle Paul mentored his spiritual son, Timothy, so the name was especially fitting, given what Paul had written to him,

> *"Don't let anyone look down on you because you are young, but set an example for the believers in speech, in conduct, in love, in faith and in purity."*
>
> *1 Timothy 4:12 (NIV)*

The Timothy School met each weekday at lunchtime in the same room we held church in at the Grand Imperial Hotel. I taught some key subjects on theology that I had studied in Bible School. We ordered fifty copies of Dake's Study Bible and told students they could keep the bible if they finished one year of the Monday-through-Friday lunchtime class. They were eager to learn more about God, his word, and what it meant to be a disciple and a leader. The classes helped to establish the core, Christ-centered, biblically based culture that we wanted to characterise the church, and is essential for national transformation and healing. That year, thirty students graduated, and many emerged as leaders in our growing church community. They valued what we invested in them. Some of those initial students have gone on to do significant things for the work in Uganda, planting churches and reaching the youth of the country. We were seeing, again, how God would accomplish good things by simple, faithful people who walked in obedience to his gentle voice.

As a family, we built meaningful relationships with the members of the new congregation. Marilyn and I were encouraged by their enthusiasm as well as the warm acceptance they extended to our children. John and

Julie Ssebutinde were some of our first Ugandan friends. They were a lovely professional couple who took a particular interest in us. They taught us much about life in Kampala. Every Sunday morning, they travelled across the punctured and littered sidewalks, pushing their young daughter in her stroller to arrive at church early to help us prepare the room for the service. They were both musical, and John accompanied us in worship on the guitar while Julie became one of our first vocalists. John was a lively, joyful character who loved to tell stories that would have us howling with laughter. Julie was a quiet, direct woman whose intellect would have been intimidating if she wasn't such a sweet and gentle person. They were the first of many friends we would make.

Over time, we grew more and more adapted to life in Uganda. It's not that life became easy. Ordinary life was challenging in those early days. Learning to cope with the breakdown of the infrastructure in a city of more than a million people was one of the more daunting things we had to do. The electricity was, to put it mildly, erratic. It would go off and come back on haphazardly. One time, it went off at our home and didn't come back for six months. The local transformer had burnt out, and it took that long to get a replacement.

The water supply was also unreliable. Often, we would return home from a day of work feeling dirty from the accumulation of sweat and dust, only to turn on the faucets and find them dry. Of course, it seemed to happen on the days we were particularly grimy. We had no choice but to eat supper and go to bed without bathing. When there was water, the pressure from the tap was so low that it would take all afternoon to fill the bathtub. Our routine was to bathe the kids first. They loved to spend their time running barefoot through the yard, playing in pools of mud, and digging up anthills, so they needed it most. Marilyn was next, and I would get in the same dirty water to conclude the ablutions.

Marilyn and I could not have survived this without the support we provided each other. Marilyn was determined to give us every opportunity to have what she considered a normal life. This led her to see our lives through the lens of possibility and ingenuity. Her resourcefulness was awe-inspiring. She learned to make pasta noodles, bake bread and provide wonderful meals with what we could get. There was huge disappointment when the electricity would go off while the bread dough was still rising or baking, leaving an inedible lump in the oven. Our supplies of flour and the other necessities that we couldn't find in Kampala were bought after an eight-hour journey to the grocery store in Kisumu, Kenya.

But Marilyn was not deterred. She kept working hard to provide things that would help us feel at home. She learned how to select cuts of meat from the fly-covered carcasses of freshly dead cows that hung at the roadside stalls, a far cry from the butcher shops and grocery stores she was accustomed to. She would mince the meat at home to make hamburgers, slicing up potatoes and frying them so that the kids could have french fries to go with their burgers. She learned how to make cottage cheese, tomato paste, and sheets of pasta because the children loved lasagna. Despite the difficulty of making a life in Kampala in those days, Marilyn slowly adjusted more and more to life in Uganda.

One Saturday, we decided to go with another missionary family to the Lake Victoria Hotel in Entebbe so the children could swim in what was then one of the only functioning swimming pools in the country. It was a classical old colonial hotel with lots of history and even served as the venue for some of the old movies about colonial African life. However, when we arrived, we were horrified to find the pool tinted a putrid shade of green, a layer of leaves and a thick film of algae on the surface of the water. At the deep end, a set of three diving boards had been built at different heights.

The kids gave each other doubtful looks. Were they going to brave the slimy pond? The children of our missionary friends were "old hands." They ran straight to the diving boards and, without a moment of hesitation, hurled themselves headfirst into the water. Our kids didn't want to be outdone by the outlandish bravery, or perhaps overt foolishness, of their friends, but they were still sceptical. They crept to the edge of the pool and, summoning up all the courage they could, plunged into the water. Breaking back through the seal of thick scum at the top of the water, they emerged, letting out a chorus of delighted squeals.

Marilyn, of course, was not too happy about the possible repercussions of a swim in that pool. She was content to enjoy a cup of tea in the afternoon sunshine as the kids played. After placing her order with the waiter, she was horrified to see him approach the swimming pool, tea kettle in hand. He got down on his knees at the water's edge and filled the pot with the same water the children were swimming in. Then he stood up and disappeared into the kitchen before re-emerging a few minutes later with tea and cake.

Marilyn was stunned. Looking at her tea, she gave her cup a gentle swirl, checking for any hidden debris that may have found its way into her drink. She weighed her options. She could reject the tea and laugh off the episode, or she could submit her resistance to defeat. Once certain that she wasn't going to choke on any flotsam, Marilyn casually sipped the tea as if the situation was entirely normal. I was stunned and impressed at how my wife had, time after time, pushed herself beyond comfort and made the best of things that she was not at all used to.

There is a joke I used to tell overseas visitors who were experiencing some of these quirky and surprising aspects of life in Africa. "You can tell how long a missionary has been in Africa by what he does when a fly lands in his soup," I would begin. The dinner guests would look up from their soup, wondering where I was going with this line of conversation.

"A missionary who is serving on his first assignment," I would continue, "well, he'll just toss out the whole bowl of soup, fly and all, and probably won't eat anything for the rest of the meal. A second-term missionary, now he's likely to be a little bit thick-skinned, and a tiny fly isn't going to put him off his soup, especially if it's an authentic tin of Campbell's Cream of Tomato. No, he'll just dig out the fly, discard it discreetly, wipe off the spoon with a napkin and then finish his soup."

At this point, everybody would share a little chuckle.

"Now, a missionary on his third term, he's probably not even going to notice there's a fly in his soup, and if he does, he'll be thankful for a change in the menu." By now, Marilyn and my kids are rolling their eyes into the back of their heads, having heard this joke a few times.

"A missionary on his fourth term, now he's an old timer. He's tough as a bag of nails and a little crazy, too. There is nothing that can catch him by surprise. This guy demands that there be a fly in his soup. And if there isn't one, he'll go looking for flies to put in there. And you know what? He'll probably catch one because he's a veteran. He's a pro."

I told that joke faithfully, and sometimes, I even got a laugh or two. I always found it to be funny because I recognised there was a certain truth to it and a good lesson that could be learned from it. To survive the constant onslaught of surprises that could unhinge confidence or unleash anger, you had to adjust. You had to adapt! I saw our young family doing just that, changing and adapting to what they faced as life in Uganda. I was encouraged by our willingness to adjust for the sake of the work God had chosen us for in Kampala, most especially Marilyn, who had grown up in a completely different environment.

Despite her seemingly endless optimism, I know living in Kampala was not easy for Marilyn early on. Things that we once took for granted consumed hours of her day, and though she was happy to do anything for her family, the amount of work it took just to make a simple meal left her tired at the end of each day. To top it all off, Kampala was no substitute for what she considered home, Canada.

After one particularly tough day, she said, "Gary, when are you going to take me home?"

I was a little stunned by her candid question, and my heart broke for the level of weariness I could hear in her voice.

"When there are 500 people in church, I'll take you home," I answered, thinking that gave us plenty of time to get used to living here.

"Great," she said sarcastically, "I guess it's going to be a long time then."

I understood her discouragement; it was easy to feel defeated by the smallest things. But we saw the potential the church had, and we were too stubborn to give up on the young, growing community. We had new friends, and the church was already making a real impact on the lives of many people. We were beginning to see the fruit of our sacrifice.

The church did grow, and far sooner than I expected. When I told her one Sunday afternoon that there were 500 people in church that day, she responded.

"Great! Can we go back to Canada now?"

I looked at her and felt my heart sink.

"I'm sorry, my sweetheart!" I replied tentatively. After all, I had no intention of leaving, and I think she knew it.

"I've changed my mind. When we hit a thousand people, we can go!" I smiled.

"I guess that means we're never leaving then, right!"

I often thought it would be amazing to have a thousand people coming to church. We would sing that old hymn, "O For a Thousand Tongues to Sing, My Great Redeemer's Praise." Somehow, deep inside, I just knew we'd get there one day. So, we just kept on serving the people and Jesus. And, of course, we did get to a Sunday when a thousand people came to church, again, sooner than I would have expected.

When I told Marilyn, she asked the inevitable question.

"Can we go home now?"

"I'm sorry, my sweetheart!"

"I know, I know," she said. "You've changed your mind. When we hit five thousand people, we can go! Right?"

Before long, we did, of course, see five thousand people worshipping the Lord and committing themselves to serving him and bettering their nation.

I let Marilyn know, and she repeated the same question. As I began what had become my stock answer, she cut me off.

"Oh, I don't really mean it, Gary. This is home. Uganda is where we belong. And besides, I've learned to like it here, too."

But this was, of course, years later. At the time, we were still just going day by day, remaining faithful through whatever came our way.

Little did we know that some of the trials on the road ahead would test the very limits of our faith and endurance.

THE START OF SOMETHING NEW

~ Reflect and Discuss ~

As you reflect on these questions and engage in discussion with others, consider the following:

1. Early Years of Kampala Pentecostal Church:

    • Reflect on what stands out to you the most when reading about the early years of planting the church in Kampala. Consider the challenges, triumphs, and God's response to Gary and Marilyn's persistent obedience.

    • Notice how God's faithfulness is evident in the midst of their obedience. Reflect on instances where God provided guidance, provision, and encouragement as they stepped out in faith.

    • How did their faith and commitment help them overcome these difficulties?

2. Reaching the Next Generation of Youth:

    • Reflect on the importance of reaching the next generation with the message of Christ, His hope and purpose. How can this impact the future of a community, church or nation?

    • Discuss the strategies Gary and his team used to engage and empower the youth in Kampala. What were the key factors that made their approach successful?

    • Consider a way you can engage with the youth in your community. What practical steps can you take to mentor and inspire them towards a positive future?

3. Inspiration from Marilyn's Attitude:

    • Reflect on Marilyn's optimism and make-the-most-of-it attitude despite facing challenges. Consider how her resilience and faithfulness in difficult circumstances can inspire and encourage others.

• Explore how we can be honest about the difficulties we face while remaining faithful and gracious in our day to day lives. Talk about the ways we can take to maintain hope and trust in God's faithfulness in the middle of trials and adversity.

These questions are designed to provoke personal reflection and foster meaningful group discussion, encouraging participants to apply the lessons and insights from the chapter into their lives and communities.

During your discussion, offer support, encouragement, and prayer for one another. Share personal experiences, struggles, and victories as you seek to navigate life's challenges with faith and grace. By leaning on God's strength and embracing a spirit of perseverance, you can find inspiration and encouragement to press on in your journey of faith.

~

137

"When we live our lives within the shadow of God Most High, our secret hiding place, we will always be shielded from harm. How then could evil prevail against us or disease infect us? God sends angels with special orders to protect you wherever you go, defending you from all harm. If you walk into a trap, they'll be there for you and keep you from stumbling. You'll even walk unharmed among the fiercest powers of darkness, trampling every one of them beneath your feet! For here is what the Lord has spoken to me: Because you loved me, delighted in me, and have been loyal to my name, I will greatly protect you. I will answer your cry for help every time you pray, and you will feel my presence in your time of trouble. I will deliver you and bring you honor. I will satisfy you with a full life and with all that I do for you. For you will enjoy the fullness of my salvation!"

King David - Psalm 91:10-16 TPT

08

~ Angels in the Night ~

"Covered by His care."

Living in Kampala that first year made us fully aware of just how dangerous the city really was. Death surrounded us. We heard the sound of the gunfire every night, sometimes in the distance and sometimes next door. People called it "popcorn" because that's what it sounded like. We never got used to it. The city was a war zone! The buildings bore the scars of battle. Every day we heard reports of theft, murder, and rape that had taken place during the night before.

Guns were everywhere. Violence had cheapened the value of life and provoked a constant and fresh fear. People lived in terror of the government soldiers and the criminal gangs who roamed in the night looking for loot. It wasn't a matter of what you would do *if* they came; it was what you would do *when* they came.

Because of this sobering reality, we taught and practised with the children how we would respond if a gang of men did come in the night. They would quickly and quietly make their beds and arrange their rooms as if we were not at home. Then, we would all climb up into the ceiling to hide. I'm sure the kids grew tired of these exercises, but they came to accept them as just another weird part of life in Kampala.

One night, Marilyn and I were woken up by cries somewhere in the neighbourhood. Marilyn sat upright in bed, grabbed me by the arm, and looked at me with terror. The screams continued, and although we couldn't make out what was being said, it sounded like a woman was pleading for mercy. Then, there was the chatter of an automatic weapon. It sounded like it was coming from the house next door. When it stopped, there was a strange silence. It lasted for only a second or two, and then we heard a harrowing wail.

We ran to the children's bedrooms and told them that it was time to hide in the ceiling. The kids made their beds. Timothy was the first up the ladder, but as he was climbing, he froze halfway up. For a moment, he remained motionless, then he turned his head and looked into my eyes.

"Are we going to die tonight," he asked.

I shuddered and replied hopefully,

"No, Timothy, we're not going to die tonight."

But Rachel read my bluff. She wasn't convinced and rephrased Timothy's question with a strange, detached tone.

"Are we going to go and be with Grandpa Dawson tonight?"

She was referring to Marilyn's dad, who had passed away some years earlier. Marilyn wrapped her arms around Rachel and tried to gather her courage.

"Everything is going to be alright," Marilyn said. "If we die tonight, we are going to be with Jesus."

Timothy, still halfway up the ladder, lifted his head and hurried into the ceiling. Rachel and James followed close behind him. When we were all up in the attic, I pulled the rope ladder up behind us. I carefully placed the ceiling panel back into place, and we spent the rest of the night hiding in the roof as we listened to the anguished cries of the neighbours.

In the morning, we learned that a gang of soldiers had gone house to house along our street. The only house they didn't come into was ours. I know that guardian angels were camped on our doorstep, there to protect us.

The Bible tells us that,

> *"The angel of the Lord encamps around those who fear him, and he delivers them."*
>
> *Psalm 34:7 (NIV)*

ANGELS IN THE NIGHT

That was what life in Kampala was like back then. Death was truly at the door. Through it all, we determined not to let fear get the better of us. We continued to live our lives, day by day, as best we could, with faith in what Jesus had called us to do and to pour ourselves into the growing church.

Every Sunday, we would load up the the car and go to the Grand Imperial Hotel to have church with those precious people. That is until the old Volvo finally "gave up the ghost" and was no longer drivable. We were without adequate transportation. The car we had borrowed, belonging to our missionary friends in Mbale, had been totally wrecked in the accident at the blind corner at Namagunga. This left us with no option but to use the Suzuki 650cc motorcycle that had arrived in the shipping container. It was a nice motorcycle, but I had no idea we would need it to transport all five of us around Kampala.

It was a squeeze, but we managed to all get on. James and Rachel sat in front and grasped the centre of the handlebars with their little hands. Marilyn sat behind me and hugged me like in the movies. I really liked that! Tim sat on the luggage rack at the back and hung on for dear life as I manoeuvred around potholes and through heavy traffic. It must have been an extraordinary sight, but the traffic police didn't seem to mind. I shudder to think that it was our family that introduced the phenomenon of boda-boda motorcycle taxis that took over Kampala's streets 15 years later. It was a workable solution for a while, but certainly not ideal.

We were thrilled when we heard that our new French Peugeot 504 Station Wagon had arrived for pick up in Mombasa on the Kenya coast. It was a very popular, comfortable, and versatile vehicle, perfect for the rough East African roads. It had been ordered months before by the mission office in Nairobi. Since the drive to Mombasa would be an arduous seventeen-hour trip, we decided that I would make the trip to Kenya without Marilyn and the kids. I would only be away for two nights, and the thought of Marilyn being left alone in Uganda with the kids wasn't all that appealing to either of us. What could go wrong in just two days?

The morning of the trip, Marilyn hugged me in the early morning darkness, and I reassured her that everything was going to be just fine and hitched a ride to Nairobi and arriving in time to catch the evening train to Mombasa. On the morning of the second day, I picked up the car and drove back to Nairobi, where I spent the night. On the third day, I got up long before sunrise and drove back to Kampala with the hope of arriving before supper. It was an uneventful trip.

It was not uneventful back in Kampala!

The first day of my absence was quite ordinary. Marilyn got Tim and Rachel ready, and friends came and picked them up for school. Marilyn cleaned the house, played with James, and tried to stay busy. She wanted to keep her mind away from the fact that she was alone in this crazy, new city. When the kids got back from school, they played with James in the yard for a while while Marilyn made supper. After dinner, Marilyn got the kids ready for bed and prayed for their protection before they fell asleep.

Lying in bed awake and alone, Marilyn listened to the sounds of a Kampala night, interrupted by the occasional pitter-patter of gunfire. She was understandably apprehensive. When I was at home, she felt, at least, some semblance of safety, but that night, alone with the three children, she couldn't shake the nervous tension. The blackness of the night covered her like a suffocating blanket. We did have a night guard, but for some reason, his footsteps outside weren't reassuring. She listened to the frogs and the crickets as if they were broadcasting her secret to the neighbourhood. She was alone with the children.

Rebuking the darkness of these thoughts, Marilyn encouraged herself. Surely, God was with her. Would he not protect her and the kids? He had done it before when the gang had gone through the neighbourhood! Eventually, her eyelids became heavy, and she fell into a deep sleep.

Relief flooded over her when she woke to the pale early morning sun and the sound of birds welcoming a new day. With the kids safe in their beds, a surge of confidence rushed through her. She knew she could conquer her fear.

That day was similar to the previous one. The kids went off to school, and she stayed busy with chores and made dinner, but when night fell, the fear returned. She put the children to bed and prayed once more for rest and protection, and they fell asleep immediately.

When she went to bed, she opened her Bible and turned to Isaiah 54 for an evening devotion. Coming to verse 13, she read,

> *"All your children will be taught by the LORD,*

ANGELS IN THE NIGHT

and great will be their peace.

In righteousness you will be established:

Tyranny will be far from you;

you will have nothing to fear.

Terror will be far removed;

it will not come near you.

If anyone does attack you, it will not be my doing;

whoever attacks you will surrender to you.

See, it is I who created the blacksmith

who fans the coals into flame

and forges a weapon fit for its work.

And it is I who have created the destroyer to work havoc;

no weapon forged against you will prevail...

This is the heritage of the servants of The Lord."

Isaiah 54:13-17 (NIV)

Marilyn had read this passage before, but living in Kampala brought her a deeper understanding. She needed God and to rely on His protection. She claimed this promise of protection as her own, planted it in her heart, and held onto it tightly. She drew strength from the promise of God's Word, which told her that despite the dangers of the life God had called her to, her family would not be harmed.

Even with this promise, she was restless. As she lay in her bed, consumed by her thoughts, she heard a knock on the bedroom window. Startled, she pulled the blanket up to her chin and clenched her fists. She drew in a breath and waited in silence. Again, there was a tap on the window, and this time, an old man's voice.

"Madam," he said, "there is danger."

She recognised the guard's voice and his Congolese accent.

"What is happening?" she asked, sitting up in bed.

"Madam, there are men who are coming here."

"Are they here now?"

"No, Madam, they are not here, but they will come."

Marilyn shuddered. Panic and fear came over her. There was silence.

She jumped out of bed and ran to Rachel's room. Rachel was fast asleep. Marilyn kissed her on the cheek and gently shook her shoulder to wake her.

"Rachel," she said. "Rachel, you must wake up now." Rachel didn't move.

"Rachel", Marilyn repeated, her voice now carrying a sense of urgency, "Wake up!"

She took Rachel's hand and began to tap it gently. Rachel's eyes opened, and she rubbed them with her fist. Looking at her mother in agitation, she rolled over as if to say, "Whatever you want, it can wait until the morning."

Marilyn gathered Rachel up in her arms. Rachel's eyes opened again.

"You have to get up, Rachel. I need you to help me wake your brothers."

Marilyn put Rachel down and stumbled into the boy's room. She reached up to the top bunk where Timothy was sleeping and gently shook him.

Timothy woke up, asking, "What's going on, Mum?"

"Thieves are coming, Tim. I need you to help me take care of Rachel and James."

"I was having such a nice dream, Mum," he replied dazedly,

While Marilyn turned to wake James, Timothy climbed down from his bed and started making it just as he had practised so many times before.

ANGELS IN THE NIGHT

"We don't have time for that now, Tim," Marilyn said. "We really need to hurry."

By now, James was awake, and everybody gathered in the main bedroom. Marilyn was unsure if there was time to get all three kids into the ceiling without my help. She locked the door behind her and looked around the room to see what she could use to barricade herself in. There was a large dressing table, a rocking chair, and some bedside tables.

"Help me with this dresser," she said to the kids.

They all gathered around, and using all of their strength, the four of them pushed the huge wooden dressing table until it was flush against the bedroom door. They gathered the rest of the furniture and packed it in tight so that it would offer more resistance if an intruder tried to break through. When they had done this, Marilyn helped Rachel and James crawl into a tiny space beneath the headboard of the bed. Tim got into bed and lay next to Marilyn, and all three children went straight back to sleep as if nothing was wrong.

With all the lights out, Marilyn lay in bed shaking like a leaf, listening to the frogs and the crickets in the darkness. She waited in anticipation for the first indication that men had arrived. Her heart beat loudly in her chest, and her gut tightened as the silence seemed to go on forever. And then she heard a scream. A series of loud pounding noises came next and then silence again.

They had to be nearby. The wait seemed to last for hours. Marilyn analysed every noise, waiting for the worst. She listened for footsteps or the sound of hushed whispers. She waited for the sound of a gun being cocked and primed to fire or for the sound of a panga cutting at the fence on the perimeter of the property. She was ready for the sound of footsteps on the roof. She listened for any clue that let her know where the men were.

More silence! With every passing second, her anxiety multiplied. For several hours, Marilyn lay in bed. Her arms were folded across her chest, and her fingers nervously tapped at her shoulder. And finally, another knock came to the window.

"Madam." It was the guard again. "They are here, and they are many."

The old man's warning was filled with terror.

"Run." Marilyn said firmly, coming to the window. "Run as fast as you can. If they catch you, they will kill you."

"Madam, God bless you." He disappeared into the night.

Marilyn was alone! Alone with her three children! Her husband away picking up a car!

She sat upright in her bed, brought her legs up to her chest, and wrapped her arms around her shins. Placing her forehead onto her knees, she thought, "So this is how my life ends."

She lifted her head and looked around the room at the furniture piled against the door. "My four-year-old son helped me move those things." she said to herself, "There's no way they are going to hold up against a gang of thieves. The front entrance is nothing more than a wooden door with a simple skeleton key lock and a couple of rusty bolts. I'm sure I could break it down by myself if I had to."

Sitting in eerie silence, Marilyn waited, listening only to the children's heavy breathing as they slept. Timothy's chest slowly rose and fell, completely oblivious to the danger that surrounded them.

"No weapon formed against you shall prevail," Marilyn whispered to herself.

Silence.

Then she heard a loud sound at the front of the house. Somebody was pounding at the door with a clenched fist.

"Woman! Open the door," a man's voice boomed. He addressed her specifically. How did he know she was alone?

"Open the door, or we shall break it," he demanded.

Marilyn sat quivering.

Again, she whispered, "No weapon formed against you shall prevail..."

"Do not make us angry, woman," his voice was strong and persuasive, but Marilyn didn't move. "It will be better for you if you open this door."

ANGELS IN THE NIGHT

Some hushed whispering followed a few seconds of silence. Again the voice cried out in anger, "We will rape you and kill your children, and then we will finish you. You cannot resist us, woman. We are many."

"No weapon formed against you shall prevail…"

Marilyn heard footsteps, and a man's shadow rushed past the barred bedroom window. The negotiation was over. She knew that many men were now surrounding the house. A loud thud came from the kitchen door at the back of the house. A few seconds of silence followed, and then there was another loud thud. The sequence repeated itself for a full minute: the sound of feet running and another thud, and another, and another. Marilyn couldn't be sure, but it sounded like a man was running and throwing the weight of his whole body against the kitchen door leading into the kitchen. But the door seemed to hold.

"No weapon…"

The slow, calculated sequence of pounding noises suddenly became a clamour of fists, elbows, and knees as several men attacked the wooden planks, seemingly increasing in frustration.

"…formed against you shall prevail…"

The door was enduring a terrifying, unrelenting barrage of blows, but still, the men could not break through. They raised their curses to the air. "Open the door or we will kill you," one man shouted. "You cannot escape."

Marilyn prayed for God to send his angels to watch over her and her children.

For two hours, she listened as the men wildly beat the door, trying to get inside. They shouted curses and threats. Marilyn continued to pray.

And then, it was quiet. Marilyn held her breath as the silence stretched out. She waited! The sounds of night returned, the whisper of the crickets and the croaking of the frogs. They seemed to be saying, "The men have gone, the men have gone.' It was now almost four o'clock in the morning. Another hour passed. Marilyn sat awake, motionless and silent. She listened to the breath of her sleeping children, and her fear turned into anger.

Her thoughts turned towards me as I slept safely in Nairobi.

"How could he bring me here to this place." she thought, the tears welling up in her eyes. "How could this 'man of God' bring his wife and three young children to this hell?"

The memory of the neighbour's harrowing screams echoed in Marilyn's brain, and tormenting oppression surrounded her.

"This place is full of death," she said to herself. "How will I survive? When Gary gets home, I am going to give him a piece of my mind, and then we will pack up our things and go back to Canada." Marilyn's anger boiled up inside.

And then, deep in her spirit, she heard a sweet, gentle voice.

"Get up, Marilyn. Get up. I didn't bring you here to be paralysed by fear. I brought you here to be filled with faith. I brought you here. You may feel that your lack is big, but My provision is bigger. You may think your weaknesses are debilitating, but My strength will see you through. You may know your faults and fears as overwhelming, but My grace is enough. Will your fear be bigger than your faith, or will your faith be bigger than your fear?"

Jesus, the great comforter and friend, was speaking words of strength and encouragement to His traumatised daughter. Was she willing to trust Him? Was her faith in her husband or her God? Was she willing to put aside her concerns for her well-being and trust in Him? Was she willing to put the lives of her children into God's hands and believe His promise, the promise he had given her that very night, no weapon fashioned against her would prevail?

Marilyn looked over at Timothy and marvelled at how the children were covered with an incomprehensible angelic peace. Not once did they shed a tear or cry out in fear. Instead, when James woke up that morning, he crawled out of his hiding place and into his mother's bed, saying, "I wasn't afraid, Mummy. Were you?"

The verses of Isaiah's prophetic words echoed in her heart,

> "All your children will be taught by the LORD, and great will be their peace."
>
> *Isaiah 54:13 (NIV)*

As the sun rose to welcome a new day, Marilyn began to feel safe again. She was grateful when the guard returned to the bedroom window unharmed. He had run for safety, jumped the fence and climbed onto the roof of a neighbour's house to watch the scene unfolding below. He counted 25 men and watched in amazement as they failed to break down the simple wooden door at the back of the house. They had tried for several hours, eventually gave up, and disappeared in a confused frenzy.

Marilyn was amazed! That many men should easily have broken down that old wooden door. She knew then that God had heard her cry for help. He sent angels to surround and protect her. She imagined two angels leaning against the door as the angry men assaulted it. She pictured the angels with their arms folded, conducting a casual conversation with each other as the men on the other side tried to unleash the very gates of hell against Marilyn and her babies.

Courage filled her heart, replacing the sense of defeat and anger. She embraced the surge of fresh faith welling up inside of her. This experience had been her own. It was a confirmation to her that God's calling on her life had brought her here to Kampala. She wasn't just following her man to Uganda because of his call. God had plans specifically for her, plans to prosper her and not to harm her, plans to give her hope and a future here in Uganda. Nobody could deny that to her now.

The sunrise brought with it a new morning and a new hope. It reawakened the realisation that even though we cannot always control our circumstances, we can control how we respond in and to those circumstances. Marilyn chose to respond with faith. God had called us to a difficult and challenging place, and with it, there would be difficulties. But He had a plan here that was far greater than anything we could have ever imagined. Our simple Canadian family had little to offer except a willingness and deep desire to be used by Him for whatever He wanted and for His glory.

I drove the new car down the steep driveway, parked in front of the house, and got out. At the door, I was greeted by a tiny little woman who is a giant of a soul, a mighty warrior of light in the Kingdom of God. She hugged and kissed the man she loved, the man she had followed to Africa, her husband, and then she told him the full story of the night her fear had been turned into faith. None of what she told me included even a hint of a desire to leave. Both of us were called to this place. We would not give up on what Jesus, the great Lord of the Harvest, had called us to do here. We would build an English-speaking church in the heart of Kampala.

~ Reflect and Discuss ~

As you reflect on these questions and engage in discussion with others, consider the following:

1. Marilyn and the Thieves:

    • Reflect on what stands out to you the most about Marilyn's encounter with the thieves. Consider the fear, uncertainty, and vulnerability she must have felt in that moment.

    • Notice how God showed Himself faithful to Marilyn, Gary, and their children that night. Reflect on the ways God provided protection, peace, and a sense of His presence amidst danger.

2. God's Call and Miraculous Plans:

    • Explore how God's call can intersect with both the evil schemes of others and His miraculous plans. Consider how Isaiah 54:13-17 prepared Marilyn for these realities, enabling her to trust God in the face of great evil.

    • Reflect on the tension between human agency and divine intervention in fulfilling God's purposes. Discuss how God can use even the darkest circumstances to bring about His redemptive plan.

3. Personal Experience of God's Protection:

    • Recall a time when you saw God miraculously protect yourself or someone you know in the face of danger or evil. Reflect on the ways God intervened, provided safety, or brought about unexpected deliverance.

    • Share this testimony with your group, allowing others to be encouraged and inspired by God's faithfulness and power.

4. Inspiration from Marilyn's Story:

   - Consider how Marilyn's story might be inspiring faith within you for the present. Reflect on her courage, resilience, and unwavering trust in God's faithfulness.

   - Explore how Marilyn's experience challenges you to trust God more fully in your own life, especially in times of uncertainty, danger, or adversity.

During your discussion, offer support, encouragement, and prayer for one another. Share personal insights, experiences, and reflections as you seek to grow in faith and trust in God's faithfulness. By leaning on God's strength and drawing inspiration from Marilyn's story, you can find courage and hope for the challenges of the present.

∼

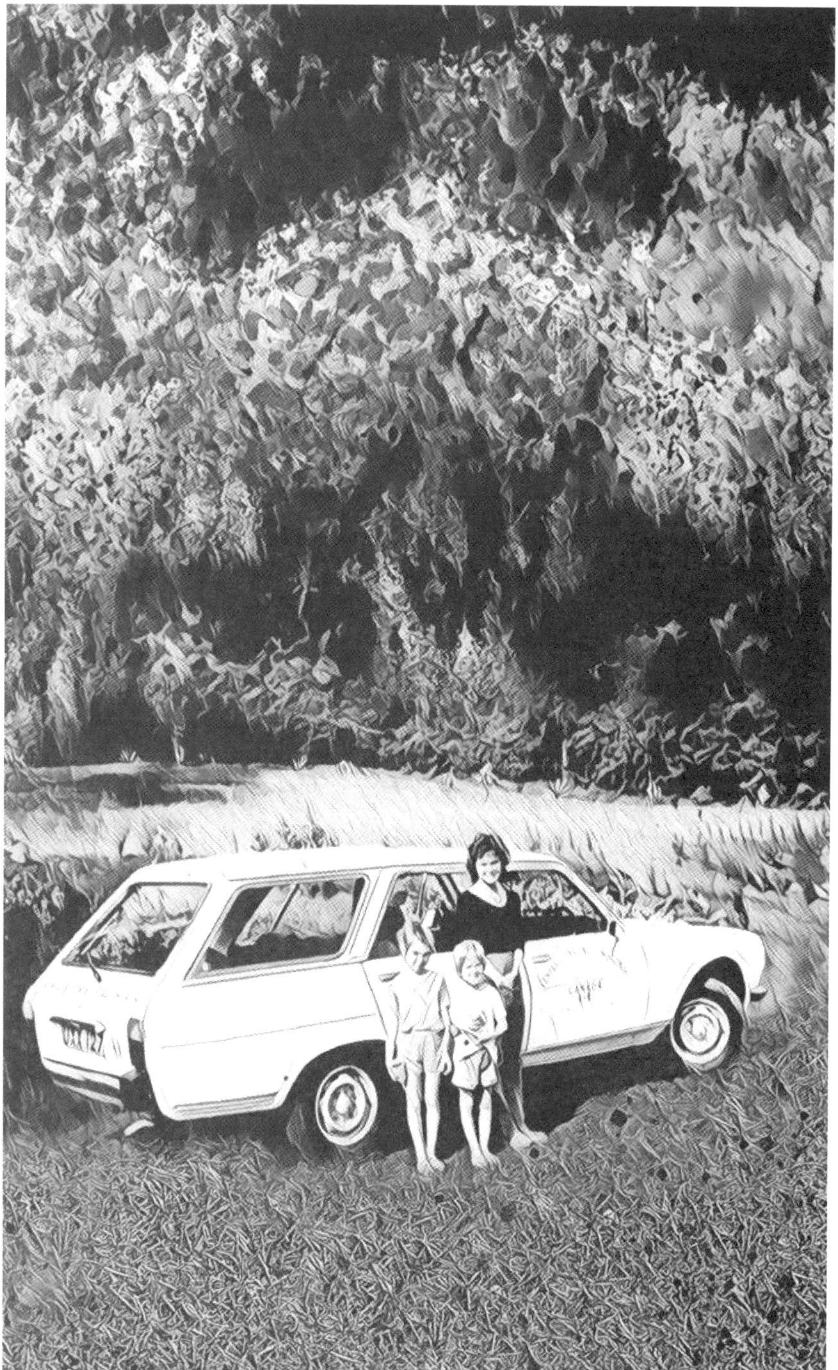

> "If to be feelingly alive to the sufferings of my fellow-creatures is to be a fanatic, I am one of the most incurable fanatics ever permitted to be at large.
>
> *William Wilberforce:*

09

Struggles in the Shadows

~ ~

"Living through Uganda's trials."

It was very evident that, in dark and difficult circumstances, Jesus had sent angels to guard over and protect our little family. We never, ever took His protection for granted but were filled with a sense of awe at the goodness of God who stood by us in the challenge of living in a war-torn land. He had promised that He would never leave us, and He had proven it.

For the next few weeks, our neighbourhood remained under attack from the same gang of men who had tried to break into our home. Nobody knew who they were as they murdered and robbed with impunity. Most thought they were government soldiers, which explained how they could get away with this kind of brutal behaviour. Others thought they might be rebel soldiers trying to create further chaos for the government. Whoever they were, they were fearless and operated without mercy.

We learned to anticipate the gunfire and though no longer surprised, we never grew accustomed to the sounds of war. Each evening, at dark, we barricaded ourselves into the small house and prayed for His protection. This carried on for weeks and always seemed to follow the same sequence: the cries, the guns, the lament. The only thing that changed was the direction the sounds of terror were coming from.

And it wasn't just our immediate neighbourhood that suffered. The whole city was affected. Milton Obote had returned as president and Amin's supporters, along with several other rebel groups, launched an insurgency that cast the entire country into chaos. Obote's government and his military were no better than the rebels. There was a complete breakdown of law and order across the nation. Conventional wisdom was that the Ugandan army was behind the violence. We found ourselves in the middle of some of the darkest moments in Uganda's history. The country's institutions were in complete disarray. There was no confidence in the government. Things were going from bad to worse. In Kampala and throughout Buganda, Obote was despised and hated because of the way in which, during his first presidency, he had treated not only the people of Baganda but also the Kabaka of Buganda, the king of Uganda's largest tribe. This led to many of the Baganda sympathising with and even joining the rebel causes.

During Uganda's colonial period, the Baganda were regarded as agents of British rule and occupied strategic and important roles in the emerging nation. The Baganda were despised by the other tribes, who did not enjoy the same privileges and felt mistreated. Many northerners felt that their best hope for any semblance of advancement was to join the army. This was the culture in which Milton Obote, a northerner, grew up.

Obote was a leading political figure as Uganda began to prepare for independence from British rule in the late 1950s. Renowned for his sharp intellect and political savvy, Obote understood the political landscape of a nation nearing independence. He positioned himself to become a dominant figure once Uganda became a sovereign state, being careful to appease the Buganda Kingdom during the years leading up to independence. As Uganda's independence drew near, elections were held to determine who would preside over the newly independent country. The Baganda realised that to maintain their position of strength, they had to form an alliance with Milton Obote's party, the Uganda People's Congress or UPC, which drew massive support in northern Uganda. It was in the interests of both the Buganda Kingdom and the UPC to work together. Together, they won the elections, and shortly afterwards, on October 9, 1962, Uganda gained independence, setting Milton Obote up as Uganda's first Prime Minister. Obote held the real power as Prime Minister, but the Kabaka held the important if only ceremonial, role of President of the Republic of Uganda.

Despite the alliance, many Baganda were persistent in efforts to separate from the rest of Uganda, leading to a crisis that threatened the newly formed government. The northerners particularly hated the culture of the Baganda in which all the Baganda would be required to lie prostrate before the king as he passed by. Eventually, with the army's backing, Milton Obote annulled the constitution and abolished all traditional kingdoms. He declared himself President with the power to rule by decree. The army, which was made up primarily of Obote's northern tribesmen, was sent to attack the King's palace. Idi Amin, Obote's military commander, led the siege. The Kabaka's palace was destroyed, and hundreds of his supporters were killed. The Kabaka managed to escape by disguising himself as a beggar, jumping over the palace walls, and fleeing across several borders until he arrived in the United Kingdom. He died in London just three years later, having failed to restore his kingdom.

Obote's actions outraged the people of Buganda and sowed the seeds of discord that Ugandans would reap for decades to come. The Baganda now regarded Obote as a foreigner from the north who had outstayed his welcome in Kampala. Obote oppressed the people of Buganda with violence and murder. His army became agents of death and humiliation, happy to exact revenge on the people in the South for grievances during the colonial era.

When Idi Amin, with the backing of the British government, overthrew Obote in 1972, the Baganda thought their deliverance had arrived, and they celebrated his ascendance to power. However, they soon realised that Amin's true ambition was to rule Uganda forever. His methods of brutality surpassed those of Obote, who was a more subtle manipulator. Amin was driven by a paranoia all too common to tyrants. He was convinced that he was surrounded by people who wanted to eliminate him. His fear drove him to eradicate any perceived threat before it could gather momentum. Hundreds of thousands of people were murdered during Amin's eight-year reign. Among them were prominent doctors, lawyers, university professors, cabinet ministers, and Janani Luwum, the Archbishop of the Anglican Church in Uganda.

Amin's rule finally came to an end after an ill-advised attack on Tanzania. His undisciplined army was no match for the Tanzanian troops and Ugandan militias, who had organised to bring down his regime. Again, the fall of the government was greeted with scenes of wild celebrations in Kampala. Tanzanian troops were treated as liberators.

The level of despair at the time of Amin's fall was so great that not even the destruction of the city nor the subsequent pillage and looting carried out by the Tanzanian victors could dampen the mood in Kampala. A military council was set up to govern while elections could be organised, but there was no consensus among the leaders as to how to unite the country.

Milton Obote, seizing the moment of confusion and disorganisation, returned from exile and took part in the elections that were held in December 1981. With his vast political experience and his sharp intelligence, he managed to manipulate the process and emerged victorious again. Obote became President for the second time, but many Ugandans felt the election was rigged and were outraged about this turn of events.

Yoweri Museveni, who had also contested the election and lost, launched the National Resistance Army and retreated to the countryside with a small group of men. They started the civil war, known as the Ugandan Bush War. Other rebel groups hoping to cash in on the mayhem joined in the fray. The struggle between the government and the countless small guerrilla armies brought great suffering. Kampala descended into chaos. Ordinary citizens bore the brunt of the violence.

This was the time and circumstances of our arrival into Kampala in November 1983. Sporadic gunfire was the order of both day and night. The infrastructure of the city was broken, with water and electrical supply intermittent and unreliable and, for much of the city, non-existent. The streets were in a state of complete disrepair. Supplies of basic needs were erratic, with many simply unavailable. Transport of goods and people was inaccessible. Guns were everywhere! Armed robbery by the invasion of houses or by hijacking of cars was a common occurrence. Military roadblocks were on every major street. Innocent pedestrians passing by were shot for not giving the soldiers the money they demanded. By sunset, everyone had returned to their homes to avoid the dangers of movement during the hours of darkness.

Obote continued his rule just as he had during his first term in office, with the brutal suppression of his opponents. He resorted to the defence of his government with ruthless military force. The economy of the nation collapsed as the army fought a costly war with the various rebel groups. The currency lost almost all its value. It was cheaper to use the paper money when responding to the call of nature than to buy toilet paper. The purchase of even the smallest of items required a bag of cash.

A joke made the rounds about a man who went to the store with a wheelbarrow full of cash. Unable to take his money into the store, he parked it at the entrance and went about gathering the few items he needed. When he went to collect his money, he discovered he had been robbed. A thief had stolen his wheelbarrow and left behind the small mountain of cash. Ugandans had an amazing ability to laugh when most other people would choose to cry, but their suffering was real.

Corruption was endemic. A total disregard for human life defined our first years in Uganda. The opposition military insurgence of Museveni's National Resistance Army (NRA) posed the biggest threat to the government. It was based and operating in a rural area 75 kilometres to the north of the capital city called the Luweero Triangle. Hoping to wipe out the rebellion, Obote sent the army into the area, systematically killing every man, woman, child and animal they found. The bloodshed and carnage left in the wake of the slaughter was total. Young boys who had been out tending the family flocks returned to their village homes to find their loved ones brutally butchered. Many of these boys and girls were recruited into the resistance army and spent the next years of their lives fighting with the NRA in the "bush war" to liberate the country.

Some years later, we passed by thousands of the skulls of the men, women and children whom the national army had eradicated. They were displayed in crude rows along the roadside or placed in a macabre grimace on vegetable stalls. Every one of them represented a life snuffed out early in a senseless war for political control and gain. Obote's brutal actions only served to galvanise the population into rallying behind Museveni's forces.

The NRA quickly grew into a viable threat to the government, and Obote responded by using the army to deal with any perceived rebel collaborators. Kampala was now full of spies. One couldn't trust a neighbour or an associate from work. Government troops routinely terrorised entire neighbourhoods in their attempts to eliminate opposition. These nightly incursions gave soldiers an excuse to loot, plunder and rape at will. Soon, Obote no longer controlled his army, but he relied on them to prolong his stay in power.

The mere sight of a soldier struck fear into the hearts of citizens on the street. By mid-afternoon, the city would begin to empty. Traders closed their shops, packed their wares into suitcases and carried them home for the evening. Every night, people barricaded themselves into their houses and prayed that they would avoid the death being portioned out all around them.

The rhythm of bullets in the night sky became the soundtrack to our lives. And though now familiar with the sensations evoked by Kampala's persistent chaos, we still lived with apprehension and nervous tension. We acquired the unkind trait of ubiquitous suspicion. We sized up strangers as they approached the car. We looked warily at the people who innocently lingered by our fence. We began to feel as if we, too, were being constantly evaluated by idlers or opportunists to gauge whether we were easy targets for theft or worse. The colour of our skin made us stand out, and just our presence in a marketplace would attract an unsettling amount of attention. We felt the constant gaze of people going about their business in the city, growing accustomed to being followed and gawked at as we walked down the street. Again, it felt like it was not *if* we would become targets of evil, but *when*.

~ They've Stolen Our New Car! ~

About three weeks after returning from Mombasa with the new, white Peugeot 504 Station wagon, I was returning home after dropping Timothy and Rachel off at school. The road was in terrible shape, cratered with potholes and deteriorating at the edges. I couldn't drive more than 20 kilometres per hour. When only three blocks from home, and as I negotiated a curve veering to the left, I was confronted with a startling scene. Standing in the middle of the road were four men armed with Kalashnikovs, each of them pointing their guns directly at me. I jumped on the brakes, bringing the car to a sudden stop.

"You have got to be kidding me," I thought. "I haven't had this car for a month."

Purposefully, they moved towards me, never taking their eyes off me and keeping their guns directed at me. I lifted my hands off the steering wheel and raised them submissively. I thought it was the appropriate response as I'd seen it done in the movies. One of them made his way towards the car window and thrust the barrel of his gun in, stopping inches from my forehead. I could smell the oil and metal of his weapon. The others positioned themselves around the vehicle, one directly in front of the vehicle and the other two on each corner at the rear.

"Well, Lord! Is this how it ends?" I thought.

"Get out of the car! Slowly!" It was the man at my window who spoke.

"Slowly," he repeated intentionally, calmly but emphatically.

I reached across to unbuckle my seat belt with my left hand, my right hand still raised.

"What are you doing?" he demanded forcefully.

I froze! "It's my seatbelt,"

Moving only the muscle that controls my index finger to point at the buckle.

"Slowly." Again, calm. Emphatic.

I reached down and unbuckled the seat belt. I felt their eyes and their weapons focused on my head.

In a time of crisis or danger, our mode of communication changes. It becomes simple and direct. Every action is justified, explained or announced. A simple miscommunication can cost us our lives, and our words become our only defence. An inappropriate tone or word could prove fatal.

"I am getting out now."

The words spilt out of my mouth while I looked the man straight into his eyes. I recognised in his face a look of determination and intent that was disturbing. He nodded and took a step back. I pushed the door open, swung my legs around, planted my feet on the dirt and stood up. My shoulders were hunched, and my hands raised, my gaze down on the ground in submission.

"Walk," he said, waving the weapon in the direction I was to take.

"Please, sir. My passport is in the glove compartment," I said. "Take the car, but just let me have my passport."

"Walk," he retorted. "And don't turn around."

I said nothing and turned away towards home, my hands still raised above my lowered head. In the immediate moments following, I imagined my death. Would I hear him shoot me as I walked away? Will I feel it? Will I see the bullet come flying out of the front of me with a piece of my spleen attached?

Dark images flooded my imagination. I anticipated the gunshot. I whispered a prayer. I heard feet crunching on the dusty road behind me. I heard the car door close and the vehicle moving towards me.

"This is it. It is over. I love you, Jesus."

The car drew up beside me. I tensed, not wanting to make eye contact with the man who was about to kill me. A hand reached out of the window. It was holding something. I couldn't tell what it was. I kept walking and squinted my eyes. The car kept pace with me for a few seconds before finally pulling ahead. The hand was still outstretched. With a casual flick of the fingers, the hand released its grip, and my passport dropped onto the dust.

I stopped, watching the car speed off, manoeuvre around a pothole, pass our house and disappear around a bend in the road. A thick cloud of dust and an eerie silence hung in the air. I don't know how long I stood there; it may only have been a few seconds, but I was stunned. I felt neither happy to be alive nor fear of death. Those emotions might come, but at that moment, I felt nothing. With a gasp, I exhaled deeply, lowered my raised hands and walked to where my passport lay on the road. I picked it up and flipped haphazardly through the pages. I looked into my own eyes in the photograph in the passport. Wow! The sounds of life around me began to emerge from the mist that had enveloped me in those moments. Birds were singing, and the sound of cars on the main road. I closed the passport, dusted it off, and tucking it into the back pocket of my blue jeans, walked home.

James was playing under the mango tree, completely unaware of what had just happened to his dad. I could see him through the fence, lost in his imaginary world of race cars and dump trucks. In that world, he was in control of the events. With his police car, he could chase down criminals and bring back goodness to the world. With his dump truck, he built fantastic cities where people could pursue and fulfil their dreams. In my world, the real one, we were at the whim of wicked men and the mercy of an immensely good God.

In my heart, I knew that our faithful God was protecting and surrounding us. Had we not come this far? But at that moment, I felt a twang of apprehension. I rehearsed what we had been through in the first six months in Uganda. Apart from the daily uncertainty of life here, we had endured a near-fatal car accident in which the car was destroyed, an assault by a gang of twenty-five violent men against my precious wife and little children, and now they had stolen our new car. I wonder what's next?

Heaviness descended on me and clouded my thoughts. Storms began to brew in my spirit.

"What am I doing here? Am I crazy?" I asked myself.

"Maybe we should just give up. We gave it our best shot and have endured as best we can. Why not just cut our losses, pack up, and go somewhere else? Of all the places God could call me to serve. And now we have no car again. It's back to five on motorbike."

I began to pray,

"Why here, God? Anywhere but here. I don't need an ocean view or a tropical paradise. Anywhere, just not here."

Surely and with a calm, strong voice, the promise God had made to me one year back rose to the surface.

"In this place, you will shed blood, sweat, and tears, but if you are faithful to me, I will be faithful to you."

The words pounded in my head, and they thrust at my heart. Blood. Sweat. Tears.

Had we not bled enough? Had we not sweat enough? And what of our tears? At this rate, we were going to be bled dry, drained of sweat and tears. We would be empty, filled with nothingness. And then I realised that this was precisely the point. Maybe all I could offer this amazingly good God was my emptiness. Any goodness, or any purpose, any success could only

STRUGGLES IN THE SHADOWS

come out of my emptiness being replaced and filled by His grace.

And I was not alone in trial and difficulty. Others had been called to give their all. Jesus himself had gone before us, sweat drops of blood and shed tears over the state of the city of Jerusalem. And what about the apostles of Jesus who had been scattered around the world after Pentecost and endured incredible hardship? What about Paul? He left behind a long list of affliction and adversity. He was flogged, beaten with rods, stoned, exposed to death repeatedly, shipwrecked, spent a day and a half in the open sea, constantly on the move, in danger of rivers, bandits, false brothers, Jews and Gentiles, hunger and thirst, cold and naked.

Who was I to complain and to feel alone in suffering?

There were those pioneer missionaries to Uganda who came from England, leaving family and comfort behind, only to die in the tropical heat from dysentery, black water fever or the spears of hostile tribesmen. The first two Bishops of the fledgling church in Uganda had died or been killed on the border before they stepped into Uganda. What right did I have to complain? Was it not true that out of adversity and tragedy, God would fashion victory and success? Yes! Absolutely yes! Our precious God and Father, our loving, gentle Lord and Saviour, Jesus, would never fail us. He would see us through and write a story to tell of His glory.

The Apostle Paul, when discussing his "thorn in the flesh," a trial he continually faced, wrote,

> *"Three times I pleaded with the Lord to take it away from me. But he said to me, "My grace is sufficient for you, for my power is made perfect in weakness." Therefore I will boast all the more gladly about my weaknesses, so that Christ's power may rest on me. That is why, for Christ's sake, I delight in weaknesses, in insults, in hardships, in persecutions, in difficulties. For when I am weak, then I am strong."*
>
> *2 Corinthians 12:7-11 (NIV)*

This is just the way God works. Even my faith, my very ability to be obedient, was a gift from Him so that I could never boast. And so, I submitted. I prayed to be washed and bathed in His grace, for my emptiness to be filled with His goodness and for my heart to be baptised with a fresh dose of divine love and compassion.

I walked into our simple house and gave Marilyn a really big hug.

~ Reflect and Discuss ~

As you reflect on these questions and engage in discussion with others, consider the following:

1. Cycle of Violence and Sin in Uganda's History:

    • Reflect on the cycle of violence, war, and oppression that has plagued much of Uganda's history. Consider how sin, including pride, greed, love of power, and vengeance, has played a continual role in the turmoil of the nations.

    • Explore how these sinful attitudes and actions have contributed to conflicts, injustices, and suffering experienced by individuals and communities in Uganda.

2. Gary's Realization of Being "Emptied":

    • Consider the significance of Gary's realization of being "emptied" in his journey. Reflect on how this experience of emptiness may have led him to a deeper dependence on God and a recognition of his own limitations.

    • Reflect on what Paul means when he writes, "For when I am weak, then I am strong." Consider how God's power is made perfect in our weakness, and how relying on God's strength rather than our own can lead to true strength and resilience.

3. God's Emptying Work in Your Life:

    • Prayerfully consider where God may be emptying you in your life. Reflect on areas where you may feel depleted, weak, or in need of God's intervention.

    • Explore how God might be calling you to open up to Him as your source of strength rather than relying on yourself. Consider how surrendering control and acknowledging your weakness can lead to a deeper reliance on God and His power.

During your discussion, offer support, encouragement, and prayer for one another. Share personal insights, experiences, and struggles as you seek to grow in dependence on God's strength and grace. By opening up to God's emptying work in your life, you can experience His transformative power and find true strength in Him.

∼

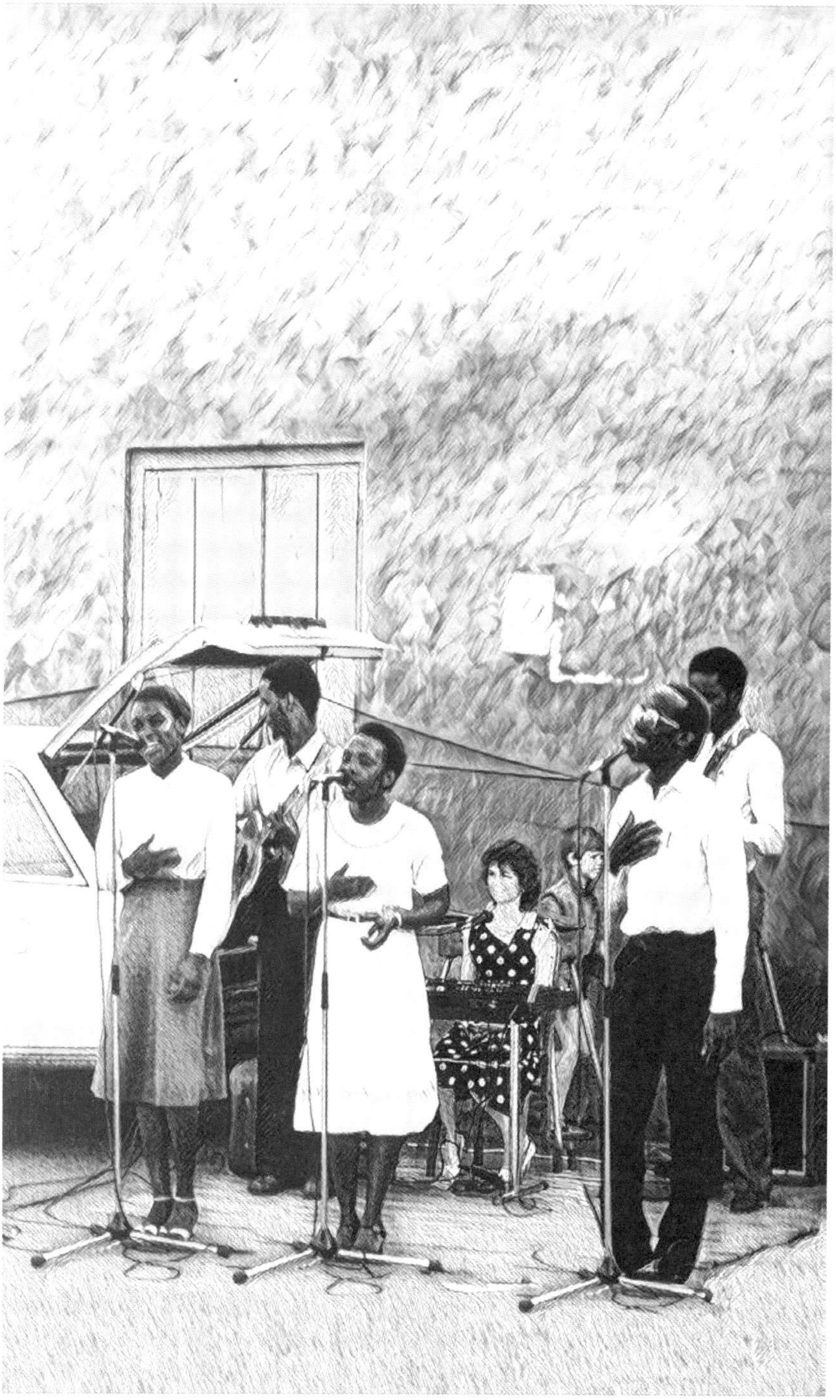

> "The Church is the Church only
> when it exists for others."
>
> *Dietrich Bonhoeffer*

10

~ Trailblazers ~

*"Igniting passion and purpose
in the hearts of the next generation."*

So now, we had no car. We hadn't been in the country for six months, one was wrecked in a crash and the second stolen. Our Kampala project was proving not only to be challenging but expensive. On top of that, the civil war showed no sign of slowing down. In fact, things were getting worse. Friends and family around the world were concerned for us.

But we had a very clear responsibility placed before us. We were to grow and establish an English-speaking church in the heart of Kampala. It was the city that controlled almost everything about Uganda. The political and financial decisions that would determine Uganda's future were made here. The education, business, culture, and legal influence were centred here. What God wanted to do was very clear to me. He had said that through this church, he would touch the city and the nation.

At that point, I didn't fully understand all the Lord wanted to do through the church we were to plant. I do remember hearing church leaders saying that they were going to change a city, a nation, or the world, and I would consider that sort of statement as arrogant. Who did this person think they were that they could have an impact on an entire city or nation? And now Jesus was saying that very thing to me.

I decided to put it on the back burner and just get on with what we were here to do. I determined to preach relevant Bible based messages that would inspire the youth to serve God unrelentingly. Marilyn and I would lead the congregation in vibrant worship that would relate to the style youth would be drawn to. We determined to start and end church services on time. We celebrated communion, baptism and prayer for the sick on a regular basis. We did our best to demonstrate consistent faithfulness and integrity as a way of life in the middle of trying circumstances. We encouraged others to do the same, as we lived together in a broken city. We modelled what I considered crucial and very much needed: a new style of leadership. We knew that if we were faithful in these things, impact on the city or nation would take care of itself, in God's time.

Having a clear and focused vision of what God wanted to do was essential and critical. The vision was to plant a church. The details of the kind of church we were to build would unfold over the ensuing years. Time would not change the vision but enhance and clarify it. Deep in my heart I knew, absolutely and without a doubt, that Jesus wanted to do something significant and big. But big things start small. The most imposing tree in the forest starts as a tiny seed. It's planted, sprouts, grows, and over time, through rain, sunshine and storm, develops into a giant that contributes to the life of the forest. All the animals, the birds and people rely on it for shelter, food and sustenance.

Marilyn and I knew that in order to do what God had called us to do, we would need help. No one can build a church alone. If the church was going to grow and have impact and influence, then we would need to empower and train others to do the work of the ministry. I had done the work of pastoral care in only two small churches. In Brockville, as a pastor to the youth, we had worked hard to disciple and train the young people of the church in evangelism and ministry. One of the highlights was taking a team of them to minister at the Montréal Olympic Games in 1976. Some of those young people went into pastoral and church leadership positions in Canada. In Listowel, a small farming community, we did the same. We mentored one of the young men, a dairy farmer's son, in the skill of leading worship. It was something Marilyn and I had a gift for. The young man took it up, even though he had no formal musical training and led worship for many years.

The Bible says in Ephesians 4:11-13 that,

> "...Christ himself gave the apostles, the prophets, the evangelists, the pastors and teachers, to equip his people for works of service, so that the body of Christ may be built up until we all reach unity in the faith and in the knowledge of the Son of God and become

mature, attaining to the whole measure of the fullness of Christ."

Ephesians 4:11-13 (NIV)

Mentoring and training ministry leaders is critical to growing a healthy local church. The biblical instructions are clear. As a pastor, my role was not just to do the work of the ministry but "...to prepare God's people for works of service..."

So, from the outset, I determined to hold classes to do just that. We started the Timothy School of Discipleship with noon-hour classes every weekday. I was looking for young men and women whom I could entrust with more responsibility as the church grew. I watched and noted those wonderful young people who were faithful, committed, worked hard and were eager to serve God.

There were times when I needed to decide on some matter affecting the fledgling church, so I gathered a few of the faithful ones who demonstrated commitment and ability and sought their advice. I made it somewhat official by calling it an advisory team. It was a precursor to what would eventually become a team of elders and deacons.

I was also determined to understand the classic culture of leadership that was popular practice in the country. I noticed that any institution or church would have a board with a chairman, a secretary, a treasurer and members of the board. I felt that God wanted me to raise a generation of young leaders who would think and act differently. Titles seemed so important to everyone. Maybe it came out of the old British culture and military background. If someone had an engineering degree and worked as an engineer, they were referred to as "Engineer John." The same was true of a doctor or lawyer. And when it came to the church, there was "Pastor Gary," "Bishop So and So," Evangelist George," "Elder John," or "Apostle Henry."

I decided that it was necessary to drop all the titles and get back to some basics. I thought it was also necessary to highlight Team ministry instead of a Board-driven mentality. Rather than a Board of Deacons, we began to refer to them as the Deacons Team. The Chairman of the board was now the Team leader for the Deacons team. I dropped the title of Senior Pastor and assumed the role of the Pastoral Team Leader of Kampala Pentecostal Church.

I felt it important to emphasise and practice that a church cannot thrive on the ministry strength of a single personality or small group of people, but through the sacrifice and service of the whole body of believers.

As I interacted with the young people who came to church and had made it home, there were a number of issues that were concerning to me about life in Uganda. One was the unreasonably elevated place education held in determining a person's value and worth. The second was the fact that so many of the young people, while outwardly respectful of their parents, had a real sense of fatherlessness. Thirdly, there was a lack of purpose in the lives of many young people. I soon realised that these matters were related.

Parents paid a high price, financially, to send their children to school. Education was not free. Government funding for schools was non-existent. The best schools, by far, were the church schools founded by the Anglican and Catholic Churches. The best of these were boarding schools that had been operated by missionaries as teachers and headmasters. The purpose of these schools was to educate Ugandan leaders who would lead the nation into a better future. It had certainly worked out that way. The cream of Ugandan society were those who succeeded in their education at the best schools. The fraternity among graduates and alumni of these schools was strong. If you didn't "make it," you were considered second class, inferior, not quite good enough. That was the way many young people looked at themselves. Fathers placed very high standards on their children, especially in light of the financial cost necessary for their education. They expected their children to perform well in school by earning excellent grades.

The problem was compounded by fathers pushing their children into preparation for careers they wanted for them, often the same career as the father. And when a son or daughter underperformed or did not meet the expectations of their fathers, the level of castigation and demeaning of the children was epic and sometimes brutal. The child was accused of not being thankful, not studying hard enough, of squandering resources. Consequently, a deep rift grew particularly between fathers and sons. Sons often saw themselves as failures, incapable of success and a disappointment to the person who they should have meant the most to. The level of angst in these young people lay festering away in their hearts sometimes developing into an unseen, but deep bitterness and a real sense of despair.

Added to that was the common practice for men to have intimate relationships with multiple women, not just their wives. Many extra-marital affairs were not conducted secretly, but often blatantly, with the second woman sometimes being brought right into the family home or a man running several households. It was not uncommon to hear of young people attending their father's funeral, only to meet, to their dismay, brothers and sisters whom they had never met, didn't know they had and who were also attending the same funeral. These young people watched the incredible trauma, rejection, betrayal, financial inequity and sometimes violence their precious mothers faced at the hands of their fathers. The bitterness ran deep.

A consequence of this was a generation of vulnerable Ugandan youth who saw themselves as inadequate, would never amount to anything, had no purpose, and little if any, hope or sense of destiny. They drifted into sexual sin in order to fill a relational gap left by emotional abuse. The guilt, depression and pain drove them to church, looking for answers and community. But they didn't want to go to the same church as their parents. Those churches were traditional in style and liturgy, and unattractive to the youth. Those churches accepted and courted what they saw as hypocritical fathers.

So, they began to explore the church life of the burgeoning number of Pentecostal churches. But these services were often eccentric and went on for hours. But as the gospel was presented, many young people received Christ and began a journey in their Christian walk that tended toward super-spirituality and negative judgment of their parents. These well intended young people would rise before dawn and pray loudly, disturbing their sleeping families. They would criticise their parents for their lack of Christian faith and zeal. This drove a deeper wedge between the children and their parents. The parents would forbid their children from attending Pentecostal churches, but the kids would find a way to go anyway.

Adding to the divide was the fact that the leadership of the traditional churches viewed the growing number of independent, Pentecostal churches as a threat as the youth gravitated to this crop of new churches. The pastors in the Pentecostal community had little or no theological training, little accountability and structure, and were largely critical of these traditional churches. I remember one weekend wanting to show *The Jesus Movie* at church, but we had no projector. The Anglican Church did, so I went and asked if we could rent it. I was informed that they had a policy not to rent to Pentecostal communities.

In this context, young people heard about what we were doing and were drawn to our new church. Though we were Pentecostal, we intentionally operated differently than both of the common expressions of church in Kampala. We preached the good news of Jesus clearly and in a contemporary way. Our music was attractive and alive. Our messages included lessons in practical Bible based living, in forgiveness and love of one's enemy, and in each person's inherent value as God's image-bearers.

I felt Jesus speak to me. "I want the church to be alive but not wild, conservative but not dead."

The prescription he gave me was a specific word of instruction for the kind of church we were to be. At the time, I wasn't fully aware of all the challenges the youth were facing, but we carefully developed a liturgy and church style that was alive, but conservative. I understood much later that this directive from Jesus was exactly what the city needed in its spiritual life. We were to be moderate in all things, not dull on the one hand, but not wild and eccentric either.

Some of the young people who were coming to church confided in me that their parents did not want them going to "...that church. It will make you mad." They were referring to the eccentricities displayed in some in the Pentecostal community. Parents didn't want this for their children. They wanted what was best for them. That's why they pushed them hard at school and cautioned them to resist what they considered to be cults.

I made it a goal to address these issues with the growing young congregation. I taught about honouring leadership and especially honouring parents, even when they considered leadership or parents were at fault. I asked the young people not to come to church if their parents forbade them to do so. I encouraged them, instead, to display an attitude of humility and submission, to serve their parents by willingly offering to do the necessary chores around the house. I pushed them to lead in spiritual activities at home gently and helpfully. I provoked them to display genuine Christian character and love, instead of judgment and criticism. I encouraged them to ask for permission to attend our services, but if the answer was negative, to show an attitude of submission tempered by godly character. I encouraged them to keep seeking permission and showing their parents that going to church made them better.

Over time, this strategy worked. Eventually, parents were dropping their kids off at our church and then going on to their church services. It wasn't ideal, as we wanted families to worship together, but young people were celebrating Jesus and new life, while developing and demonstrating Christ-like character at home. Years later, it was a delight to meet parents who would thank me for pastoring their children, for helping them be better kids and for keeping them out of trouble. It was a matter of persistence to this principle over an extended period, but the reputation of our church, known as Kampala Pentecostal Church, grew to be respected and valued in the city. It was no longer considered one of those crazy churches.

I was also delighted to learn that many of the young people came from homes of people in the community who had significant influence in politics, business and other segments of society. As I interacted with these young people and, consequently, with their parents, I noticed that they were beginning to have a positive influence at home and in their schools. We became known as that "young people's church." I was only thirty-one years of age at the time. Some said that as a church full of young people, we were just a fad and would, at some point, fade away. But God had placed a dream in my heart. We were to build a church community, in order to disciple for Christ the next generation of leaders.

Another factor that attracted youth to the church was the opportunity we had to visit schools, colleges and the University. We were invited to preach to the students. Most weekends, we packed up the car, took some of the youth from church along with us and headed off to a school. We led in worship, sang some special songs and then delivered a Gospel message to the students.

God moved, people were giving their lives to Christ, were growing in maturity and faith, and our community was starting to thrive. And through it all, God continued to remind us that this was not about how impressive we were or what we would accomplish.

He beat this gentle drum in our hearts and minds over and over. "You are not going to touch this city, this nation." He would clearly say, "My church is! It is going to be the people that I raise up among you, my people, that I will use to bring healing, hope, and transformation to Kampala and

Uganda."

We embraced this promise. Our community represented a small start, but we knew God wanted to do something significant. He wanted us to plant the seeds of change into the heart of a young nation. We were beginning to understand in a new light what Jesus meant when he said,

> *"The kingdom of heaven is like a mustard seed, which a man took and planted in his field. Though it is the smallest of all seeds, yet when it grows, it is the largest of garden plants and becomes a tree so that the birds come and perch in its branches... The kingdom of heaven is like yeast that a woman took and mixed into about sixty pounds of flour until it worked all through the dough."*
>
> *Matthew 13:31-34 (NIV)*

We were witnessing the small beginnings of a church that would touch the city and touch the nation for Christ. Things were beginning to grow.

~ Reflect and Discuss ~

As you reflect on these questions and engage in discussion with others, consider the following:

1. Demonstrating Godly Character through Submission to Parental Leadership:

    • Reflect on the importance of demonstrating godly character by submitting to parental leadership, even when we may consider our parents to be wrong.

    • Consider the biblical principles of honour and respect for parents, as outlined in Ephesians 6:1-3 and Colossians 3:20, and how obedience to parental authority reflects our obedience to God.

    • Discuss practical ways to honour and submit to parental leadership, such as through respectful communication, prayerful consideration of their guidance, and seeking reconciliation and understanding in disagreements.

2. Role of Members in Church Ministry according to Ephesians 4:11-13:

    • Explore Ephesians 4:11-13 and its teachings on the role of members in church ministry. Consider how God has gifted individuals within the church for the purpose of building up the body of Christ.

    • Reflect on the diverse gifts and roles mentioned in the passage, such as apostles, prophets, evangelists, pastors, and teachers, and how each contributes to the growth and maturity of the church.

    • Discuss the importance of unity, service, and mutual edification among members as they fulfil their respective roles in ministry.

3. Impact of the Church in Building God's Kingdom:

    • Reflect on Jesus' parables of the mustard seed and the yeast in Matthew 13:31-34 and what they teach us about the impact of the church in building God's Kingdom.

    • Consider how the mustard seed, though small, grows into a large tree, and how the yeast leavens the whole batch of dough. Reflect on the transformative influence of the church in society and the spread of the gospel message.

    • Discuss how the church, like seed and yeast, spreads the message of God's Kingdom, brings about spiritual growth and transformation, and permeates every aspect of community life with the love and truth of Christ.

During your discussion, offer support, encouragement, and prayer for one another as you seek to apply biblical principles in your lives and ministries. Share personal experiences, challenges, and victories, and commit to growing together in faith and obedience to God's Word. By embracing godly character, fulfilling our roles in church ministry, and being agents of Kingdom impact in our communities, we can glorify God and advance His purposes on earth.

~

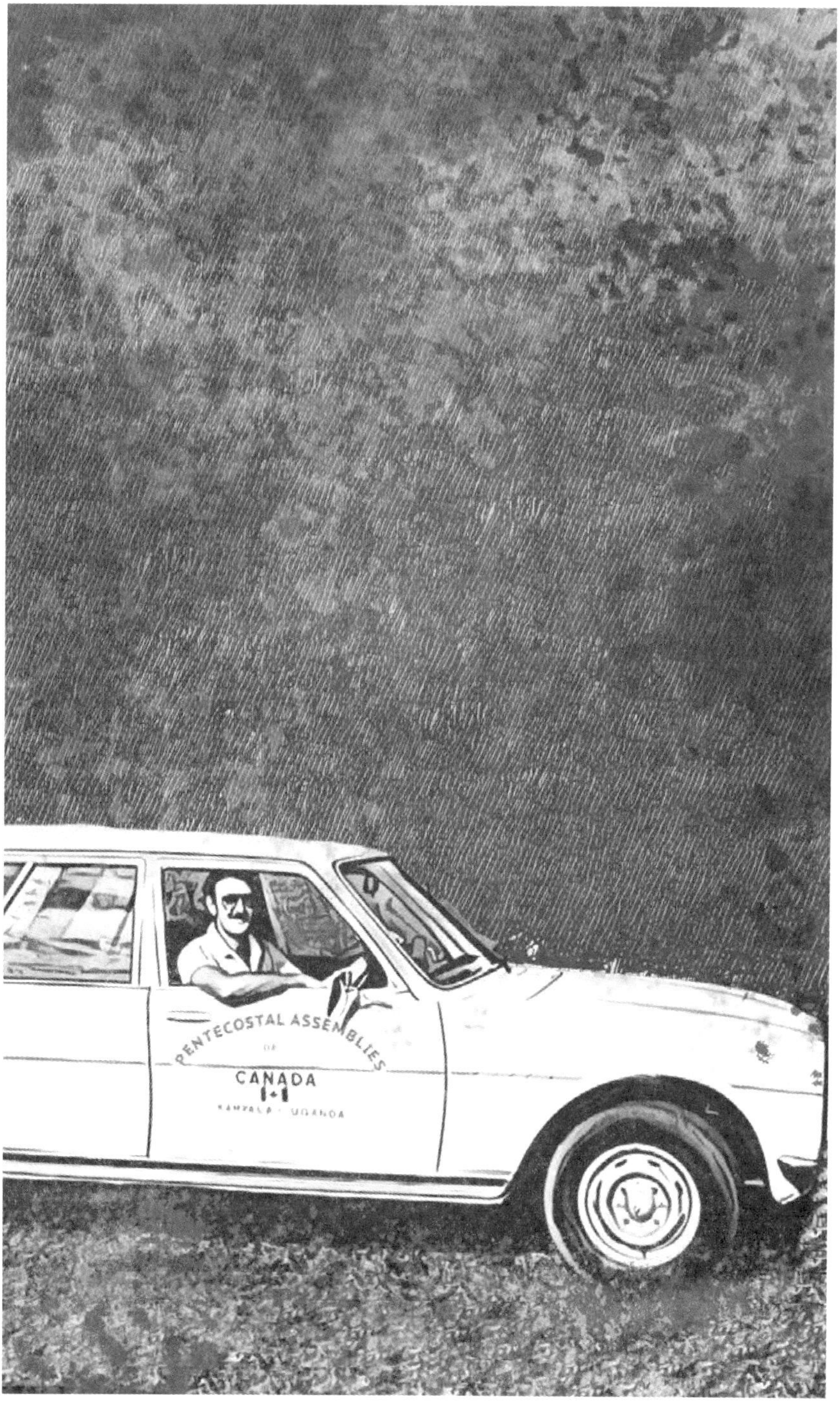
PENTECOSTAL ASSEMBLIES
CANADA

"Real Christians revel in desperate ventures for Christ,
expecting from God great things
and attempting the same with exhilaration."

C.T. Studd

"When you believe in angels
you have friends in high places."

Author Unknown

"If God has determined to stand with us,
tell me, who then could ever stand against us?"

The Apostle Paul - Romans 9:31b TPT

11
~ Beyond Belief ~

"Supernatural intervention."

The two years we held church at the Grand Imperial Hotel were during a time of great national insecurity and uncertainty. Kampala was a tough place to live in. Every day was a day for potential disaster. Each time we drove out of the gates of our home, we wondered if the car would be stolen from us at gunpoint. Each night, as we headed off to bed, we wondered if this would be the night thieves would invade the house. Random gunfire at any time could mean being caught up in crossfire. It wasn't a matter of *if* but *when* disaster would strike.

Everyone living in the city was going through the challenges of surviving in a time of war, uncertainty and general mayhem. Almost daily, we heard reports of people we knew who had been robbed, beaten or killed. I think that for us to be there, identifying with those precious people and going through the same challenges together with, and alongside them demonstrated that we genuinely cared for them. In fact, we did more than just care for them as an act of duty to God. We loved them. They won their way into our hearts. They became family to us. We loved them enough to walk with them in the trials and challenges they were going through.

This is what the divine Christ, Jesus, the Son of God, did in taking on human flesh. The incarnation of Christ was a very clear demonstration of God's love for humanity. He showed his love for us by sending Jesus to walk with us and to model how life should be lived. He showed his love for us by taking the place of judgement and conviction that we deserved because of our wrongs, our sins and our rebellion against God. He showed His love for us by dying in our place. And the glory of the gospel, is that death could not hold him. He rose from the grave as a clear demonstration of the sovereign power of His Lordship over all.

He loved Uganda with such a deep passion and devotion that He sent Marilyn and me, and our three young children, as ambassadors of the Kingdom of Heaven, to declare the purposes, plans and will of our wonderful Lord and Saviour. Our vision to plant the church was a noble one that was very much needed. Our purpose became more and more clear as time unfolded. The Church, as Christ's body on earth, was to be the agent of Heaven, calling individuals and community to personal and corporate surrender to the sovereignty of Christ over all human affairs. This is what bringing healing to the city and nation is about.

We felt the reciprocal love of the people, but what we wanted was for them to love God, and for that to translate into personal and community transformation. So, as tough as it was, we considered it a great honour to serve in Kampala during those tough times. We determined that whatever it cost, we would remain faithful to the call God had put on us to be here in Kampala. We would persist, one day at a time, to do the work of God. We knew that what God had said in His word was true.

> *"You are not your own; you were bought at a price. Therefore, honor God with your body."*
>
> *1 Corinthians 6:19b-20 (NIV)*

As followers and disciples of Christ, we did not get to choose what to do with our lives. We belong to Jesus. For us, that meant living in Kampala. The apostle Paul understood this and wrote,

> *For none of us lives to himself alone, and none of us dies to himself alone. If we live, we live to the Lord, and if we die, we die to the Lord. So, whether we live or die, we belong to the Lord."*
>
> *Romans 14:7-8 (NIV)*

If being in Kampala meant suffering, then that is what we would do and not grumble about it.

Perhaps we have lost, in our contemporary expression of Christianity, the truth that life is not about our comfort and ease. It's not about our prosperity but about our commitment to faithfully serve the Lord who gave himself fully for us and to seek, as a priority, His Kingdom.

Paul, in his suffering, wrote to the Philippians from a jail cell and said,

> *For it has been granted to you on behalf of Christ not only to believe on him, but also to suffer for him..."*
>
> *Philippians 1:29 (NIV)*

We would trust God to take care of us. Psalm 91 is a promise from God of His wonderful protection for those who take refuge in Him. We may face trying and difficult circumstances, but we do not fear the terror that stalks at night nor the arrow that flies at noonday. It does not come near us. If God is our refuge, then no harm will overtake us, and no disaster will come near our tent. And then there is this amazing promise,

> *God sends angels with special orders to protect you wherever you go, defending you from all harm."*
>
> *Psalm 91:11 TPT*

I have no doubt that there were times when God sent angels to protect us from harm. The Bible tells us that angels are ministering spirits sent to serve those of us who are the followers of Jesus. (Hebrews 1:14). We may never be aware of their presence, but they are present in situations when we need divine help.

~ Angels Again! ~

There were several other missionary families also serving in Kampala during those very difficult and trying days who we would visit from time to time for fellowship and encouragement. On one visit, they told us of angelic protection they had experienced that very week. They had gone downtown to pick up some supplies. Stan parked the car behind a pick-up truck and went into the store, leaving Marion in the car. As she waited, she was interrupted by a commotion. Soldiers dragged a man in the direction of the pickup truck. The man was being dragged out of a store beside the car, shouting and resisting the soldier's attempts to muscle him into the truck. One of the soldiers beat the man on the head with his rifle, and then, picking him up, they dumped him into the open back of the truck. The man resisted again and tried to get up and jump out of the truck. One of the soldiers leaned over the edge of the truck and, boom, boom, shot the man several times. Marion watched as his body jerked at the impact of the bullets slamming into his torso. She slumped down in her seat, her heart beating rapidly. The soldiers got into the truck and drove away.

Marion gulped and felt the shock of what she had witnessed rise up in her.

A prayer formed in her mind.

"Lord! We can't stay here any longer. This is too much!"

Stan returned to comfort her, and they drove home. In their distress, they cried out to God in prayer later that evening.

"This is too difficult, Father! If you want us to stay, Lord, please give us a sign."

The next morning, they gathered for early morning prayer and worship with their staff. The security guard asked if he could tell them what he had witnessed the previous night while watching over the property. Seated by the gate at midnight, he was shocked to see two big men dressed in white, both on horses, ride up to the gate. He had never seen a horse before but knew they were horses from pictures in a book. He stood up! The men and horses disappeared. So, he sat down! The horses and riders reappeared. So, he stood up! Again, the horses disappeared. So, he sat down, and the horses reappeared.

"I better just sit and watch, he thought."

The men rode right through the closed gate. One of them circled the house. The other rode through the walls of the house and then re-emerged. He watched as they rode back out through the gate and on down the street. Stan and Marion realised the supernatural protection of God over their lives in the middle of difficult and trying circumstances, and stayed in Uganda for several more years.

On a visit to the northern part of Uganda several years later, I met a fiery Ugandan evangelist at one of the meetings. He was known for his zeal in winning people to Christ and had a joyful, effervescent spirit and a broad smile. He told me of how, in the bad days of President Idi Amin's regime, the churches had been banned from meeting. Amin had converted to Islam and wanted Uganda to become a Muslim state. The evangelist refused to stop preaching the gospel to the villages he was assigned to. Several years after Amin had been deposed and exiled, a man came up to the evangelist after a meeting. He had come to Christ and wanted to let the evangelist know that he had been a soldier in Amin's army. One of his assignments had been to waylay the evangelist after a meeting, and kill him. They waited beside the path for the preacher to pass by them on his bicycle. As he approached, they emerged from the bushes, ready to kill him. To their amazement, running on the path beside the cycling evangelist, who was singing a song of worship, were two enormous men dressed in white. They brushed the soldiers aside, and the evangelist rode on oblivious to the ministering spirits sent to serve him.

None of us will ever be fully aware of the wonderful protection and miracles God has worked for us as we serve him. As we lived in Kampala in those early days, we knew that we could never have made it without the knowledge of his goodness and care.

~ The Car Comes Home! ~

We had wrecked one car, and the brand-new one that I had picked up in Mombasa had been stolen. There was no money for another vehicle, so an old Volvo station wagon that was not being used in Nairobi was made available to us.

No one ever got their car back once it was stolen, but that didn't stop us and the wonderful people at church from praying for the miracle return of the car. For months, we prayed. One morning, while sitting in my office at home, I received a phone call from the police, asking for Pastor Skinner. The officer on the phone informed me that they had found our stolen car and wanted to return it to me. Would I come down to the station to set up the details? Of course, I would. Arriving at the station, I made my way up to the police commander's office, was kindly welcomed in and given a seat beside his desk. Then he told me what had happened in finding the car.

At the time the relationships between the army and police were not cordial. The police had discovered that the army commander in the barracks in the city of Masaka, 120 kilometres southwest of Kampala, was driving our car. And then he revealed the details. The car had been stolen by members of the rebel army that was working to overthrow the government of Milton Obote. They had used the vehicle in a bank robbery in Masaka. I imagine it was a way of financing the needs of the rebel forces. The army in Masaka was made aware of the robbery as it was taking place, rushed to intervene, and, in the ensuing battle, recovered the car. The commander of the army barracks kept the vehicle for his personal use. After all, it was brand new, in great shape, and he didn't know who it really belonged to. The police knew of the robbery and decided to recover the vehicle. They approached the army commander, who was compelled to return it. The police had made arrangements for us to drive the two hours southwest of Kampala to the barracks at Masaka, and the car would be returned to me.

The next day, we drove down with the expectation of getting the car back. As we were nearing Masaka town, I saw our car pass us in the opposite direction on its way back to Kampala. I'm not sure the policeman with me believed me when I told him that I thought it was my car I had seen going back to Kampala, so we continued on to Masaka.

When we arrived, we were told that the commander had an urgent meeting in Kampala and had used the vehicle to get there. However, we could return the next day, and he would hand it over to the police, who would return it to me. He also informed me that the car had been involved in a small accident and the commander had spent several hundred dollars on repairs. He was happy to give the car back, if we would reimburse him for the repairs. I laughed and said that he owed me rent for using the car for several months. It was his turn to laugh!

"Bring the money," he said, and we parted.

The next day, we returned. I decided not to argue the point about money for repairs and brought two hundred dollars with me. They handed me the keys to the car, and I drove it to Kampala, worshipping Jesus all the way home. Our good and gracious God had provided us with another miracle. The people at church were jubilant and celebrated with us at the wonder of our Father God.

We were delighted to have the car back. It was so much better than the Volvo and a whole lot more comfortable than the five of us on a motorcycle. God had shown himself faithful to his word. He had said that he would never leave nor forsake us. He had promised that He would be with us wherever we went. His presence and protection were constant and reliable.

The news of the miracles God was working on our behalf began to spread around. There was a general feeling that this man of God from Canada had God on his side. I couldn't agree more. He had kept armed men from attacking the family while I was away. He had put angels around us when the same gang had gone through our neighbourhood looting and raping. Now we had the car back. It was a fine batch of miracles from a good God.

Of course, God was on our side.

~ Reflect and Discuss ~

As you reflect on these questions and engage in discussion with others, consider the following:

1. Surrendering to God's plan for your life:

    • Discuss the implications of 1 Corinthians 6:19b-20 and Romans 14:7-8 in regard to surrendering our lives to the plans of God.

    • What does it mean to honour God with our bodies?

2. Suffering for the cause of Christ:

    • Reflect on the meaning of Philippians 1-29 about suffering for Christ. How does the message of abundant life in Christ and suffering for Christ work in tandem in bringing about the purpose of God for our lives.

    • Consider some of the ways you have suffered for Christ. How can we support one another in the trials we have to endured as followers and disciples of Jesus.

3. Divine intervention as we serve Christ:

    • God provided angels and miracles as the church was being planted in Kampala. Recall and discuss times in your life when God protected and provided for you as you served Him.

During your discussion, offer support, encouragement, and prayer for one another as you seek to discern and follow God's call in your lives. Share personal experiences, challenges, and insights, and commit to walking alongside one another in faith and obedience. By embracing compassion and empathy, recognizing the transformative power of God's Kingdom, and fostering community support, you can cultivate a deeper understanding of God's call and faithfully respond to His leading.

191

"The greatest legacy one can pass on to one's grandchildren is not money or other material things accumulated in one's life, but rather a legacy of character and faith."

Billy Graham

12
~ No Easy Answers ~

Though God was beginning to work wonderfully at church, we had to face the difficulty of living in a war zone. This proved to be particularly traumatic for the children. We heard the repetitive sounds of gunfire throughout the night, felt the anxiety of the community, and, to the degree they were able, the children understood the danger of living in this new place. Our son tells of an early memory while riding in the car one day. He watched shoppers casually step over a dead body as they entered and exited a general store.

It is difficult to put into words the impact scenes like this and others can have on anyone, let alone a young and impressionable child. Marilyn and I began to realise that the sacrifices we were willing to make in obedience to God's call to live in Uganda extended, in a very real and significant way, to our children. They had no choice in the matter of moving to and remaining in Uganda. They had been inserted into a volatile, unstable community and, as a result, witnessed what no child should ever witness: horrific violence. They had to reconcile with the fact that their parents had placed them in dangerous circumstances and brought them into and kept them in this fractious environment. We learned, later on, the weight they carried to "keep it all together" in front of others and to present themselves as "good" missionary kids, never complaining but remaining positive in light of the extreme difficulty they lived with daily. The burden of that kind of pressure was immense.

Understanding this aspect of our call cannot be remedied by appealing to easy, flippant answers or by quoting Bible verses out of context. Explain to your four-year-old why God wants them to live in difficult circumstances, and you will come to the awareness that any attempt to downplay or rationalise suffering is a disservice to the complexity of our lives and vocations on this fallen earth.

Each of our children has a different perspective on their childhood in Uganda. Out of honour to them, I will not go into detail about those perspectives, but the simple truth is that our children experienced real trauma as a result of our willingness to subject them to living in an unstable, war-torn African country. There is no skirting the matter of trauma. We cannot just shrug it off and hope for the best. Yes, we could edit out the immense challenges our children faced, the real long term influence it had on them, and it would be an omission that would make the story in these pages far tidier. But to ignore and leave out this part of the narrative would lack transparency that we believe to be critical and necessary for us to acknowledge, and important for you to understand. There is, unfortunately, a cost to discipleship and to obedience and understanding it and reconciling yourself to it does not come easily.

As the Ugandan civil war raged on and the political situation continued to degenerate, we felt less and less safe having our children in the country. The simple act of driving our kids to and from school became more and more precarious, given we were expatriates and because, at the time, we owned one of the few cars in the city. There were times that Marilyn and I were unsure that we would be able to pick them up from school because of street fighting going on in the area. The reality of keeping our children in school and in the city became too tenuous for us to feel comfortable with. We were faced with a painful decision. Do we leave Uganda or explore other options.

One option was to home-school the children. Thinking that over carefully, we realised it was not a viable option. Another was to send the children to boarding school in Kenya. Other parents were doing this. Not only was the boarding school option safer but acceptable, even desired within the British and Ugandan framework of education. The rural farming community and missionaries whose posting meant they lived in out-of-the-way places found it necessary to use the boarding school option. I attended boarding school as a child in Zambia. I did not find it easy. It was traumatic. My father had also attended boarding school while his parents served as missionaries to Kenya in the 1940s. It was not our first choice, but we had survived the ordeal.

We began to explore this as an option, though with gut-wrenching agony and travail. Reluctantly, we decided to enrol them in a very good school in Kenya. In September of 1984, we drove across the border into Kenya and took Timothy to boarding school. He was nine years old. To this day, sending our little boy off to another country to spend nine months out of the year away from the family remains the hardest, most painful decision Marilyn and I have ever had to make in order to be obedient to the call of God on our lives and ministry.

Saint Andrew's School, a renowned international boarding school in Turi, Kenya, was safe, well-run, and would provide a high-quality education. We had little doubt that Timothy would be well taken care of, but to be separated from the family at such a young age was certainly not going to be easy for him. It would not be easy for us either. The three-month school terms were interspersed with a one-month holiday at home.

Once a month we could attend the school for a visiting Saturday. It was an arduous 10-hour trip over horrific roads from Kampala to Turi. The crossing at the border post between Uganda and Kenya was never a simple matter. We would spend Saturday with Tim, only to travel back to Kampala in time for church on Sunday morning. James and Rachel continued to be with us in Kampala.

That year, while Tim was away at school, the security situation in Uganda deteriorated even further. There was a total breakdown of any law and order. Soldiers had little or no discipline and roamed freely day and night, terrorising the community. The school Rachel and James were attending was forced to close. If we were to remain in Kampala, we felt compelled to send them to join Timothy at Saint Andrew's School. Rachel was eight, and James was six. We were encouraged that children from the Pentecostal Assemblies of Canada mission in Uganda would also attend the same school. We made the painful decision that Rachel and James would join Timothy in Kenya the following September.

~ Evacuation ~

Milton Obote's government and presidency, at the time, became more and more ineffective. In July of 1985, while Timothy was at home on a school break, Obote was overthrown in a military coup led by Basilio Olara-

Okello and senior political statesman, Tito Okello.

The British Embassy was now caring for Canadian citizens in the country and immediately ordered an evacuation of all British Commonwealth citizens in the country. We were asked to report to the British High Commission the following morning and would be led by a military escort to the Kenya border post at Busia. We arrived the next morning and drove out of the city in a convoy toward Kenya. Armed British soldiers in military Land Rovers accompanied about a dozen other vehicles. The 170-kilometre journey should have taken about 4 hours to complete, but every 20 kilometres, we were stopped by a Ugandan army roadblock. These military checkpoints were notorious as opportunities for soldiers, many of whom were drunk, to extort money and goods from passengers as they travelled. We were asked to sit quietly in our vehicles as the British soldiers leading the convoy negotiated with the soldiers manning the barrier.

Our nerves were frazzled each time the leading sergeant was approached by one or several of the government soldiers. They would stroll up to his truck, and we watched as they talked. It would end with a bit of laughter and then a wave of the arm to indicate that we were free to proceed. We smiled and waved politely to the soldiers as we passed by. This happened several times, and we began to relax as we got closer to our destination.

However, at one roadblock, the banter and usual laughter didn't happen. Instead, the Ugandan soldiers who met the convoy raised their weapons and ordered the sergeant out of his vehicle. They stayed back on the side of the road as he emerged from the Land Rover and raised his arms above his head. They demanded that he lie face down on the road. I can still picture it in my mind all these years later. The British sergeant had short brown hair and a neat khaki uniform with short trousers. He wore knee-high socks that were pulled up and complemented his dark brown boots very nicely. He took several steps forward and, with hands still raised, went down first on one knee and then the other. He lowered his hands and clasped them behind his head as he lowered himself and lay flat on the ground with his face down.

Our frazzled nerves returned!

The Ugandan soldiers spoke animatedly among themselves. One of them walked toward the prostrate sergeant, his gun swinging at his side and ordered him to get up. The sergeant released the grip on the back of his head, lifted it and then pressed his hands into the ground, pushed himself up onto his knees, lifted one leg and stood up. He took a step back, stood to attention and saluted. The Ugandan soldier saluted back. The British soldier spun on his heels, snapped to attention again and returned to his truck. He got in, and with a wave from the soldier, we drove on. We followed, smiled and waved at the soldiers as we passed by.

A single thought flashed through my mind.

"Pretty impressive of the sergeant, indeed!"

We reached the border post, where it was obvious that we were expected. The convoy pulled up to a line of British soldiers. One of them stepped up to Marilyn's door and then the back door for the children. He opened them both, stood back and when they were out of the car, he spoke to them.

"Would you walk quickly and join the others gathered over there?" He pointed to a row of tables that had been set up. As Marilyn and the children were led away, the soldier leaned forward through the front door. And spoke to me.

"Kindly follow the convoy back, where you will be cared for by our soldiers overnight in Uganda. You will be able to drive across the border in the morning."

He closed the door, and the convoy drove back into Uganda.

There was no table for Canadians. Marilyn and the children were led to the one for Australians. A delegation met them and arranged for them to be driven to Nairobi. They ended up in a van with the Australian ambassador as their host. They were able to stay at one of the small hotels on the way and ended up at the Mission guest house in Nairobi. It was full and couldn't accommodate them, so one of the missionary families in Nairobi hosted them.

I drove with the military escort, which included the British Ambassador, to a school in the town of Busia on the Ugandan side of the border. The soldiers were well prepared and set up camp on the football pitch. They bought a goat, butchered and roasted it over the coals on a huge fire they built. We ate and spent the evening chatting and laughing around the fire.

Everyone decided to have a good time in spite of the circumstances.

The soldiers tuned into the BBC radio for the nightly British newscast. We all listened as they mentioned the coup in Kampala and that foreign nationals had been evacuated across the border to Kenya.

"Oh! Well done, chaps," the High Commissioner commended his soldiers as he went around the circle, patting each of them on the shoulder.

I slept in the car that night, and early the next morning, we were escorted through the border post, and I drove on to Nairobi and was reunited with my precious, little family. Marilyn showed me an article on the front page of the Kenyan newspaper about the coup and evacuation. The lead picture was our three children sitting at the border, waiting to go on to Nairobi. I think they thought it was a great adventure.

It was too insecure back in Kampala to return, and we were concerned about what was happening to the church and the members we had left behind. They hadn't been able to be evacuated as we had. How were they coping? We would try to contact them, although this was difficult as phone service was erratic or non-existent in Kampala. We decided to spend some much needed time together as a family, and to monitor the situation back home. The problem was that we couldn't afford an extended stay in Kenya. Canadian missionary friends who were visiting Kenya, heard of our plight. John approached me and told me that a friend in Canada had given him two thousand dollars and that it was for someone he would meet in Africa. He would know who it was when he met them.

"Here! This is for you and the family." He put the money into my hand.

The Lord had given us what we needed, just when we needed it. We were astonished and so grateful. Now we could spend three weeks with the family at the beach on the Kenyan coast and camping in the National Park at Masai Mara. Those days swimming and watching Africa's amazing wildlife were rejuvenating before we had to do what was difficult, but necessary. We took the children to begin the new school year in Turi.

~ A High Price To Pay ~

To say that we did not question or agonise regularly over the decision to send the children to boarding school in Kenya would be a lie. Nor is it true that any of us, children or parents, came out of this arrangement unscathed. The whole scenario was by far the most difficult thing we had to do in order to fulfil our call to plant an English-speaking church in Kampala. Many times, since then, Marilyn and I have struggled with whether we did the right thing or not. Certainly, it was a choice that left us and our children with scars that we still carry today.

Our good and gracious Lord has been nothing but faithful to us. He has graciously used us to see advancement in His Kingdom in ways we could scarcely have dreamed of or imagined. We cannot simply brush aside the good things He has done in so many precious Ugandan lives. We cannot overlook the impact of what He has done in Uganda and in the lives of so many others around the world. But neither can we lightly use that good work as justification for ignoring, as irrelevant or insignificant, the real wounds inflicted on our children and on us as parents.

And even though the decision to send the kids to Kenya did shield them from much, such as the January 1986 Battle of Kampala only four months later, it could not protect them from the inevitable trauma of life in Uganda. They did experience difficult situations prior to, in, and as a consequence of attending boarding school.

The reality is that there is a cost associated with obedience to the will and call of God. Jesus himself paid the ultimate price to bring about the salvation and hope we experience by faith in Him. It did not come without cost. Jesus himself struggled with this cost as He agonised in prayer with His Father in the garden of Gethsemane hours before His brutal death on a Roman cross. He wanted the cup of suffering to pass, if it was possible, but then surrendered to the will of the Father. And what was that will? Pay the price. It will be worth it.

Jesus clearly elucidated the cost of discipleship in the gospels. We are all called to take up our crosses and to follow or imitate Jesus in obedient self-sacrificial service. (Matthew 16:24-26) We are called to seek first the Kingdom of God and His righteousness, and all the other things of life will be cared for as well. (Matthew 6:33) We will never accomplish the great things God wants to do through us until we come to a place of full surrender and pay the necessary price.

How can we ignore the example of an army of early missionaries who went to the dark and difficult places on earth to share Christ, and establish the Kingdom of God? On distant shores, far from home, many buried their young wives and little children who had died of disease or conflict in doing God's work. How can we forget their burden and the immense cost? Their self-sacrificial service changed the world. How dare we think we can change our world and win the war for the control of the nations by preaching and pursuing a gospel of prosperity, ease and comfort.

There was a time when the missionary call was honoured and valued by society. Missionaries and their sacrifice were considered heroic, dignified and appropriate. Today, the missionary call is vilified as an evil intrusion and insult to the cultures of others. All of that is promoted by the perverted culture of Western human secularists who bombard the nations and cultures of the world with their twisted lifestyles, foul language, sexual perversion, ridicule and marginalisation of Christ and His magnificent moral code through vile movies, music and godless education. They are free to change culture but insist that Christ's Church may not!

This is a tragic inconsistency that has been embraced by the world we live in. We are not ashamed to continue to remain faithful to the message of the Bible, knowing that the life of Christ and what He teaches is one of freedom, hope, wellbeing and fullness. We are commissioned and called as salt and light, to preserve and illuminate the darkness of this world with the love, truth and transforming power of Jesus.

And what is truly sad is that there are some in the Church who feel the same way about World Missions and missionaries, as does this hostile world. Even the very title "missionary" is being abandoned for some less insulting and acceptable title.

I am not ashamed to openly declare that our goal is not only the declaration of the gospel, the planting of churches, the theological training of mission workers, and the compassionate demonstration of the gospel through acts of charity and kindness, but also the transformation of a godless, wicked, corrupt culture into a culture that honours and reflects the righteous character of Jesus. We are called to make disciples of the Nations. If you like it, then join the battle and pay the price. If you don't like it, then get used to it. This is not our world; it belongs to Jesus. We have a Great Commission from the King of Heaven Himself and are his agents of transformation. We go without seeking earthly permission and will pay whatever it costs to lift up the King of Heaven and Earth, Jesus.

There is a price to be paid in the battle for the souls of people and nations. It may result in personal trauma, a trauma our family knows all too well by our first-hand experience of it and our willingness to plant an English-speaking church in Kampala in extremely trying circumstances. To exclude and not mention the reality of the price we and our children have paid would be a disservice to this account and to you. To be silent on this matter would be an affront to the very real sacrifice and cost that our family paid in our journey of faith and obedience.

In sharing all this, Marilyn and I hope that our honesty might help you understand not only the weight of the sacrifices we and our children made as a result of our call, but also to express to our children gratitude for the price they were required to pay.

We also share this to encourage you in light of the price you are presently paying or will pay to be faithful to the Master. As we each follow God's call on our lives, there will be wrinkles that cannot be ironed out with clichés and trite theological "answers" that do not address the full complexity of the hurt we and those we love face along the way.

The ache and the ambiguity of this season of our lives are a vital component of our family story. It is a very real part of the narrative of each member of our family, as we each uniquely experienced and responded to it. We acknowledge the scars of trauma and seek to heal and reconcile these difficulties within ourselves, with one another, and with God. I would be lying if I said that the lasting impact of these traumas in the lives of our children didn't elicit more than one wrestling match between God and us.

There is no avoiding these complex and perplexing elements of life. Trying to explain them away or shrug them off is not helpful. Our lives will be punctuated by times when we are confused about what God is doing and why certain things play out the way they do, times in which sound theological explanations will not seem fully satisfactory. Instead, we must come to God, balancing our trust in him with full authenticity, knowing that he is not afraid of our challenging questions and that we can turn to our good Father in Heaven, bringing and surrendering to Him our hurt, our confusion and even our anger.

In this, we join King David in radically honest prayers of lament, one of which reads,

> *O Lord, how long will you forget me? Forever?*
>
> *How long will you look the other way?*
>
> *How long must I struggle with anguish in my soul,*
>
> *with sorrow in my heart every day?*
>
> *How long will my enemy have the upper hand?*
>
> *Turn and answer me, O Lord my God!*
>
> *Restore the sparkle to my eyes, or I will die.*
>
> *Don't let my enemies gloat, saying, "We have defeated him!"*
>
> *Don't let them rejoice at my downfall.*
>
> *But I trust in your unfailing love.*
>
> *I will rejoice because you have rescued me.*
>
> *I will sing to the Lord*
>
> *because he is good to me."*
>
> *Psalm 13 (NLT)*

David models, for us, a prayer that is both vulnerable and authentic while embracing hope and trust that God will, in the end, make things right. His cry does not dismiss or explain away his pain, but it does express a trust that pain will not have the final word.

For Marilyn and me, this is a challenge to trust that what God has called us to, will lead us to hope and rest in His sovereign goodness. At the same time, we decidedly resist the urge to minimise or negate our pain or the pain of our children.

God is a far greater Father to my children than I ever could hope to be, and I trust that He, in part now, and in completion in the future,

> *"...will wipe every tear from their eyes. There will be no more death or mourning or crying or pain, for the old order of things has passed away."*
>
> *Revelation 21:4 (NIV)*

~ Reflect and Discuss ~

As you reflect on these questions and engage in discussion with others, consider the following:

1. Difficulty in Sharing:

    • Reflect on what is most difficult for you about what is shared in this chapter. Consider any aspects of your own story that may be challenging or confusing to share with others.

    • Explore the importance of sharing the most difficult and confusing elements of our stories. Discuss how vulnerability and authenticity can foster deeper connections with others and create opportunities for healing and growth.

2. The Cost of Discipleship:

    • Read Matthew 16:24-26. What does Jesus mean when he requires us to take up our cross and follow him?

3. David's Prayer of Lament in Psalm 13:

    • Consider what stands out to you about David's prayer of lament in Psalm 13. Reflect on the raw honesty and vulnerability expressed in David's words as he wrestles with feelings of abandonment and despair.

    • Explore how this sort of authenticity before God can play a role in ultimately strengthening our faith. Discuss how acknowledging our struggles and doubts allows us to bring them before God, trusting Him to meet us in our pain and provide comfort and reassurance.

3. Personal Experience of Lament:

    • Reflect on an event, season, or situation in your life that awakens lament. Consider the feelings of grief, loss, or disappointment that arise in these moments.

    • Explore how you might share this lament honestly with God and others for the sake of healing and hope. Discuss the importance of creating spaces for lament within your faith community, where individuals can express their pain and receive support and encouragement from others.

During your discussion, offer support, empathy, and prayer for one another as you explore the complexities of your own stories. Share personal experiences of lament and moments of struggle, trusting in God's presence and provision amidst the challenges of life. By embracing vulnerability and authenticity, you can cultivate deeper relationships with God and others, leading to greater healing, hope, and spiritual growth.

~

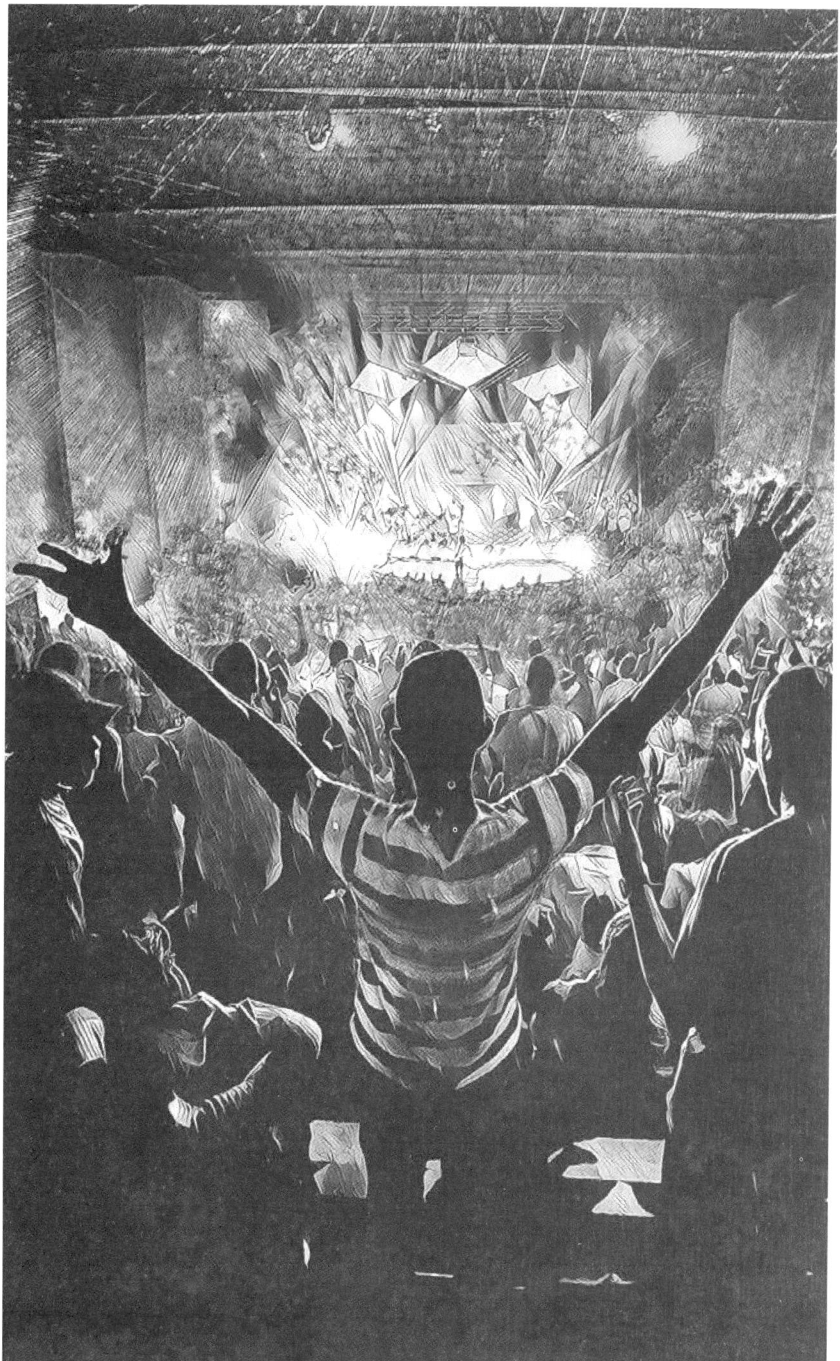

"And we know that in all things God works for the good of those who love him, who have been called according to his purpose."

The Apostle Paul - Romans 8:28, NIV

13

~ Reel to Real ~

"Embracing faith in an old cinema."

The space to meet in the hotel was too small to accommodate those who were coming to church each Sunday. We needed room to grow, so we began to look for a suitable place that was bigger than the Crystal Suite at the Grand Imperial Hotel. It would only seat two hundred people, and we were bursting at the seams. Each room or hall we found was too small or run down to meet our needs.

"Have you considered The Center?" someone suggested.

We discovered that "The Center" was the largest public auditorium in the country. It was an old movie theatre on one of the key intersections in downtown Kampala. It had been known as the Norman Cinema, named after the owner, a well-known businessman and Indian immigrant, Norman Godhino. He built the beautiful theatre the same year that I had been born, in 1952. The first movie to be shown, in what was at the time an opulent structure, was the Ugandan premier of the epic film The Robe, a fictionalised story about a first-century Roman military officer whose unit served in Jerusalem during the crucifixion of Jesus. The cinema's main auditorium was furnished with 1400 plush, fold-down seats, and the entryway was fitted with beautiful chandeliers and grand staircases. The modern architecture and unique design were completely new to Uganda at the time. Beyond the main auditorium were many adjoining spaces and rooms designed for a variety of uses. They would serve nicely for the smaller meetings and gatherings the church needed. The building was a broken shell of the magnificence it had once been, but a perfect fit for our growing community.

My subsequent enquiries as to who owned the building came as a bit of a shock. I found out that the army was occupying and using the building. Before Amin had taken power, Ugandan citizens of Indian heritage, referred to as "Asians", made up a large ethnic minority in Uganda. They had come to East Africa in 1895 as labourers to build the new railway line from Mombasa to Lake Victoria. Because of their acute business savvy, many of them now owned and controlled much of Kampala's businesses and property. In 1972, President Idi Amin expelled the Asian community from the country, allowing them to leave with just the clothes on their backs. Their businesses and properties were portioned out to his cronies, who didn't know how to operate them. They fell into disrepair and ruin as a result of greed, neglect and ineptitude.

The Norman Cinema was no different. The army was now occupying it and using it as a detention centre for political prisoners. Government soldiers lived in some of the adjoining rooms. When rebel soldiers or suspected collaborators were caught, this was one of the places they were brought to. They were interrogated, beaten and even killed in these rooms. There was no way we were going to get this building. It would take a miracle!

I vividly remember walking into the main theatre through one of the side doors that entered the building off the parking lot. Marilyn stood beside me. We gawked up at the high ceiling and expansive hall. The place was a mess. A single 100-watt light bulb hung down from the ceiling. The roof leaked so badly that you had to have an umbrella inside when it rained. The walls were streaked with water stains. The theatre seats were ripped and torn. The huge screen that stretched across the full width of the back wall hung in tatters. There was a rickety, old wooden platform at the front below the screen. I imagined that there were bats, cats, rats and elephants living underneath it. A small television was perched on the front of the platform. About twenty-five people were watching Bruce Lee demolishing somebody.

I groaned!

"What a waste of a beautiful building."

The words tumbled out of my mouth as I looked around and then down to Marilyn. I looked back up at the hall and had what I now know was a vision. The entire scene mutated before me. I saw the place renovated, full of light, the walls painted in pastel colours, a new platform, the old screen gone. But the best part was that it was jam-packed, full of young people, their arms raised and swaying together, as one, from side to side, as they sang a song of worship to Jesus. Tears filled my eyes, and I knew that this building was to be our new church home.

"This is it, Marilyn." I said. "This is the building God wants us to have."

I had no idea how, but I sensed in the deepest part of me that, somehow, we would get it! So, we did what we knew we had to do. We prayed! I clung tenaciously to the vision I had seen of the building full of worshipping young people. I shared the vision with just a few prayer warriors in the congregation, as I didn't want the soldiers in the cinema to hear that we wanted to take over their building. We prayed for weeks and then months. Nothing changed. We persisted in asking for the miracle we needed. For a full year, we prayed.

As 1985 came to an end, the security in the country deteriorated even further. The soldiers of the NRA liberation movement, led by Yoweri Museveni, were closing in from the southwestern side of the city. That side of the country was already under their control. With each passing day, the frequency of gunfire increased. Almost every expatriate had left the country in anticipation of the imminent battle for the city. The Canadian consulate did not have an office in Uganda, so the few Canadians who were still in Kampala were being cared for by the American embassy.

We were surprised by a visit to our home from the ambassador of the United States to Uganda. He informed us that the battle for the city was expectant and fast approaching. His family and most of the embassy staff had been evacuated. He was left with only marines to guard him. While he could not force us to leave, he advised us to seriously consider the wisdom of staying.

We were certainly ready to leave as the situation was dire, but we felt compelled to pray and ask God what he wanted us to do. His answer was clear. He wanted us to stay. But there was more! He wanted me to ask the army to let us use the Norman Cinema auditorium for two weeks of special services. But there was even more!

"You will enter it and not leave it. I am going to give it to you!"

While I didn't hear the words with my ears, they were as clear and vivid in my spirit as though I had heard them with my ears. I was overcome with a sense of joy and a little trepidation at the prospect of approaching the army commander with a request to use the facilities for two weeks.

Reluctant at first, he agreed, especially since I told him that we'd clean the place up and do a little painting.

Our young church was excited at the prospect, and enthusiastically, many joined us to help clean and restore the auditorium in preparation for the meetings. What a job that was! It was filthy and disorganised. The toilets were a stinking mess, with many of them blocked. Christopher Komagum, one of the young people who later became my assistant pastor, tells of how we unblocked one of the toilets. We looked at each other with puzzled looks as we stood in front of it. I shrugged, rolled up my sleeves and worked my hands into the slimy mess that was clogging the toilet. With a little effort, I was able to pull out a mass of the fetid stuff, and the toilet pipes were cleared. Chris went over to a basin nearby and vomited.

It was a bonding time for many of us as we spent a week together cleaning up the facility. Some of the people that were there all those years ago are still with the church all these years later. One of them was Mrs. Ruth Mayanja Nkangi. I wasn't aware of it at the time, but her husband was an extremely important political figure in the country and had held ministerial positions in several Ugandan governments. He was also at one time, the Katikiro, or Prime Minister of the Buganda Kingdom. And then there were the ordinary, simple young people who all came together with a single purpose: building Jesus' Kingdom.

Marilyn and I invited Ken Bombay, a Canadian evangelist and pastor, to come to Kampala and speak at the week of meetings. I must admit that we were surprised and delighted that he agreed, especially at such short notice, and because it was still a dangerous assignment. He would fly in on a small, chartered flight into the Entebbe airport, which was closed to regular commercial air traffic. We set mid-January 1986 as the date for the meetings.

As anticipation grew, God affirmed again, that once we entered the place, we would not leave. It would be ours!

> *"...the land on which your feet have walked will be your inheritance."*
>
> *Joshua 14:9 (NIV)*

I had no idea how that could happen, but we were ready for whatever God planned to do.

The week of special meetings finally arrived. Everything was set in place. The auditorium was as ready as we could make it. Ken and his wife Joan arrived on Sunday morning, which was to be the very first time we met for church in the building. I drove out to the airport at Entebbe and watched the small plane as it landed and pulled up to the dilapidated terminal. The only other aircraft were a few military planes. The door to the small aircraft opened up, and sure enough, Ken and Joan stepped out onto the runway and made their way toward the terminal.

As I watched them walking toward me, I began to weep. To think that they would be willing to come to war-torn Uganda and help us by preaching God's message to a nation in turmoil broke my heart. I embraced them and thanked them for coming. Ken is a large, full-of-life character with a wonderful sense of wit and humour. He smiled, and we went to the car to drive the 35 kilometres back to the city and to the building we had spent so much time getting ready for this.

We pulled up into the parking lot at the cinema and went into the auditorium. I was overwhelmed as I saw the seven hundred and fifty people who had come to worship and hear God's word. They were singing! It was a hymn!

> *Great is Thy faithfulness, O God my Father;*
>
> *There is no shadow of turning with Thee;*
>
> *Thou changest not, Thy compassions, they fail not;*
>
> *As Thou hast been, Thou forever wilt be.*
>
> *Great is Thy faithfulness!*
>
> *Great is Thy faithfulness!*

> *Morning by morning, new mercies I see;*
>
> *All I have needed Thy hand hath provided:*
>
> *Great is Thy faithfulness, Lord, unto me!*

Again, I wept!

The goosebumps of joy tingled all over me as I took in what I was witnessing: a miracle of grace, love and provision. The church was alive and well in the middle of a national crisis. It was incumbent on us to just step forward faithfully, day after day, doing what Jesus had called us to do here: serve the English-speaking church we had planted in the heart of the city.

The characters in the Bible had a vision from God and, through great difficulty, had ploughed forward. God had never abandoned them but proven himself faithful. He brought them through every situation and led them on to success.

Joseph had endured rejection, abandonment, slavery, deceit and prison, and still God used him to bring about His purposes, "...the saving of many lives." (Genesis 50:20, NIV)

David was another Bible character who was called, chosen, appointed and led through great difficulty on his journey to become king over God's people and build a great nation.

If God could do it for them, then He would do it for us. He had a plan! He had a purpose for Kampala, for our new church community and we were the ones He had chosen to do it through. Wow! What a privilege! What an honour! I sensed God wanted to write a little bit of history and use us in the process. We just had to remain faithful, no matter what the challenges or obstacles were. He would see us through! He would do what we couldn't! He would bring about His purpose!

And so, with a burning faith in our loving and kind God, we went into that week of meetings. We planned to hold the weekday services over the noon hour and into the early afternoon. It was too dangerous to have evening services. And besides that, there was a curfew at 7pm. Everyone was to be indoors after that, or risk being shot.

The meetings went well, with hundreds turning up each day. God was doing good things in the hearts of the young people who gathered. Each day, we would return home in the late afternoon, but the atmosphere was tense. The battle for Kampala was intensifying. We heard the rapid chatter of gunfire and watched the military helicopters floating above the city. The city was abuzz with rumours.

"The rebels are coming! The rebels are coming."

The downtown area would evacuate at the speculation, with everyone scrambling to get out of the city to the relative safety of their homes. This had happened periodically. No one really knew when the final incursion into Kampala would take place. In this atmosphere of tension, we were holding services in the auditorium.

From Monday to Wednesday, things went well, but on Thursday, all hell broke loose. We were in the auditorium for the noon hour service when we saw hundreds of soldiers of the national army trudging past in full battle fatigue outside the side doors of the auditorium. This time, it wasn't a rumour! The battle for Kampala had started in earnest.

We closed down the meeting with prayer for safety and sent everyone home. The retreating soldiers were stopping any vehicles that were passing. Throwing out the occupants and filling the vehicles with looted possessions they were stealing from the shops, they were driving out of the city, heading east and north away from the advancing rebel army.

How were we to get home in this chaos? I had parked our car, a Peugeot station wagon, inside the building for safety. In preparation, I painted a small Canadian flag on the two front doors. I had also fashioned a Canadian flag from a small pillowcase and tied it like a flag to the radio antennae. We all got into the car, and my instructions were clear.

"If soldiers try to block us, I will not be stopping. We are going to get home. Put your heads down and pray."

We drove out of the city center, heading for home. The soldiers had set up roadblocks and were commandeering the vehicles that tried to pass. As I approached each roadblock, I acted as though I was the Canadian ambassador. I looked directly at the soldier manning the roadblock and saluted! Each time, they stood back, saluted, and we drove through! We made it home safely. We took time to thank the Lord, and then endured three days of warfare for the city of Kampala.

Innumerable rounds of artillery fire and the constant booming of the big guns that were set up on the hills of Kampala bombarded us. Thousands of people, fleeing the city on foot, passed by our gates, heading out of the city on side roads.

By Saturday, things were quieter, and we were getting bored sitting at home. The BBC radio was up to date on what was happening. We tuned in regularly to hear the latest news. The incoming National Resistance Army occupied the city. We decided to walk a few blocks down the road and check in on some missionary friends to see how they were faring. They had a great view over the city from their veranda, and they told us how they had witnessed much of the battle, the big guns booming, the tracers lighting up the evening sky.

As we sat chatting, a small group of military vehicles rushed by on the road below. We could see them clearly. A soldier in the lead vehicle saw us, leaned out of the car and opened up with a burst of gunfire aimed directly at us. We heard the bullets whizzing past us and overhead. Dropping to our knees, we crawled into the house. No one was hurt, but we were shocked at what had happened. When things had calmed down, we carefully walked back to our house.

By Sunday, the fight was over. Yoweri Museveni, the leader of the NRA, spoke to the nation from the government-run radio station, announcing the fall of the government and the installation of a new regime. I decided it was necessary to go downtown and check up on what had happened at church. Several young people, including Chris Komagum, had stayed in the building to look after things as best as they could.

What I witnessed was the aftermath of war. There were the dead bodies of both soldiers and civilians littering the sides of the road. Some were decapitated, the head lying beside the bloated corpse, which was covered with flies. There were burnt-out vehicles, many of the buildings pockmarked with holes from the gunfire and shelling. A few hardy citizens were out and, with a dazed look, taking in the scene.

I arrived at the auditorium to find Chris and the other young people safe and still there. Chris then told us how the rebel soldiers had approached the building as they were clearing the city of government troops. They must have known it was used as a detention and interrogation centre and were ready to storm into it. Chris waved a white towel out of a window and welcomed in the soldiers, who, after checking, had moved on.

And here is the wonderful, God honouring truth. We have never left that building. We stayed as the occupants, and God fulfilled his promise!

Now, every Sunday, I witness with my eyes what I saw in that vision the first day I walked into that broken building. It is fully renovated, full of light and packed to the doors with worshipping young people, not once or twice but multiple services every Sunday.

It is in this building, once a movie theatre and now a church, that we have seen tens of thousands of people commit their lives to Christ and be filled with the Holy Spirit. Inspired by the preaching and teaching of the Word of God they have become followers of Christ, a new generation of Ugandans, disciples bringing transformation to the city and nation. It is in this building that we have conducted thousands of weddings and funerals, dedicated a multitude of babies, held vibrant concerts of musical celebration and witnessed the wonderful healing works of a good God.

Yep! With the help of King Jesus, we have written a little history!

~ Reflect and Discuss ~

As you reflect on your own story and engage in discussion with others, consider the following:

1. Experiencing Miracles through Obedience:

    - The miraculous provision of the Cinema for the home of Watoto Church came as a result of Gary and Marilyn's active obedience and faith.

    - Recall a time when you heard God ask you to do something, and having obeyed, you experienced a miracle. Reflect on the circumstances surrounding that experience and the impact it had on your faith.

    - Consider how obedience to God's prompting can lead to unexpected blessings and supernatural interventions in your life.

2. Learning from the Early Years of Watoto Church (KPC):

    - The Cinema was broken but God showed it as fully renovated and full of worshipping young people. God does not see things as they are but as they can be. He does not see our brokenness but our potential. Discuss the implications of this in our lives as Christians.

    - Consider how faith and obedience can release the potential in us.

During your discussion, offer support, encouragement, and prayer for one another as you reflect on your own stories and seek to grow in faith and obedience. Share personal experiences, insights, and aspirations, and commit to walking alongside one another in your journey of faith. By embracing hope, trust, and obedience, you can experience God's transformative power and fulfill His purposes in your life and in the world.

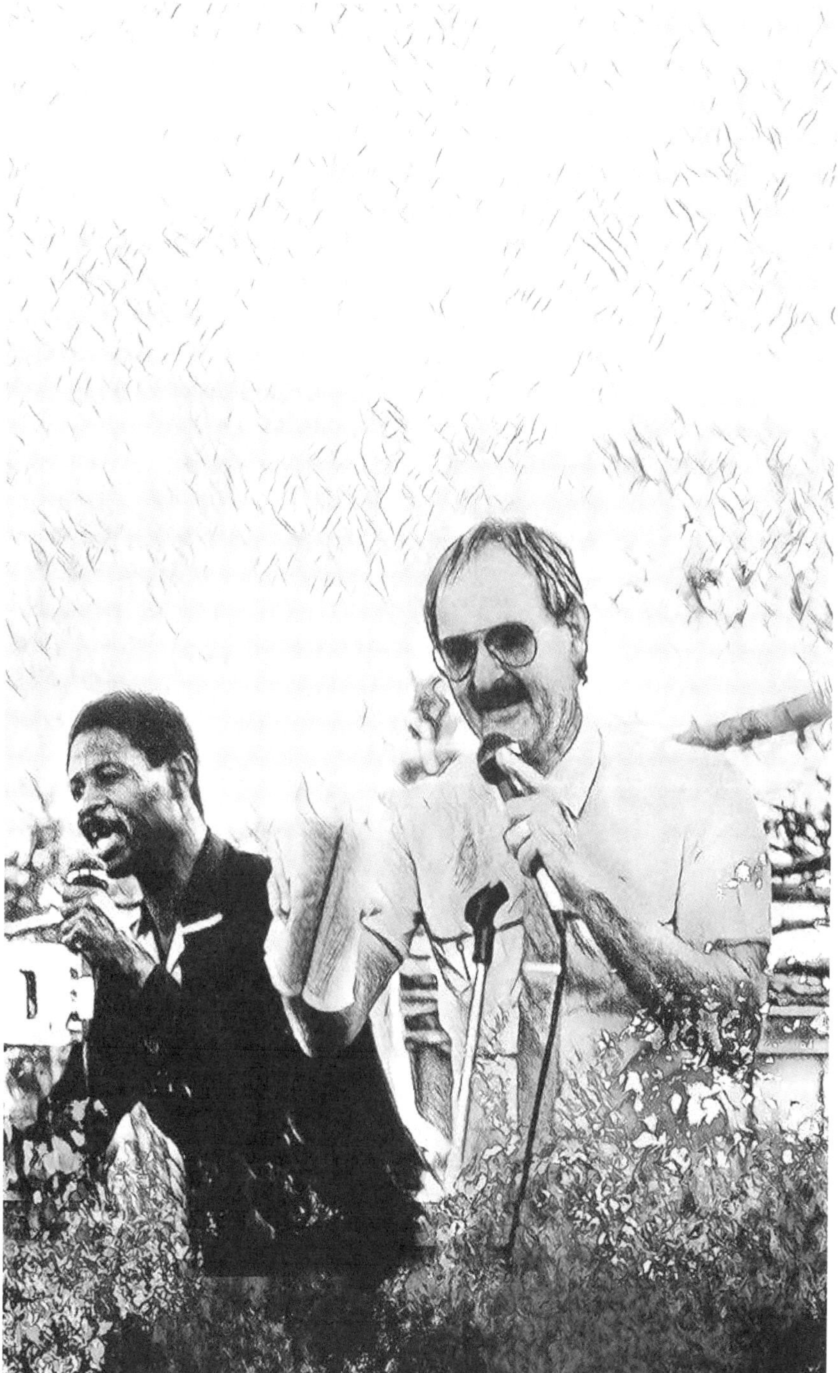

> "Yesterday is gone.
> Tomorrow has not yet come.
> We have only today.
> Let us begin."
>
> *Mother Teresa*

14

~ A Courageous Stand ~

"Defying false prophets and danger."

We were in the building, but it wasn't ours. We were the current squatters and decided to make the place home. I knew that God had promised to give us the building, so we appointed a lawyer to help us get clarity on the ownership and the possibility of purchasing the building. The government had decided that in the interests of developing the economy, the previous Asian owners who had been ousted by the Amin regime, should be given an opportunity to return and repossess their properties. If that happened, it could open the door for us to purchase the property from the rightful owners.

The lawyer let me know that this was a precarious matter, especially as it was a key building in the heart of the city. There was no other building in the city more suited for our purposes. What we needed was another miracle.

I shared with the Missions Department of the Pentecostal Assemblies of Canada what we were trying to do and that, as things fell into place, we would need to secure a loan in Canada to make it happen. I wanted them to have time to mull this over. Meanwhile, the lawyer pursued the matter in Kampala. Our role now, was to do the things we knew we were called to do, grow and build the new church.

Nothing of great value, nothing of lasting impact, just happens. It takes hard work! It takes time, persistence and patient intentional strategy to accomplish and establish great things. It means getting up every morning and getting on with what Jesus has for you for that day, especially when you have no idea what that could entail. You plan, prepare, execute, expect a miracle, and never give up, no matter what comes your way. But Jesus is in charge of it all. It is His work, His Church and His plan, so you have to hear from Him and get on with what He asks you to do without holding back, no matter what happens.

The following years meant that we had to do just that: get on with it no matter what. They were traumatic years. History told us that a new political regime did not mean that peace was going to come to Uganda. It was going to take an undetermined time for things to settle down and for any semblance of order to re-emerge. In a country replete with guns, decommissioned soldiers, rampant unemployment, endemic poverty and a broken infrastructure, violence and theft become, for many, a way of life. Armed robbery and home invasion continued unabated. Even though the new government was settling in and establishing itself, there was a constant swirl of political intrigue and uncertainty about what was really happening in the city.

The Anglican Church of Uganda had organised a year-long Greater Kampala Mission, a series of evangelistic activities to preach the gospel and help rebuild a sense of order and peace in the country. The concluding large gathering was to be held in the month of April, at the main Kampala city square in the heart of the city. I was deeply honoured by the invitation to be one of the speakers at the three-day event. The other speakers were well-known and highly respected Anglican clerics, Bishop Festo Kivengere and the Rev. John Wilson. The week prior to the event, one of our dear church members, who seemed to have an ear to the ground when it came to what was happening in the country, asked to see me. He had heard that several people had been targeted to be assassinated over the next few weeks. One would be a politician, one would be a lawyer, one would be a clergyman, and another a white man. My role in the community was beginning to become fairly well known, hence the invitation to speak at the city-wide event. Church colleagues were so concerned for my well-being and, thinking that I might be targeted, encouraged me to leave the country for a short while. I was not in favour of leaving. I wanted to participate in the occasion at the city square as it was a wonderful opportunity to not only preach the gospel but to develop a budding relationship with the Anglican community.

The next day, we heard that the lawyer who was looking into the potential purchase of the building had been killed at his home. It had been a violent, brutal and senseless murder. Again, I was urged to leave the country for a while. Still, I resisted.

That afternoon, we held a Bible study in the Timothy class, a small hall in the building that we used for our discipleship and mentoring lessons. As I was speaking, I began to feel a very powerful presence of wickedness in the room. It was palpable and a warning of imminent danger, and seemed to be directed toward me. Someone in the room had come with foul and evil intentions. I stopped, paused, reflected on what I felt in my spirit and then calmly, but boldly and with firmness, informed whoever had come into the room with evil in their heart and with the purpose of harm to be warned that they could not fight God and win.

The following day, Tuesday, we drove to the city square to participate in the gathering. Fifteen thousand people were assembled to hear the Word of God preached. As I parked the car just above the platform on the north side of the square, another very strong impression settled down in my spirit. I hesitated, wondering what to do.

"Marilyn," I spoke to my dear, little wife sitting beside me.

"Marilyn, something is terribly wrong. There is an evil presence here. I feel so deeply that one of us participating here is going to die."

"Maybe we should leave." She was deeply concerned.

"No! I don't feel it's going to be me, but someone is going to die."

We held hands, whispered a short prayer, stepped out of the car and participated in what was a powerful and wonderful presentation of God's Word and love for the city and nation. We then returned home.

I had invited Rev. John Wilson, one of the other speakers at the city crusade, to preach at our Sunday morning service later that week and was very excited at his willingness and the fresh new relationship with the Anglican community that this demonstrated.

On Friday morning, we received the tragic news. Two gunmen had killed Rev. Wilson as he was returning home the previous evening. It was a senseless, bloody and violent murder. The full import of what it meant for us to be in Kampala during those days settled down heavily on us. And yet there was this unshakeable, deep, inner conviction and a calm, unwavering certainty that God had something He wanted to accomplish in the city, and I knew that He wanted to use us. We also trusted that in the face of real danger, He would protect us. We determined to put our hand on the plough and consistently, faithfully and with a dogged determination just get on with the day-to-day, week-by-week, month-by-month work of building the new church.

A high level of insecurity continued, but the end of the open conflict brought a tenuous peace to the city and the southern part of the country. It turned out to be a rather eventful number of years for us.

The first was moving into the old cinema. The second was a series of murders of people close to us. The third was the whirlwind of church deception caused by a so-called "prophet" who had come to Uganda from Nigeria.

He aimed to exert spiritual leadership and influence out of the mayhem and division among the church community. He would speak at one of the local "Pentecostal" churches, where he would perform strange "signs and wonders." He was held in great awe by many, and his presence and activity in the churches in Kampala was causing quite a buzz. It was evident to me that he had malicious and malignant intent.

He sent an emissary to serve notice to me that he would be coming to our church on the upcoming Sunday, and I was to let him preach and do his thing. I politely informed the messenger that "the prophet" was not welcome and would not be given a platform. Moreover, if he showed up, the police would be waiting to escort him off the property. The delegate expressed his shock, informing me that I could not speak this way to "the prophet" or threaten him. I politely informed him that I had just done that very thing. He was now given leave to deliver my message back.

When I arrived home that evening, a deputation of about eight pastors was waiting for me at the gate. I welcomed them in, and we sat down in our small sitting room. One of them, as spokesman, wanted me to know that they had come with a message for me directly from "the prophet."

A quiet irritation rose inside me! With a gentle confidence, I looked intently into his eyes and answered him.

"I am not receiving messages from prophets today."

I looked around the room.

"I am ashamed of you men for your conduct and disgraceful alliance."

And then a greater holy anger, born of the Holy Spirit, swelled up in me.

"Not only that, but Jesus will not allow this conduct and activity against His people to continue. In fact, I have a message for your 'prophet.' You can notify him that he is touching and hurting the apple of God's eye, the church, the bride of Christ. He is in grave danger. If he does not stop, God will remove him to protect His Church."

With a calmness I didn't know I had, I informed them that they were free to leave.

It was a Thursday evening, and the following day, after our noon-hour discipleship school meeting, we drove to the border and crossed into Kenya to visit our children at St. Andrew's School. It was an arduous trip, as the road in Kenya was bad, and the road in Uganda was horrendous. Once each month, we made the ten-hour journey and broke it up by staying in a small hotel on the Kenya side. We would finish the excursion the next morning, arriving at the school for a very special eight-hour time with Timothy, Rachel and James. After the wonderful time with the kids, we would drive the ten hours back, most of the way to the border, rising early the next morning to finish the trip and arrive just in time for church. We did this for years. It was a thrill to be with the kids but a huge strain to keep up the schedule, as we felt compelled to make both the kids and the church a priority.

I had completely forgotten about "the prophet." As soon as we arrived at church, one of the members came up to us.

"Have you heard about 'the prophet'?"

"No!" I replied. "We've just got back!"

"On Saturday morning, he woke up, walked out of his house, stretched in the morning sunshine and dropped dead."

I didn't know what to say. I just stood there with a dazed and shocked look. And then an awe, a holy fear, and an amazing love for our good, good

Father God filled my soul. You simply don't mess with Him, His people and His Church!

We decided to take a short furlough back to Canada. Paul and Gloria Willoughby filled in for the few months that we were away. It was a time to reflect and rest from the constant and arduous presence of danger and insecurity that we lived under in Kampala. It was a time to connect with family and friends, and prepare to return to Uganda. It was also a time to hear from Jesus, more of what, specifically, He wanted us to do in the place He had called us to serve.

One day, while I was away, preaching in the Maritime provinces of eastern Canada, God spoke to Marilyn. He took her to Isaiah 58, and the magnificent truth of that passage was revealed and opened up to her. It's about true fasting, not just living out the rituals and practices of religion, which the Jewish people did so well, but practising love, justice, righteousness and kindness to all but especially to the marginalised and poor of the community.

> *"Is not this the kind of fasting I have chosen:...*
>
> *If you do away with the yoke of oppression,*
>
> *with the pointing finger and malicious talk,*
>
> *and if you spend yourselves in behalf of the hungry*
>
> *and satisfy the needs of the oppressed,*
>
> *then your light will rise in the darkness,*
>
> *and your night will become like the noonday.*
>
> *The LORD will guide you always;*
>
> *he will satisfy your needs in a sun-scorched land*
>
> *and will strengthen your frame.*
>
> *You will be like a well-watered garden,*
>
> *like a spring whose waters never fail.*

Your people will rebuild the ancient ruins

and will raise up the age-old foundations;

you will be called Repairer of Broken Walls,

Restorer of Streets with Dwellings.

Isaiah 58:6,9b-12 (NIV)

Marilyn called me on the phone, and we talked about what she sensed Jesus wanted us to do when we returned to Kampala. We were to keep building a great church, and through that church, we were to care for the destitute and the marginalised, but specifically look after the orphaned children of the land he had commissioned us to.

From that passage, we felt that, in doing this, the Lord would bless us and meet our needs in a sun-scorched land (Uganda is that). Our light would rise in the darkness, and he would guide us. Not only that, but we would fix, both spiritual and physical, broken streets, walls and foundations.

It is so important, even critical, that we hear from God! When we do, we can move forward with confidence and faith. We can be assured of His provision and protection. We can live with a loving but holy boldness.

As we spoke on the phone, I felt the "yes" of Jesus in what Marilyn was sharing with me. We prayed and surrendered ourselves once more to what Jesus was calling us to do. A fresh enthusiasm for our return to Uganda beat in our hearts.

Before returning to Kampala, we had the honour of preaching at a church in Toronto where the pastor was a good friend of ours. At the end of the service, he approached me and asked if I would receive a prophetic word of encouragement from one of the gentlemen in the church. He assured me that he knew the man well and I would be safe hearing what he had to say. I agreed!

A kindly-looking man walked up to me and, putting his hands gently on my shoulders, looked intently into my eyes and smiled.

"God wants to set you in a large place and bless you. I see you rising to stand head and shoulders above those around you. But what I see, most clearly, is that you will be a father to thousands, surrounded by many children."

I thanked him, and we parted, but I knew that Jesus was speaking to me about what He wanted us to do. We were to continue planting, building and growing an English-speaking church in the heart of Kampala, one that would touch the city and nation with the love and compassion of Jesus.

A significant facet of the plan was to rescue the vulnerable, fatherless children of Uganda.

~ Reflect and Discuss ~

As you reflect on your own story and engage in discussion with others, consider the following:

1. Remaining Hopeful and Persistent in Difficulty:

   • Reflect what it means to remain faithful and to persevere over an extended period especially through difficult times. Consider the implications of hard work, planning and persistence as you do God's work.

   • Consider some biblical examples of faithful persistence, such as Joseph and David.

   • Share a time when you struggled to remain hopeful. Discuss the circumstances and emotions you experienced during that challenging period.

2. Following God's Leading

   • God spoke to Marilyn about caring for the poor and marginalized of Uganda. He did so from His Word in Isaiah 58.

   • Reflect on a time when God spoke to you from His Word. Recall the circumstances and how you responded.

   • Discuss the importance of being open to God's leading and allowing Him to work through you in unexpected ways. Consider how you can surrender to the Holy Spirit's guidance and step out in faith to fulfill God's calling on your life.

During your discussion, offer support, encouragement, and prayer for one another as you reflect on your own stories and seek to discern God's will for your lives. Share personal experiences, insights, and aspirations, and commit to walking alongside one another in faith and obedience. By embracing hope, using your passions for God's glory, and trusting in the power of the Holy Spirit, you can experience transformation and become instruments of God's grace in the world.

∼

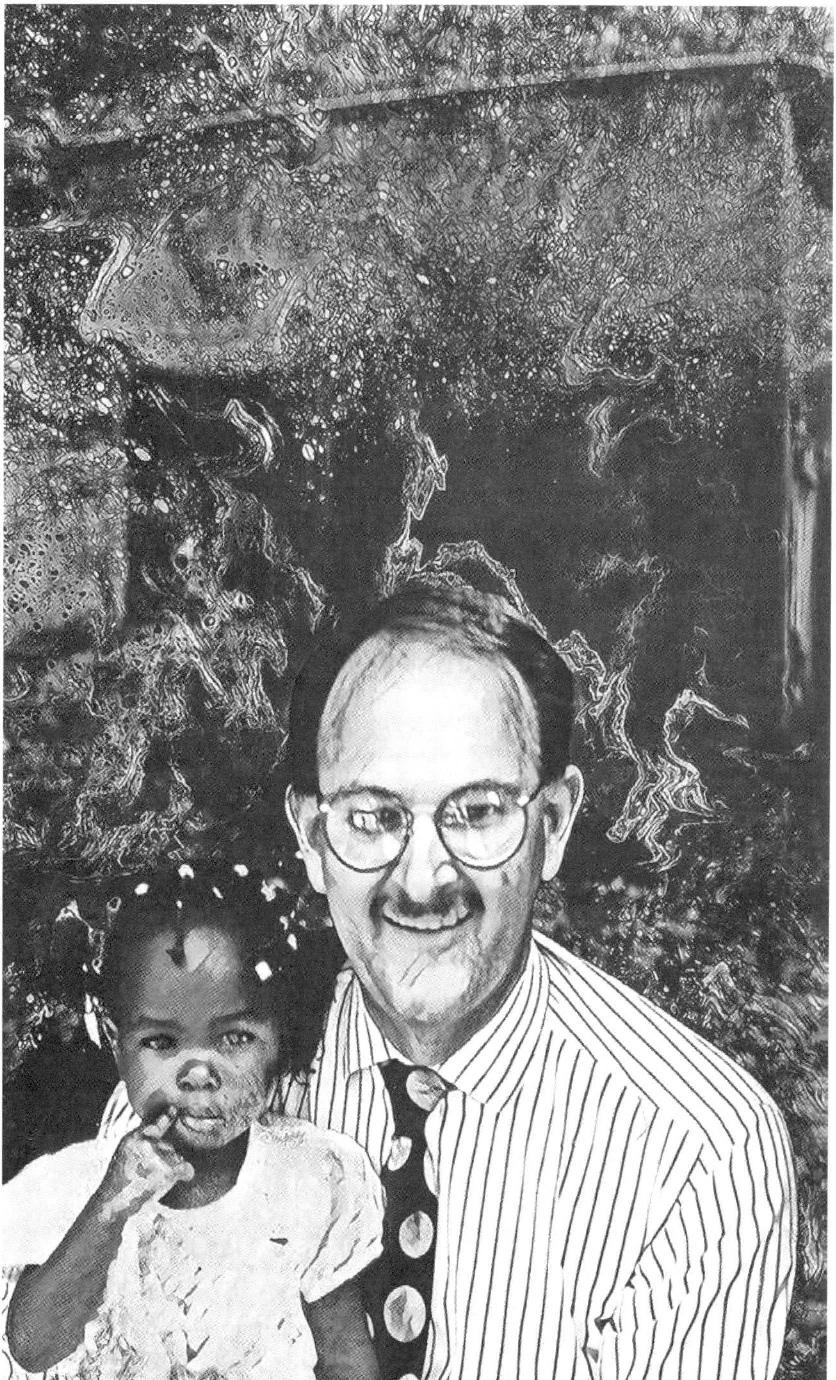

"Children are the true wealth of a nation."

John F. Kennedy

15
~ Silent Epidemic ~

"The heartbreaking legacy of HIV/AIDS."

Herbert, a fine young man who was attending our church, stepped off a sidewalk and was hit by a passing bicycle, opening a deep wound in his leg. Three days later, he died, his body was unable to fight the infection that coursed through him. Herbert's life was cut short by what we soon found out to be an infection with HIV. More and more people began to succumb to this new, strange disease that everyone was calling "slim," later known as AIDS.

HIV/AIDS hit Uganda like a bomb. In the early 1980's it had been creeping silently into the population. By the mid-1980s, the number of deaths began to increase dramatically. Infection was evident by dramatic weight loss, vulnerability to common diseases and simple infection, followed by death. Over the following years, funerals were a common event that disrupted normal life. Fear gripped the populace, accompanied by a strong stigmatisation, as it became known that the primary cause was sexual relations with an infected person. The pandemic became a dominant factor in the social life of the region.

The church and the new government, with mutual compassion and support, met the response to the crisis. The President and his wife led from the front in addressing the issue by bringing the church together in a campaign to raise awareness and teaching on the matter. The ABCs of HIV prevention was developed as an effective program by the government, churches and support groups, who joined forces to confront the dilemma. The three pillars of Abstinence, Be Faithful (Monogamy) and Christ were taught openly and in schools, the media and churches across the country. So dire was the problem and successful the effort in addressing the issue in Uganda that the international community came alongside to finance the effort but changed the "C" from Christ to Condom.

This caused no small amount of consternation among the Christian community who had initiated the program and felt that a commitment to Christ and his purpose for our lives sexually was critical. The use of condoms might help, but a genuine surrender to Christ and his way of living most definitely would. The need for intervention, however, was so prevalent that the Church felt compelled to continue the campaign in spite of the pressure to promote the use of condoms. There was a strong emphasis placed on making a commitment to sexual purity until marriage. Tens of thousands of young people signed a pledge called "True Love Waits" to keep themselves as virgins until marriage or to recommit themselves to abstinence until marriage.

Over the next number of years, hundreds of thousands in Uganda and across Africa succumbed and died of the virus. The impact on the community was significant as the pandemic touched almost every family. It was devastating to watch as young wives lost their husbands and as children witnessed the death and burial of their parents. It was heartbreaking to watch as mothers and fathers buried their sons and daughters. And it was never an easy death, with infectious diseases sometimes brutally marring the sick as they wasted away in death.

The significant consequence was not just in the deaths of the infected, but also the jarring impact on those left behind, especially young children left orphaned as a result. It became commonplace to hear of child-headed households. Teenagers were left to care for their siblings. The extended family was stretched to the limit as uncles, aunts, and grandparents assumed the responsibility for the parentless children.

And then I had an encounter that changed my life, and the course of what God would do through our church.

The church we had planted in Kampala was thriving and growing. We had also helped to plant a number of local language churches in rural communities near Kampala. One of the churches was in the small town of Luweero, 75 kilometres north of the city. We visited the little church, situated in the heart of President Milton Obote's killing fields, an area called the Luweero Triangle. The army, in an act of brutal revenge and anger at the perceived support for the rebel army in that region, massacred every living thing they could find within the confines of a triangle formed by three small towns.

On the road north, we passed roadside stalls, which usually sold bananas, cabbages, tomatoes and incredibly sweet Ugandan pineapples. It was a shock to see displayed not fruit and vegetables but hundreds of human skulls laid out in a macabre grimace of neat lines, a gruesome reminder of what had happened, and a firm determination to never let it happen again. I stopped at one of those gruesome museums, and as I held a skull in each hand, I wondered about the life of the human being that had occupied this skull. My heart broke for the people of Uganda, who had suffered so much at the hands of corrupt political systems and evil despots.

After the church service, we had lunch with the young pastor and his family. The subject of the devastation of AIDS in the area came up in the conversation. The massive trauma and death caused by political and military conflict was evident around us, but was now replaced by the devastation of an incurable disease that was snatching away more precious lives.

Just a few weeks later, one of the men in the church who worked for a well-known para-church agency asked us to accompany him to Rakai, in southwest Uganda, to witness the gruesome impact AIDS was having on the community. He took us to the home of a widow who lived in one of the villages. She was 79 years of age. She had seven children. Six of them had died of AIDS, and the seventh was dying of the infection. She led us around the back of the house to the banana plantation. There, among the bananas, were seven graves, one for her husband, one for her daughter and five for her sons, all taken by "slim." Children of every age surrounded her, the youngest of them clutching tentatively to their grandmother's shabby dress, looking up at us with big, sad but beautiful eyes. There were twenty-three of them, her grandchildren. She was caring for them alone.

I will never forget her words to me as the tears welled up in her weary old eyes.

"I am an old woman. I can no longer dig to grow food. Soon, I, too, will die! Who will look after my grandchildren?"

What could I say? Here was a situation so bleak you can hardly imagine it really happening. I took her frail, calloused old hands into mine, looked deeply into her eyes and told her that God would never abandon her children.

A short time later, in a time of personal devotion, Jesus spoke to me.

"Gary! I want you to look after my children!"

He didn't say, "the children." He said, "My children."

I knew what he meant. He wanted me to lead the church in the compassionate intervention of Uganda's bereaved, broken, battered and most vulnerable parentless children. Children who, through no fault of their own, had been left fatherless, alone and in desperate need. Children who did not have enough to eat, wore ragged old clothes, did not attend school, and had little or no hope of finding solutions to their dilemma. Children who had no hope for a secure future. Children who would lie down on a simple grass mat in the stillness of an African night and cry at the pain of their plight.

I must confess that I argued with God. I told him that I didn't want to look after children. I wanted to preach, to pastor, to grow the church he had helped us start. His words to me were direct and clear.

"I did not send you to Uganda to do what you want! I sent you to Uganda to do what I want! Look after my children."

For months, God took me on a journey through the bible. He showed me how much he loved the poor, the hurting, the homeless, the abandoned, and the refugee. And then He affirmed his special love, the unique place in his heart, for the widow and the fatherless.

The words of Psalm 68:4-6 leapt off the page, and as I read them were embedded into my soul.

> *"Sing to God, sing in praise of his name,*
>
> *extol him who rides on the clouds;*
>
> *rejoice before him—his name is the LORD.*
>
> *A father to the fatherless, a defender of widows,*

> *is God in his holy dwelling.*
>
> *God sets the lonely in families,.."*
>
> *Psalm 68:4-6 (NIV)*

I became fully aware that He, Jehovah God, is the God of the heavens, and He is the God of the ditch. He's the God of the universe in all of its splendor and He's the God of the slum. You cannot separate who He is in His holy, awesome person in heaven from who He is in the middle of any crisis on earth. He is present here in the centre of whatever we face in our day-to-day lives.

I felt so strongly that He didn't want us to build an institutional orphanage with dormitories, where children were just a number in the system but a community with homes where each one of them had names, faces, and a future. We were to provide them with family. We were to infuse them with belonging, with dignity, with a future and hope. We were to show them that they were precious and had extreme value to a Heavenly Father and to us.

He took me to the scripture, the Bible, God's Holy and Precious Word.

> *"Religion that God our Father accepts as pure and faultless is this: to look after orphans and widows in their distress. and to keep oneself from being polluted by the world."*
>
> *James 1:27 (NIV)*

The Lord hit me with a sledgehammer of simple truth. All my preaching and church building was nothing if I would not help those He called His own, those who He loved with a passion and wanted to rescue through us. How big and beautiful the church, how magnificent our worship and preaching, meant so little, if we did not care for the those that mattered to Him, the suffering, marginalized and vulnerable around us. Nothing about my religiosity impressed God. Our denominational heritage was not what mattered to Him. Our theological education and training, important as it was, were not paramount. What He was looking for is how much we lived like Jesus and cared for the lost, the least and the lonely in the place He planted us.

So, I gave up fighting with God; I surrendered to His will and decided, with all my heart, soul, mind and strength, we would do whatever it took to rescue and change the lives and the future of the children and the widows of Africa. With intention and definite purpose, I would build this young church to be a vibrant and living witness to the wonder of Jesus, the Lord of Life. We would be his hands and feet, going and giving loving service to those most in need. We would demonstrate the gospel not just by what we said but by what we did.

Watoto Childcare Ministries was born.

A visit with a little old lady in a Ugandan village was a life-defining moment. It was a spark God, our loving Heavenly Father, ignited and fanned into a burning fire in my soul for justice and righteousness to the least, to the lost and the lonely.

I often think of how that moment changed, not only our lives, but the trajectory of our ministry, and has given life and hope to so many.

~ Reflect and Discuss ~

As you reflect on your own story and engage in discussion with others, consider the following:

1. Responding to Community Crisis:

    • Reflect on how Gary and Marilyn, along with their church, responded to the HIV/AIDS crisis in Uganda. What were some key actions they took to address the community's needs?

    • Identify a current issue in your community that needs attention.

    • What specific steps can you take to help address this issue, and how can the group support you in this effort?

2. Biblical Guidance for Personal and Community Crisis:

    • Consider the impact of scripture (Psalm 68:4-6, James 1:27) on Gary's decision to care for orphans and widows. How did this scripture influence his actions and ministry?

    • Discussion: Share how a particular scripture or piece of wisdom has influenced a significant decision in your life. How did it guide your actions?

    • Discuss the role of biblical instruction in addressing personal and community crises.

    • How can faith in God through biblical instruction help us respond to personal and contemporary community issues?

During your discussion, offer support, encouragement, and prayer for one another as you reflect on your own stories and seek to discern God's will for your lives.

Share personal experiences, insights, and aspirations, and commit to walking alongside one another and with your local community in faith and obedience.

∼

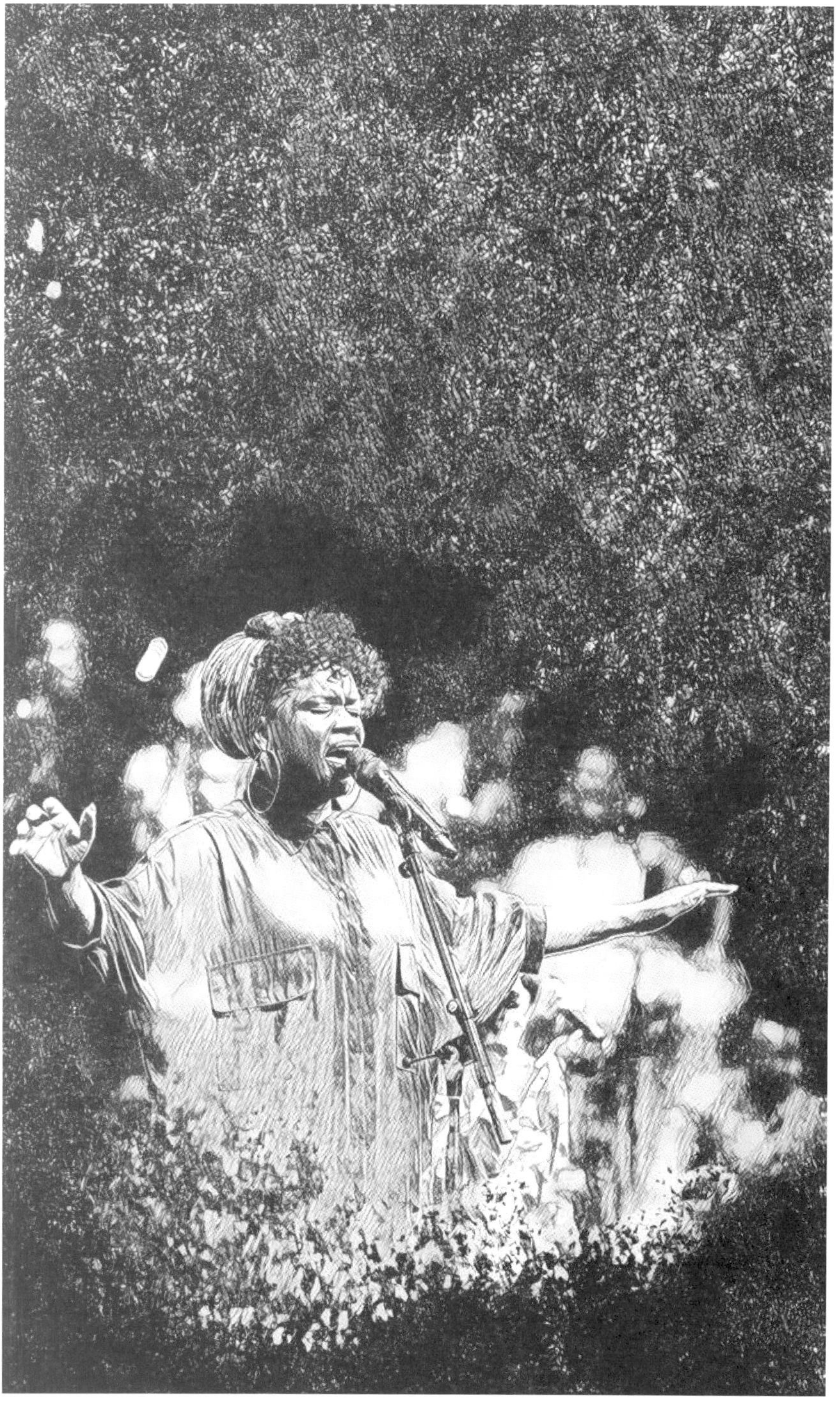

"All of life is a sacred act of worship."

Gary Skinner

"...whatever you do,
do it all for the glory of God."

The Apostle Paul - 1 Corinthians 10:31 (NLT)

16
~ In the Line of Fire ~

"Faith over fear equals worship."

It would take several years to develop a ministry to care for the orphan children of Uganda. I knew, however, deep in my heart that this was what God was calling us to, and at the right time, it would all come together. Until then, we had so much to do to see the church grow and establish itself in the city.

In 1991, we returned to Canada for another short furlough. My brother Dean and his wife Wendy filled in for a number of months. They were followed by Roy Davis, a Canadian pastor who also blessed the church with his unique ministry. The congregation grew and matured as we continued to be faithful to His call for us to build a vibrant church in the heart of the city.

~ Put Your Heads on the Table ~

Unfortunately, on our return to Kampala, we had another one of those traumatic home invasions, typical of those early days in Kampala. We were sitting down to enjoy a family supper when three gunmen walked into the open kitchen door and into the dining room. They were wearing black plastic bags on their heads with ragged holes cut out so they could see and breathe. It felt surreal as if it was some sort of slow-motion dream.

"Everyone put your heads on the table." The order came from the man obviously in charge.

We all complied, with Timothy almost plopping his head into the bowl of chili we were supposed to be enjoying.

One of the men walked around to stand behind me and pressed a revolver into the back of my head. He spoke.

"All your money, dollars, shillings, pounds, get it right now."

I answered slowly and deliberately.

"I'll give you everything we have, and then you can go."

Man in charge said, "Don't let him talk to you like that! Just shoot him."

"Money! All of it. Right now!" Pistol man poked the gun more firmly against my head.

We always kept a few hundred dollars at home. We called it "thieves' money" and kept it at hand for just a moment like this. It might get ugly if we didn't have anything!

"It is in the filing cabinet, in the office."

Slowly rising to my feet, my hands raised in submission, I turned and walked into the office. When I reached the cabinet, I realised it was locked, and the key was in Marilyn's purse.

Not good!

"I'm sorry! It's locked, and the key is in my wife's purse."

I felt the pistol rammed against my head as he spoke.

"Get on the floor. Lie between the doorposts. There."

He motioned with the gun to the door leading from the office into the bathroom.

I got down on the floor.

The third man had ripped some electrical cable off a light. He tied my hands behind my back in what I later learned was called the bowtie. The chord was wrapped just above the elbows, pulling them painfully together behind me.

The gunman sat on me with the pistol jammed into the back of my head.

One of the men brought Rachel and Timothy, laid them on the floor in the office near me and tied them up, too. The other one took Marilyn into the bedroom.

Also not good!

Thankfully, they only collected the keys. He brought her to the office and roughly tied her up as well, pushing her onto the floor.

They opened the cabinet and collected what money we had. Man in charge looked at Marilyn and demanded more money.

"We don't have any more money," she replied.

He told her to get up. Of course, it was impossible, tied up the way she was at the elbows. He grabbed her arm and roughly pulled her to her feet. The electrical cables cut into her arms.

Man in charge shoved his face up to Marilyn's, looking intently into her eyes.

"More money now," he demanded.

"That's all the money we have," she said.

He pressed his face closer to hers.

"Maybe you don't understand. Give us more money right now, or I'm going to shoot you."

Some kind of boldness came over my pretty little wife as she answered.

"You can shoot me if you like, but you won't get any more money. That's all we have."

I didn't think it was the wisest response. You don't invite someone to shoot you. Besides that, the gun was at the back of my head, not hers.

The man in charge spoke to the man sitting on my back and holding the pistol to my head.

"Shoot her husband."

Oh great!

I heard the gun cocked and then a click. Nothing.

"Shoot her husband," he said again.

Another click... Another nothing!

"I said shoot her husband and shoot him now."

A third click, and a third nothing.

"I can't shoot him," man on my back replied. "I can't shoot him."

Marilyn's man spoke again.

"Are you people Christians here?"

"Of course," she replied. "We're pastors."

The men's mouths dropped open, and a blank look of confusion descended on them. Picking up what they had collected, they ran out of the house.

Silence settled in the room. Now what? Is it over? Where is James? I called out to him.

"James! James! Are you there."

James came into the room. He untied us, and we all hugged! We went into the sitting room and sat down, relieved but trembling.

"James! Where were you." I asked.

"When they came in, I curled up on the dining chair and, pulled the tablecloth over me and lay quietly. I guess they didn't see me."

"What were you thinking, my boy?"

"I knew there were three of them. I heard everything that was going on. I heard them say they were going to shoot you."

"What were you going to do?"

"Well, if they had, I was going to lie still and count three people going out. Then, I was going to get up and call Grampa in Canada and say, "Grampa, they just shot Mom and Dad, Rachel and Tim. Can you come and get me?"

As I write this, all these years later, I am filled with a mix of emotions. One is such huge gratitude to a wonderful Father God for stopping a gun from going off and for sparing us the terrible trauma of what that would have meant for all of us as a family. Two is such a deep awe and love for my precious little wife and our three amazing children for having to live through this situation so that we could walk in obedience to his call. Third, if the Lord would do this to protect us, what more does he want to do in and through us?

We went back to the table and finished the now-cold chili. In life, you must accept the reality of what happens and get on with what you're supposed to be doing.

~ A Culture of Worship ~

One of the important things we did in those early days was to establish a culture of worship.

Worship is the oxygen of the Kingdom. Worship is a way of life and releases the favour and blessing of God into our lives. Worship is much more than just what happens with singing voices and instruments in a church building on Sunday. All of life is a sacred act of worship. But the musical celebration, the dance, the exhilaration and exuberance of a congregation lifting their united voices in praise to King Jesus, is one of the most powerful and important things we do. It is also a dynamic witness to anyone who is not yet a believer and finds themselves in the middle of corporate worship. Worshipping Jesus with music is a vital part of building and growing a vibrant, healthy local church. From the first days of the Kampala Pentecostal Church, we led people in worship.

History is replete with amazing Church music that celebrates Jesus. The greatest music ever written is worship music. When we worship, Jesus always shows up. He lives in the praises of His people. When we worship, the presence of Jesus fills the atmosphere. The glory of God is tangible, and in that presence, anything is possible.

Both Marilyn and I are blessed to be musical. Marilyn has formal piano training, and I, well, I just feel it deep in me and sing with a guitar. We met in a Christian rock and roll band, fell in love, married and went into pastoral ministry. We've been leading worship most of our lives. Worship with music is a core component of who we are and what we do. We have been influenced not only by growing up in church and experiencing worship regularly, but also by the revolution of worship music that we were immersed in as young people.

The Jesus Movement of the 1970s significantly influenced church worship music. Young Christians with long hair and strange clothing wrote and sang contemporary-styled music that made its way into congregational worship. The classic style of liturgy, which God had used for centuries, was transformed by guitars and drums. Classic theology didn't change, but the way we expressed it in modern youth-styled musical worship did. Jesus still showed up, doing His wonderful work of transforming sinners into saints.

By the 1980s, the young people Jesus had drawn to himself during the Jesus movement were leading thriving churches. Contemporary worship was an emphasis in these churches. New and powerful songs were released and made their way around the Christian world.

As we led our fledgling congregation in contemporary worship, young people were attracted like bees to honey. It was fresh and unique in Uganda. A more informal expression of adoration to God, with worship music that was compelling, upbeat and done with excellence, was liberating to so many who felt constrained by what they had grown up with. The Lord was meeting them right where they were. They could reach out to Him as an emerging generation of youth, and He would embrace them with His Holy Spirit. This kind of worship became a vital element of the culture of the church we were growing in the heart of an African city. And it went from strength to strength.

One of our pastors tells of how, as a university student, he was interested in a certain young lady. She was a Christian and attended our church, so he followed her to a Sunday morning service. He can show you where he sat in the packed hall and watched and listened to worship and Christian celebration like he had never seen or heard it before. He decided this was going to be his church. And that was before he had given his life to Christ. He kept coming back, overwhelmed by the presence of Jesus, as He was lifted up in the worship of His people. He surrendered to the message of God's love and became a follower of Jesus. He found Jesus, but the girl wasn't interested in him. He went on to get more and more involved in church, eventually responding to a call to serve Jesus in ministry. Worship, church and, most of all, Jesus transformed his life.

I remember another young Muslim man who had never been inside a church tell of how, as he walked by on the street outside the building, he heard music, was drawn in, stepped into the auditorium and then stood with mouth agape as he listened and experienced a sensation he had never felt before. It was the magnificent presence of Jesus flooding the atmosphere with love and grace, as in unison, God's people worshipped. He sat down, listened to a Bible message and surrendered his life to Christ. Wow!

I became aware that at every gathering, there was to be worship, followed by the Word, that would open up the hearts of people to receive the wonder and work of God. It's become a way of life for us.

Ugandans have a natural affiliation with music. They learn to play instruments quickly and skillfully. Their vocal talents are unusual. Over time, the power of worship filling the church grew stronger. As we worshipped, the sound of praise was as full in the congregation as they sang, as it was from the platform and all the sound equipment. It was accompanied by dance and waving and jumping, all joy-filled acts of worship to Jesus. Everyone was involved in the worship, not just those on the stage. It was electrifying, passionate and focused.

Visitors who came, over the years, in their thousands, from all around the world were captured and enraptured by the richness and power of the church in Kampala at worship. It was a very important factor in drawing young people to church, where they could become part of our loving, Christ-focused community and be trained as the next generation of Ugandan leaders, with a dream to bring healing to the city and the nation.

Marilyn trained a choir. They would help lead in the worship. We held the first of our annual Christmas Musical Celebrations in 1984, the year we started the church. It was called "The Reason for the Season." Each year, the presentation became more and more elaborate. Our passion and desire has always been to exalt Jesus by celebrating His birth and what it means to human history. In time, it became so popular we had to run the event over eight days with multiple presentations each day. Each Christmas season now, tens of thousands pack out the downtown auditorium to revel in the majesty of Jesus' birth, celebrated with dynamic music, drama and worship. So many came that we had to make it a ticketed event, or the chaos to get in would be crazy. The tickets were always free, but you needed one to get in.

~ Incense ~

Our first trip out of Uganda with musical worship was by a team we called "Incense." We wanted our worship to be a sweet smell to the Lord and to those who heard it.

> *"May my prayer be set before you like incense; may the lifting up of my hands be like the evening sacrifice."*
>
> *Psalm 141:2 (NIV)*

It consisted of ten young adults who were faithful in the worship ministry. We visited Rome first, singing in a very conservative Pentecostal church. The men sat on one side of the church and the women on the other. The ladies were all to be jewellery and make-up-free and to have their heads covered. As I came onto the platform with the pastor, I looked down at our team, the ladies with their heads wrapped in tourist-style shawls. I was so overcome by the humour of the sight I had to fight off laughter. The Italian Christians watched this unique group of Africans worshipping with joy, delight and movement. It was very different to what they were accustomed to. As we were singing, I leaned over to Anita, one of the singers beside me and said,

"Anita! Anita! Your hips!"

"What's wrong with my hips," she asked.

"They're moving!"

She looked at me as though I'd lost my mind. Of course, her hips were moving; she was worshipping!

At the end of the presentation, the pastor got up and thanked us. Would the congregation like to hear another song? They clapped. I thought they must have liked it, even if they were so very conservative. The pastor asked us to sing again, the only hymn we had sung. We did. He announced the benediction, and with one motion, off came the head coverings, and the men and ladies came together across the aisle like they hadn't seen each other for a week, filling the auditorium with banter and joy.

They took us out for a meal after the service, and all had wine. Our Ugandan Christians couldn't figure it out. No make-up but lots of wine! Don't you just love this marvellous thing called the Church? It's diverse, cuts across so many nations and people groups and is the hope of the world.

Since 1996, well over a hundred Watoto Children's Choirs have toured the globe. The music we prepared for the choirs was crafted to tell the story of redemption and hope for those in need, but what was most important is that it was framed in that special style of Ugandan worship. It wasn't created to be merely a musical presentation but a dynamic celebration of worship by rescued children. It was vibrant, passionate and accompanied by dance and African clothing. It was designed to be filled with the joy and wonder of the goodness of God, expressed in energetic but authentic celebration and praise. And my, how it was enthusiastically received by people all around the world. The choirs went, literally, around the world to every continent, lifting up the glory of Jesus and His love with worship. They were invited to sing and celebrate in thousands of churches, parliaments, castles and state houses all around the globe. Many thousands received Christ, were encouraged in their faith and became partners in rescuing vulnerable children and women in Uganda.

Worship is a core value to life and releases the favour and blessing of God. That certainly was true for us. One blessing was that the Sunday morning service was so full it was necessary to start a second service at eight in the morning.

~ We Bought the Building ~

Another blessing is that we were able to finally buy the theatre we had so miraculously occupied five years earlier. The Godhino family, who owned the building, returned to Kampala with the government's blessing to reclaim their properties. It was a tense time when they informed us that we would have to vacate the building. But, with a loan provided by the churches of the Pentecostal Assemblies of Canada, we were able to negotiate the purchase and never did have to move out. God had been faithful to His promise. He had given us the building. What a thrill to see a building designed to show movies be a place for the church to gather, celebrate Christ and declare His Word. It was a place for Ugandan youth to find the destiny that the Lord had placed upon them. It was now, truly, our home. The church, over a number of years, was able to pay back what was not an insignificant amount to purchase the property. The Lord brought it all together in a wonderful demonstration of the power of the Missions program of the Church in Canada. We will always be grateful for the kindness and generosity of the church in Canada.

~ Heavenly Mist ~

A third blessing was demonstrated in a way I can never forget. Each year, to thank the Lord for his blessing for the past year and to anticipate and ask for his favour for the new year, we would hold an all-night celebration on December 31st, the last day of the old year. It was a time of worship, prayer and preaching just to love our wonderful King Jesus. That particular night, as we reached the midnight hour, what I can only describe as a visible heavenly mist settled down on the auditorium. The presence of Jesus was overwhelming. In fact, it was so palpable and so close that a holy hush rested on all of us as we stood with uplifted hands to the Lord. We stood in silence and bathed in the intimate presence of Jesus.

It was a loving embrace and a kiss from heaven on that precious gathering of Ugandan worshippers. I also felt that there was much more that He wanted us to do as we moved boldly and with faith-filled expectation into the future together.

~ Reflect and Discuss ~

As you reflect on your own story and engage in discussion with others, consider the following:

1. Importance of Worship in Life:

    • Reflect on why worship is such an important part of life. Consider how worship connects us with God, expresses gratitude and adoration, and fosters intimacy with our Creator.

    • Discuss how worship shapes our perspective, attitudes, and actions, influencing every aspect of our lives and relationships.

2. Life as an Act of Worship:

    • Explore what Gary means when he says that all of life is an act of worship. Reflect on how worship extends beyond formal religious practices and encompasses our daily activities, interactions, and attitudes.

    • Discuss how viewing all of life as worship transforms our understanding of spirituality and encourages us to live with intentionality, integrity, and devotion to God.

3. Lessons from Jesus' Conversation with the Woman at the Well:

    • Consider some of the key lessons from Jesus' conversation with the woman at the well in Samaria (John 4.) Reflect on Jesus' teachings about true worship, spiritual fulfillment, and the nature of God's kingdom.

    • Discuss how Jesus challenges cultural and religious

norms, emphasizing the importance of authenticity, sincerity, and faith in worship.

• Explore how Jesus' encounter with the woman at the well inspires us to seek genuine encounters with God, embrace our identity as worshippers, and share the message of salvation with others.

During your discussion, offer support, encouragement, and prayer for one another as you explore the significance of worship in your lives and seek to deepen your relationship with God. Share personal experiences, insights, and aspirations, and commit to pursuing a lifestyle of worship that honors and glorifies God in all things.

~

255

"True spirituality that is pure in the eyes
of our Father God is to make a difference
in the lives of the orphans, and widows in their troubles,
and to refuse to be corrupted by the world's values."

James, the brother of Jesus – James 1:27 TPT

17
~ A Place Called Home ~

"Where love builds family, futures, and dreams."

Over the next couple of years, we refined the process of Childcare. Our first two homes were small, rented houses on the edge of a slum in the city and attached to a Luganda-speaking church that was part of the Pentecostal Assemblies of God, Uganda, the fellowship of churches we belonged to. We had a good relationship with the pastor and his church, and as the children were coming from the slum communities, we felt it would work best this way. For a variety of reasons, it did not work well at all. So, we moved the project to another church in a different part of the city. That didn't work any better. We then decided to try going to a small rural community 75 kilometres to the northeast of Kampala, where there was a good Luganda church. That also didn't work.

One of the ladies in our church had a husband who had died when Uganda Airways Flight 775 crashed in Rome in 1988. She had received compensation and wanted to donate six acres of land near the centre of the city to the church. We decided to use the land to build our first "Watoto Children's Village." We built twelve little houses, and, as the lady who had given the land was called Olive, we called it "The Olive Gardens." The children were enrolled in a nearby school. They could be a part of our church, which was within walking distance of the "village." It worked well as we learned how to care for more and more children. The "Olive Gardens" was near the University, and over time, the environment was not the most conducive for what we wanted to accomplish with the children. It was also too small for the number of children we were beginning to care for, so we purchased a 25-acre piece of land, 15 kilometres along the road leading out of Kampala to the western side of the city. Here at the Buloba Village, we built 40 homes with the children going to a nearby school. This also worked well. The children were happy and well cared for.

Later, as hundreds more children came into our care, we added a second village at Bbira and then a third at Suubi by purchasing 255 acres on the main roads out of Kampala to the southwest and west side of the city. Watoto Suubi has grown into a vibrant community with hundreds of homes.

Each house is home to eight children and a loving mother. The mothers are unemployed Christian women from the city and area. They come through a rigorous selection process and then undergo a time of training before they serve as mothers to the children. Mothers are an important component of the process of caring for children who come from such difficult backgrounds. Each of the mothers has their own unique story, and it is a wonderful thing to see them radiate with the purpose they find in caring for the children. It is such a thrill to see the bonding in the little families as they mature in the safe and healthy environment of the Watoto Villages.

To call them villages is a reflection, somewhat of any rural community in Africa. They certainly are not a collection of mud huts in a circle. What they are is a rural neighbourhood and community of family homes. The homes are simple but functional, three-bedroom houses with a kitchen, living room and bathroom. It's a home that is certainly better than most Ugandans live in. A dining room table and chairs serve as a focal point for meals and family time together. Modest but comfortable furniture fills the living room. Each child has their own bed with a mattress and comfortable linens. A secure and loving family home is the environment in which every child grows and matures as any child should. The houses are arranged in a circle of eight, with a ninth beside them. This ninth home is for the senior mother of that group of nine homes. She oversees the care of that cluster of homes, encouraging and caring for the mothers of the cluster, helping them with issues they might face as they serve the children.

~ Home, Not an Institution ~

Over the years, there has been growing criticism of placing vulnerable children in an institutional orphanage environment. Watoto has been included in this criticism by some who have never been to one of our beautiful communities. It is a lively, bustling neighbourhood of family homes filled with children who live in a family. The children grow up with a real sense of family. They see and interact with the other children as genuine siblings. Even though the mother may not be their biological mother, she is still a real mother in their lives. Time and time again, we have seen this in our interaction with the children.

I visited the Suubi Village for a Sunday morning celebration and church service. There was a young lady who told us her story. She had grown up in the village, and as a teenager, she became pregnant and left the village because of the shame she felt as a result of her choices. Life did not go well for her. Her Watoto mother, not her biological mother, but her mother, nonetheless, rented a small home for her near the Watoto village. She just loved her, affirming and accepting her. The young lady was invited to attend a Saturday evening fire-side service for the teenage children on the village. She didn't want to attend, feeling the other children might not accept her. The village pastor encouraged her to attend, which she reluctantly did. There, around the fire, she listened to the stories of the other teenagers and what they were going through in the process of just growing up. She recognised and identified with their struggles and mistakes, realising that she was not alone in navigating the challenges of life. She found the courage to tell her own story, only to find love and acceptance around the fire that night.

At the church service that morning, I had the privilege of dedicating her baby girl to Jesus with hundreds of mothers, children, teachers and workers of the village watching. She had found real family and belonging. No, Watoto certainly isn't an institutional orphanage. It is a community of people who are learning to deal with the challenges that life has thrown their way, most through no fault of their own.

We had lunch with one of the families, and then, as we were driving out of the village, something wonderful happened, something that made this point even more clear. One of the house mothers saw we were leaving and came out of her home with several of her teenage children in tow. She had a baby in her arms. They waved for us to a stop and came up to the vehicle.

"Oh, Pastor Gary, Auntie Marilyn, I couldn't let you leave without meeting my new little granddaughter." She held out the little bundle of life.

And here's what makes it such a beautiful story. The baby was the child of the daughter she had raised on the village, in her home. Her daughter had married one of the fine young men of our church. The baby was the fruit of the marriage. As is customary in Ugandan society, a daughter after giving birth, moves back into her mother's home for the first three months, and grandma helps in raising the baby and helping the new mother through the process. They were all there, celebrating family life. No! Watoto Homes, designed to rescue Uganda's most vulnerable women and children, are not an institution. It is a family!

Each village has a nursery, primary and high school within easy walking distance for every student. Sports and music facilities provide an opportunity for the children to develop their unique passions and skills. A technical department in the high school caters for the training of children who will go into a vocational career. At the heart of the "village" is the church auditorium. Its design makes it a multi-functional hub for worship, celebration, banquets, conferences and activities for the surrounding community.

A Watoto Childcare Team of employees work to ensure the smooth operation of the community. Everything that a child needs to develop into a responsible Christian disciple and a reliable citizen of Uganda is provided for them in a healthy, secure social environment. All their natural physical, emotional and spiritual needs are met in the homes, schools, medical clinics and churches. Food, clothing, and medical care are things they never have to worry about. The most important thing they learn is that God is their Father, loves them and has a purpose for their lives.

~ Rescue, Raise, Rebuild ~

As Watoto Childcare Ministries expanded to care for thousands of Uganda's most vulnerable children, it became clear that we were to do far more than just rescue orphans. We were to rescue vulnerable children, raise godly leaders and rebuild a nation. Those three words have become so important to us.

God loves to take the weak to do great things. He takes the despised and marginalised and raises them to significance and influence. It was burned into my soul that we were to raise leaders. What Africa and the world need is godly, servant leaders who model their leadership after the world's best leader, Jesus. As we grew the church and expanded the leadership base, we were not just to lead but model, motivate, mentor and multiply leadership in those we had the privilege to lead. We spoke openly about this in the "villages" and at church. We reiterated to the children repeatedly that God was, in a special way, their Father. He had a plan, purpose and destiny for them. He had chosen them to participate in bringing healing to their nation through the calling and careers they would fulfil one day as adults. We gave them a dream of a better life, a better community and a better nation.

Church is about loving and reaching people where they are in their pain and disappointment. In their poverty, in the injustice and insecurity of life, Jesus is the answer, and Jesus makes His presence known through the lives of the people He calls the church.

~ Patient Persistence~

It is important to be aware that what has transpired and come together in such a wonderful work is actually the result of the dedicated, focused and intentional service and ministry of so many over many years. It is not possible to have a transformative work take place over a brief period or even a few years but over a protracted period of unrelenting persistence. It takes time, consistent faithfulness and commitment to a specific set of goals and strategies for something of value to be established.

Villages that care for vulnerable children don't just spring up out of the ground when we find property and put up a few buildings. It takes years to see a village become a fruitful neighbourhood for the community. It takes decades of hard work in a consistent, day-by-day effort to accomplish results with lasting value. Raising parentless children to be leaders takes a whole generation of pushing forward with an unrelenting passion and tempered zeal.

Building a church or business, a school, nation or institution, in fact, developing and establishing anything effective that has a positive and enduring impact, requires a grand and noble vision that is realised by those with staying power. It takes teamwork. No one does it alone! Rebuilding infrastructure, reshaping culture and fashioning a better future requires long-term persistence, an unswerving resolution to keep moving forward through any difficulty, trial and opposition that we may face. Any journey will have obstacles along the way that will delay, sidetrack and hold us back from accomplishing what God has called us to do. But we must never give up!

This has been our personal experience. Every obstacle is an opportunity for God to show Himself great. The stumbling blocks before us are the steppingstones for the way forward. The victories we win never come without a fight. Battles won are faith builders that call us to step up to a fresh challenge and gain new ground. Discouragement must not find a home in our hearts. We may feel discouraged, but that is normal. It is also the reason why God always spoke words of encouragement to those in the Bible record who were called to do something for God and the country. Fear will paralyse us, and faith will motivate us. Winners never quit, and quitters never win. Never, ever give up! God wants to write some history, and He will use anyone willingly to hear His call, commit to it and then step forward without wavering.

To be honest, there were a thousand times when both Marilyn and I were bone tired or facing challenging issues or unkind opposition, and we just wanted to give up. As we stood side by side and hand in hand, we knew that Jesus had commissioned us with a specific calling and enablement. He, Himself, stood with us, held our clasped hands in His nail-scarred hand and whispered that we were to keep going. He would never leave us or forsake us.

The vision He birthed in us was crystal clear and focused. It could not be completed without staying the course, no matter what transpired along the way. And we were never, ever alone. He was with us, and so were a lot of good people within whom God has also birthed this same vision.

~ Reflect and Discuss ~

As you reflect on your own story and engage in discussion with others, consider the following:

1. Role of the Church in Social and Community Development:

    • Reflect on whether the Church has a role in social and community development. Consider how Jesus' teachings and actions demonstrate a concern for the marginalized, oppressed, and vulnerable in society.

    • Discuss how the Church can actively engage in social justice initiatives, poverty alleviation efforts, and community development projects to demonstrate God's love and compassion for all people.

2. Fulfilling the Call of God in James 1:27:

    • Explore how we can effectively fulfill the call of God found in scripture (James 1:27, Ephesians 1:22-23) Reflect on the essence of true religion, which involves caring for the widows and orphans and keeping oneself unstained by the world.

    • Discuss practical ways in which individuals and churches can live out this call by advocating for justice, providing practical assistance to those in need, and fostering spiritual growth and transformation.

3. Sponsoring a Needy Child:

    • Sponsoring a needy child or woman through Watoto Church or another ministry can change the life and destiny of that child. Discuss your personal experience of sponsoring a child if you have done so.

    • Discuss the implication of financial generosity and

support toward the cause of world missions and compassionate ministry.

During your discussion, offer support, encouragement, and prayer for one another as you explore these important questions and seek to align your lives with God's purposes. Share personal experiences, insights, and challenges, and commit to living out your faith with boldness, compassion, and perseverance. By seeking to fulfill God's call in James 1:27 and actively engaging in social and community development, you can be agents of positive change and transformation in the world around you.

~

SPONSOR A CHILD

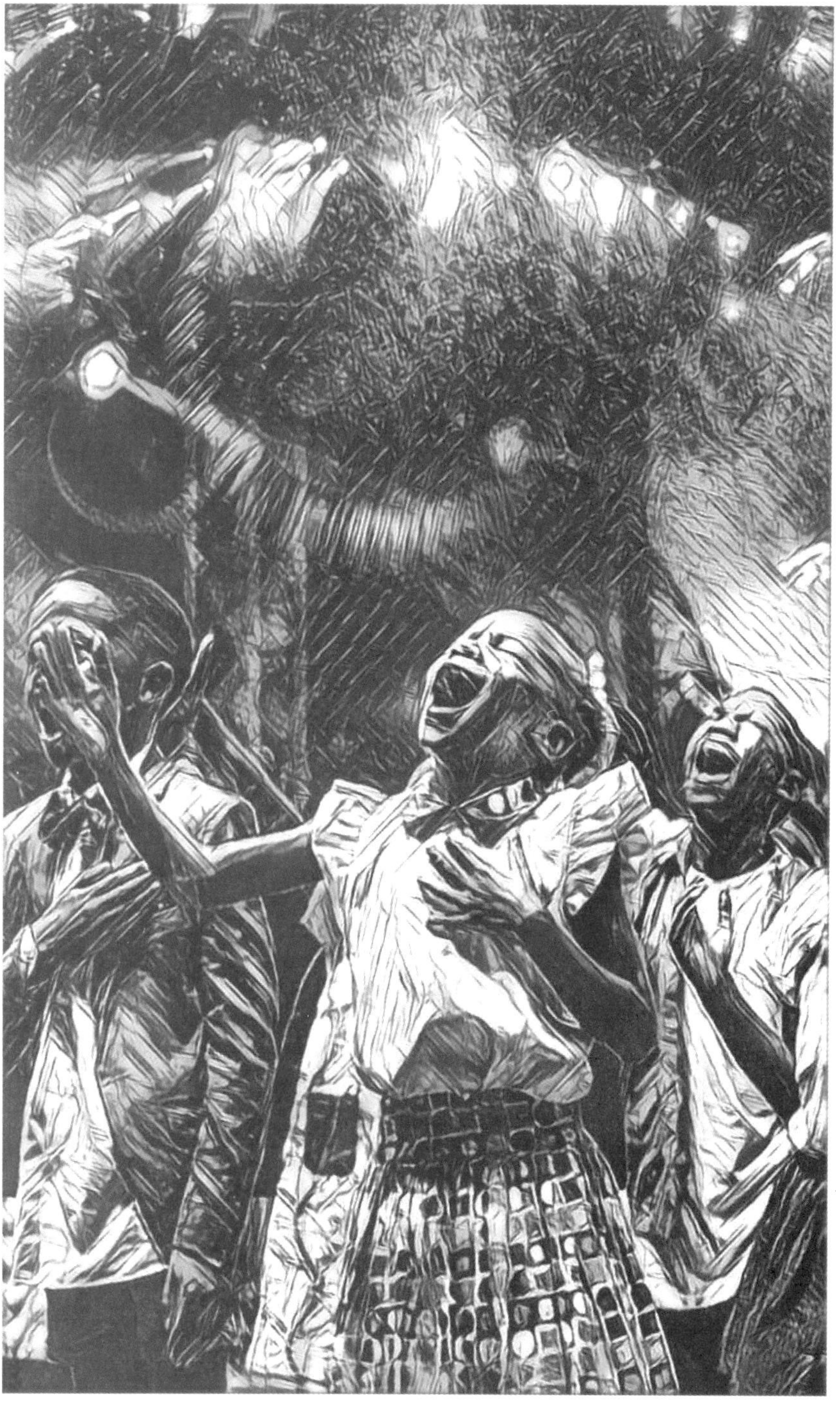

"You have built a stronghold by the songs of children. Strength rises up with the chorus of infants. This kind of praise has power to shut Satan's mouth. Childlike worship will silence the madness of those who oppose you."

King David - Psalm 8:2 TPT

18
~ The Songs of Children ~

"Powerful praise from little hearts."

One day, in a time of devotion, Jesus told me he wanted us to put children in a choir and take them around the world. We were to tell a glad story, not a sad story, a story of hope and redemption, not misery. We were to speak up on behalf of those who could not speak for themselves.

I talked to Marilyn about what Jesus wanted us to do. Our immediate thought was to take a choir to Canada, the country that had sent us to Uganda. We knew lots of churches and pastors there and were sure it would be a blessing to the churches in Canada.

The leadership of the mission declined. Caring for orphans was what other organisations did, not us. Church planting and Bible Schools were the priority. Orphan care was not the emphasis we had as a mission. The final decision was that we could take the choir and raise funds in other countries but not Canada. I must admit I was surprised and not a little confused by this, especially as I felt it was what God wanted us to do. Again, I knew that submission to leadership was critical and the right thing to do, so, albeit reluctantly, I agreed to not bring the choir to Canada.

Where should we go? The great United States of America, of course, but we knew few people there and had little or no relationship with pastors and churches there. You have to understand that this became a massive faith venture for us. We were to put a choir of twenty orphaned children together, develop a great musical concert, fly them halfway around the world, and tell a story of hope and redemption. Who would set up an itinerary? Where would we stay? Could we get concerts in the middle of the week? How would we finance a choir tour? Would it work, or are we nuts? You also have to understand that we did have one thing going for us. The choir was not our idea! I blame Jesus entirely for the whole concept. If He wanted us to do this, then he would make a way.

Marilyn went to British Airways with a proposal. Would they give us thirty tickets to the States on credit? She was sure they would say no, and we could be done with this madness. They said yes! What city in the States would she like to go to? She hadn't thought that far! Did they have a map? They did! Chicago looked like it was in the middle of the country. Let's go to Chicago! Okay! Hey! I'm not making this this up. It was either faith or foolishness, and I now know it wasn't foolishness.

The following months were a time of learning and preparation. We put together a concert and chose twenty children and eight young adults to accompany them as caregivers. We wrote and practised the music and dance. We made uniforms. We recorded the concert on tape in a very makeshift studio. The electrical power was so erratic we would have to suspend the recording until it returned. Sometimes, it came back in ten minutes, only to go off again in ten minutes. Sometimes, it came back hours later. You just never knew. The sound insulation was blankets, so we would have to start over if a dog barked, a rooster crowed, a motorcycle drove by, or it started to rain. Fun! Fun! Fun!

Going on British Airways meant going through London, so why not start the tour in Great Britain? Jeff, one of the young men who came to the church, had returned to the U.K. to study. Jeffrey had lost both of his parents to AIDS the same week. He believed in what we were doing and was delighted to set up some concerts in London. He approached a well-known motor coach company that a wealthy Christian businessman owned to enquire if he would help with a bus for the tour. At first, he declined but later changed his mind and provided the bus for the tour around England. That was a real gift as the cost of transport for thirty people in a bus was significant.

Rev. John Wood of St. Ann's Anglican Church in Tottenham, London, helped set up the tour. He had spent time in Uganda and was delighted to help. The church hall became home for three weeks. We had school presentations during the day and concerts some evenings and on the weekends. We called the presentation a "Concert of Hope." It was a great success. Children who had heard the choir at school would invite their parents to church on Sunday.

~ I Can't Stop Crying ~

One Sunday, after a concert in an Anglican church in North London, some of the children were standing with me at the front of the church to meet and pray with those who wanted to meet the children. A young mother came up to us. She was carrying a baby in her arms, and a girl of perhaps seven stood beside her. The mother was crying. I looked into her eyes and asked how we could help her.

"I don't know what's wrong with me! I can't stop crying. I've never been inside a church before but my little girl, Lucy, heard the children sing at her school and begged me to bring her to hear them again here at the church. From the minute we walked into the building and then the children began to sing, I started to cry, and I can't stop. I don't know what's wrong with me."

We shared the love of Jesus with her and prayed for her and her children to come to know and love Jesus.

~ It's Not About the Money ~

We were ministering to people and having real impact, but I must admit that the offerings were not good. I didn't think we would be able to pay all the bills.

One weekend, we drove down to Brighton, on the south coast, to do a day camp in the Anglican Church. On Saturday, we held the camp for the children, and then on Sunday morning, a "Concert of Hope" in the church. The children were hosted in the homes of church members. After the morning concert, the vicar thanked the people for bringing their children and attending the concert, and asked if they had any spare coins to drop them in the bag on the way out. They would pay for the day camp, and what was left over would be given to Watoto. We received all of two pounds and fifty pence in the offering, and I remember complaining about it with Jesus on the way back to London on the bus. Jesus spoke so clearly to me.

"You think you're here to raise money. You're not! You look after the ministry; I'll look after the money."

The next morning, a Monday, we were singing in a small school and about forty children were listening. I always shared a simple, child-friendly gospel message as a part of the concert. As I was speaking, I noticed two little boys wearing turbans in the middle of the children who were seated on the floor. They were both gently crying and wiping tears from their eyes. I heard Jesus whisper again.

"You think you're here to raise money. This is why you're here."

Shortly after returning from that first Watoto Children's Choir tour to England and the USA, we received a letter from Rev. John Wood at St. Anne's. He asked if we remembered the weekend church camp in Brighton. Oh yes, we remember! It was the two-pound-fifty church. He went on to let us know that one of the host homes had just finished settling the financial matters of their late mother's estate and had sent Watoto a gift of twenty-five thousand pounds. I heard a soft voice in my head,

"You look after the ministry; I'll look after the money."

I have never forgotten that tender rebuke from Jesus. It became central to what the choir tours were all about. We were to tell the redemptive story of Watoto and not focus on the money or the size of an offering as the children ministered. We wanted listener's interaction with the choir to lead them to Jesus and His wonderful, healing love. We were to leave behind a beautiful spirit of worship and ministry with those we had the privilege to sing to. Jesus would look after the money.

We flew on to Chicago without a clue as to where we would spend the first night. After landing and getting everyone somewhat settled, I called a pastor of one of the Assemblies of God Churches. I knew that he had some Canadian connections. I told him who we were and that we needed a place to stay. Would he be so kind as to let us sleep in the church hall that night? They were so gracious and immediately agreed and used their church's Sunday School bus to take us to the church.

The next day, they offered to drive the choir the 380 kilometres to Detroit for the only concert we had booked. It was for the Sunday morning services at the Brightmoor Tabernacle. The pastor was Cal Ratz, the son of one of my favourite Bible School teachers. The church was large, with several thousand people on a Sunday morning. The children gave it their best and then greeted the people in the foyer after the service. We had made cassette tapes of the concert and had a few African curios for people to buy as a memory of the concert. We were shocked at the generous size of the offering and the large amount of tape sales.

I remembered, again, Jesus' words to me. He would look after the money, but what was important was that Jesus, the great Healer, was glorified.

~ Wherever This Bus Takes Us ~

We now had enough money to buy our own bus. I went to a bus dealer and picked out a bright orange school bus that would take us where we needed to go. I had made sure I had the appropriate license to drive, and we spent the next three months taking the choir wherever the doors opened. It was a wonderful journey of faith, not knowing from day to day where we would be next.

One day, after boarding the bus, Marilyn asked me,

"Well! Where are we going today?"

"We are going wherever this bus takes us!" I replied.

Off we drove, not knowing what the day would hold. But Jesus never let us down. We sang at school assemblies, and a teacher would be the wife of a pastor in the community. They would call the people for an impromptu concert that evening and then host the children. We would sing outside a MacDonald's Cafe, and they would give us a meal for the children. Sometimes, a stranger would ask us who the kids were. We would tell them, and they would offer to pay for lunch. Of course, as time went on, we became far more organised, but it was a leap of faith in simple obedience to Jesus' call for us to "put a choir together, take them around the world and tell a story of hope." It was a faith trip that launched the Watoto Children's Choir.

Once back in Uganda, the finances raised while on the U.S. tour served not only to pay off the airfare, buy the bus, and meet the other costs for the tour but also to fund the building of the first six homes at the Olive Gardens, our first Watoto Village.

The choir tour became a yearly tradition. The same children never travelled twice, giving other children the opportunity for a trip of a lifetime. Through it all, we never forgot the principles God taught us on that first tour: to step out in obedience even when you are unsure how God will answer, to listen for and follow the leading of the Holy Spirit, to focus on the ministry and let Jesus worry about the money.

In the beginning, Marilyn and I would go on every tour, leading the group, but after a few years, it seemed important that we step back from leading the choir and entrust the responsibility to young adult leaders we had trained on those earlier trips.

~ The White House ~

On one of those tours, the team leader received a call while travelling on the bus in the Washington D.C. area.

"We're phoning on behalf of President George Bush." the voice on the other line said. "The President would like for the children to come and sing at the White House."

Thinking it was a prank, he simply said, "Yeah, right," and hung up.

A few minutes later, he had another call, this time from the Ugandan ambassador to the U.S.

"Did you just get a call from the White House and hang up?" The ambassador asked.

"I did get a call from someone saying they were from the White House," he answered, his heart now beating a little faster.

"It was the White House! You will receive another call from them in a few minutes."

They did call back, and a visit to the White House for the following day was set up. We later learned the circumstances that brought about the invitation.

The choir had performed at a large Episcopal Church in Washington D.C. on a previous tour and was scheduled to return to the same church. A woman in the church whose husband was a significant member of the government and who had attended the concert the year before wanted to do something to continue to support the children.

"Honey," she asked her husband, "how would you like to do something for the Holy Spirit this morning?"

She mentioned the choir and that they would be at their church again in a week or so. Would he consider reaching out to a friend at a newspaper that had an audience all across the States? He agreed, and a significant article about the choir appeared in the newspaper that week.

The First Lady, Laura Bush, came across the article.

She knew that the President of Uganda, Yoweri Museveni, was in Washington that week to receive an award for his good work in addressing the AIDS crisis in Uganda. It would be perfect if the choir could sing for both presidents at the occasion, to be held at the White House, the official American presidential residence.

You can't make this stuff up! Clearly, God was at work!

The next day, the Watoto Children's Choir performed in the Rose Garden at the White House for President George W. Bush, members of his staff, members of the diplomatic core and President Museveni.

After the event, First Lady Laura Bush invited the children into their private residence, served them cookies and let them play with the presidential dogs.

A year later, President Bush and his wife held an official tour across Africa. Their last stop on the trip was to Uganda. The President wanted to address the HIV/AIDS issue while in Uganda. Marilyn received a phone call from the American embassy in Uganda, asking if the choir would accept an invitation from the President to sing at the event. Of course, we were delighted and honoured to participate.

The choir made all the preparations, including a special song arranged by our son Timothy, blending the Ugandan National Anthem with the famous song "America the Beautiful."

Sitting at the event was a unique and special experience for Marilyn and me, especially since we were seated next to the Secretary of State, Condoleezza Rice. The children sang and worshipped, and, of course, as always, a heavenly presence filled the atmosphere. It was obvious from the President's response that he wanted another song. The kids then sang the special rendition of the Ugandan National Anthem and "America the Beautiful."

The President and Laura Bush both were moved, wiping their eyes as they listened. Forgoing his scheduled meet and greet with the rows of seated diplomats present at the event, he walked directly over to the children and shook hands with the littlest girl in the front row. She looked up confidently into his eyes and leaning down, the President wrapped his arms around several of them. I'll never forget the sight of several tiny black hands clutching onto the back of the President's suit jacket. The click and clatter of cameras from the gathered press captured the moment. The President stood, smiled, thanked the children and turned to the assembled dignitaries. He saluted and simply walked out, leaving behind ambassadors and dignitaries, many with dazed looks at not having had the chance to greet one of the most important men on earth.

There was a buzz at the end of the event as people began to disburse. A few moments later, an embassy official came over to Marilyn and me. He had escorted the President back to his big, black, shiny limousine to reboard Air Force One and return to the USA. He wanted to let us know that the President had specifically asked that we receive his thanks for bringing the choir to the event.

Psalm 113:7 says of God that,

"He picks up the poor from out of the dirt, rescues the forgotten who've been thrown out with the trash, seats them among the honoured guests, a place of honour among the brightest and the best."

Psalm 113:7 MSG

The children sang once more, several years later, for President Bush at the Washington prayer breakfast, "seated among the honoured guests."

It has been such a great delight and privilege to send the Watoto Children's Choir all around the world. These precious children, rescued from despair and raised to celebrate King Jesus, have ministered by their dynamic worship music to millions around the world. They have performed "Concerts of Hope" in tens of thousands of churches of every denomination. They've had the privilege to perform with notable celebrities. They've travelled around the planet to sing for parliaments and palaces, kings and queens, presidents and prime ministers and important members of government.

But the most important guest at every concert is Jesus, the King of Kings and the lover of our souls. He is the reason we sing; we worship and do what we do. He is the theme of our music and the focus of our worship.

Without Him, it's just noise. With Him, it's life changing.

~ A Scottish Tattoo ~

The choir were invited to sing in Scotland at the twenty-fifth anniversary of the motor coach company that had so generously provided a bus for the tours in the U.K. and Europe. The concert was held at an old Scottish castle. Celebrity guests, politicians and business people enjoyed a sumptuous banquet. As the choir went up to sing, a well-dressed Scottish gentleman approached me as I stood watching from near the back.

"Watch this," he said.

We listened to the sweet celebration of African children as they worshipped Jesus in song and dance, getting that aristocratic crowd up on their feet to join them. The presence of Jesus filled the banquet hall, as it always does when the children worship Him. The Scottish gentleman leaned over to me.

"This is what I want at my Tattoo."

I had no idea what he meant by a choir at a Tattoo.

"We would be most honoured to do so." I replied.

I handed him a business card and asked if he would coordinate it with the Watoto Office in London.

A year later, the children participated in the Royal Edinburgh Military Tattoo. The event is a grand performance of international guest performers, highlighted by Scottish bagpipes, military music, marches and fun. It has been held for over seventy years and takes place on the esplanade in front of the majestic Edinburgh Castle. Two hundred and twenty thousand people attend each year, with millions more watching on television.

We were permitted to sing one of our Watoto songs, so we sang one that honoured King Jesus. The highlight of the concert was to be Elton John's "Can You Feel the Love Tonight." Sheila Tugume and Dennis Kiima sang the solo parts, the children joined in on the chorus, and then the thunderous sound of rank after rank of marching soldiers on their bagpipes, drums and crashing cymbals filled the atmosphere.

Marilyn had explained to the children that the song was written by a man who wrote about human love, but as they stood on that square and lifted their voices, they were singing about the greatest love of all, the love of Jesus.

"Sing to the people about His love," she encouraged them.

Marilyn and I were privileged to be seated in the royal enclosure for the event. It was filled with many of the cream of British society. As the children raised their voices to the accompaniment of the musical instruments, the glorious presence of Jesus descended on that huge crowd. I wept! So did Marilyn! And we watched as those important people pulled out their handkerchiefs to wipe the tears from their eyes. The singing of children worshipping Jesus brought heaven down.

Alexander Tee, a very senior, well-received and highly respected British evangelist, had served Jesus all his life. The previous year, he had visited us in Kampala to speak at the church and the Watoto Villages. I received a letter from him shortly after the Tattoo. He told me that he had been watching it faithfully for many years on his television. He wanted to thank me for sending the children to sing at the Tattoo. He told me of how, for the very first time in all the years of watching it, he had seen Jesus honoured at the event. He also wanted me to know that he had wept with joy and love as the presence of Jesus filled his room as he listened to the children sing.

I thought again of the verses God had put in our hearts about His purpose for the choir. It was from Psalm 8,

> *"You have built a stronghold by the songs of children.*
>
> *Strength rises up with the chorus of infants.*
>
> *This kind of praise has power to shut Satan's mouth.*
>
> *Childlike worship will silence*
>
> *the madness of those who oppose you."*
>
> *Psalm 8:2 TPT*

~ Not a Financial Gimmick ~

The Watoto Children's Choir has never been a fundraising gimmick.

Yes! Many millions of dollars have been given to support the noble work of rescuing and raising Ugandan orphans to be future leaders. The concerts have, first and foremost, been a way of telling of the goodness of God and his love for the lost, the lonely and the least. It has also been a platform to see thousands of people receive Christ.

It has been a school of discipleship and leadership for the children and the adult caregivers as they serve Jesus in cross-cultural settings. Some of our pastoral team developed their leadership skills by leading choir tours. It has been a tool to inspire churches around the world to be actively involved in the practical ministry of compassion in their towns and cities. Tens of thousands of Christians from around the world, in Asia, Europe, and South and North America, have faithfully sponsored a child, making it financially possible to rescue vulnerable children.

As a result, we have built Watoto Children's Villages, where hundreds of single-family homes have been built for the children to live in. They grow up and mature in healthy families in a safe and secure environment. The houses were built by the generosity of churches who had hosted the choir, many of whom sent teams to construct them. We have constructed quality schools for children of every age in each of the villages. Medical clinics provide health care for the Watoto community and the people of the surrounding area. Sports and music programs develop the creative and worship skills of the children, some of whom have gone on to represent their countries in national events.

We have established agricultural farms and developed a sustainable food program for the villages. Vegetables, eggs, chickens and fruit from our farms supplement the diet of the children. Goat farms provide the very best substitute for mother's milk for the infants in the baby's homes we've set up. Most of the children who now travel with the children's choir were rescued as abandoned and vulnerable babies.

As a consequence, Watoto Church has rescued over 5000 children and 1500 babies, giving them a chance to become all that Jesus created them to be.

This is what Jesus meant when he told me to plant an English-speaking church in the heart of the city of Kampala, and through that church, he would touch the city, and he would touch the nation. And here is the wonderful, good news. The full story of the impact on and in these children has yet to be told.

~ Reflect and Discuss ~

As you reflect on your own story and engage in discussion with others, consider the following:

1. Watoto Children's Choir Beyond a Musical Concert:

    • Reflect on how the Watoto Children's Choir has been more than just a musical concert to raise funds for the Childcare ministry. Consider the testimonies shared, the personal stories of transformation, and the message of hope and redemption communicated through the choir's performances.

    • Discuss how the choir's ministry goes beyond entertainment to inspire compassion, raise awareness about the needs of vulnerable children, and mobilize support for sustainable community development initiatives.

2. Role of Worship in Leading People to Christ:

    • Explore how worship plays a part in leading people to Christ. Reflect on the power of music, prayer, and corporate worship experiences to create a conducive environment for encountering God's presence and experiencing spiritual transformation.

    • Discuss how authentic worship can soften hearts, open minds, and draw individuals into a deeper relationship with God, ultimately leading them to accept Jesus Christ as their Lord and Savior.

3. Impact of Attending a Watoto Children's Choir Concert:

    • Share personal experiences if you have attended a Watoto Children's Choir concert. Reflect on the impact it had on you, both emotionally and spiritually.

- Discuss how the testimonies, songs, and performances of the choir members touched your heart, challenged your perspective, and inspired you to action or deeper faith.

During your discussion, offer support, encouragement, and prayer for one another as you reflect on your own experiences and insights related to the Watoto Children's Choir and the power of worship in leading people to Christ. Share how these experiences have shaped your understanding of ministry, compassion, and the transformative power of God's love. Commit to being ambassadors of hope and agents of change in your communities as you continue to walk in faith and obedience to God's call.

~

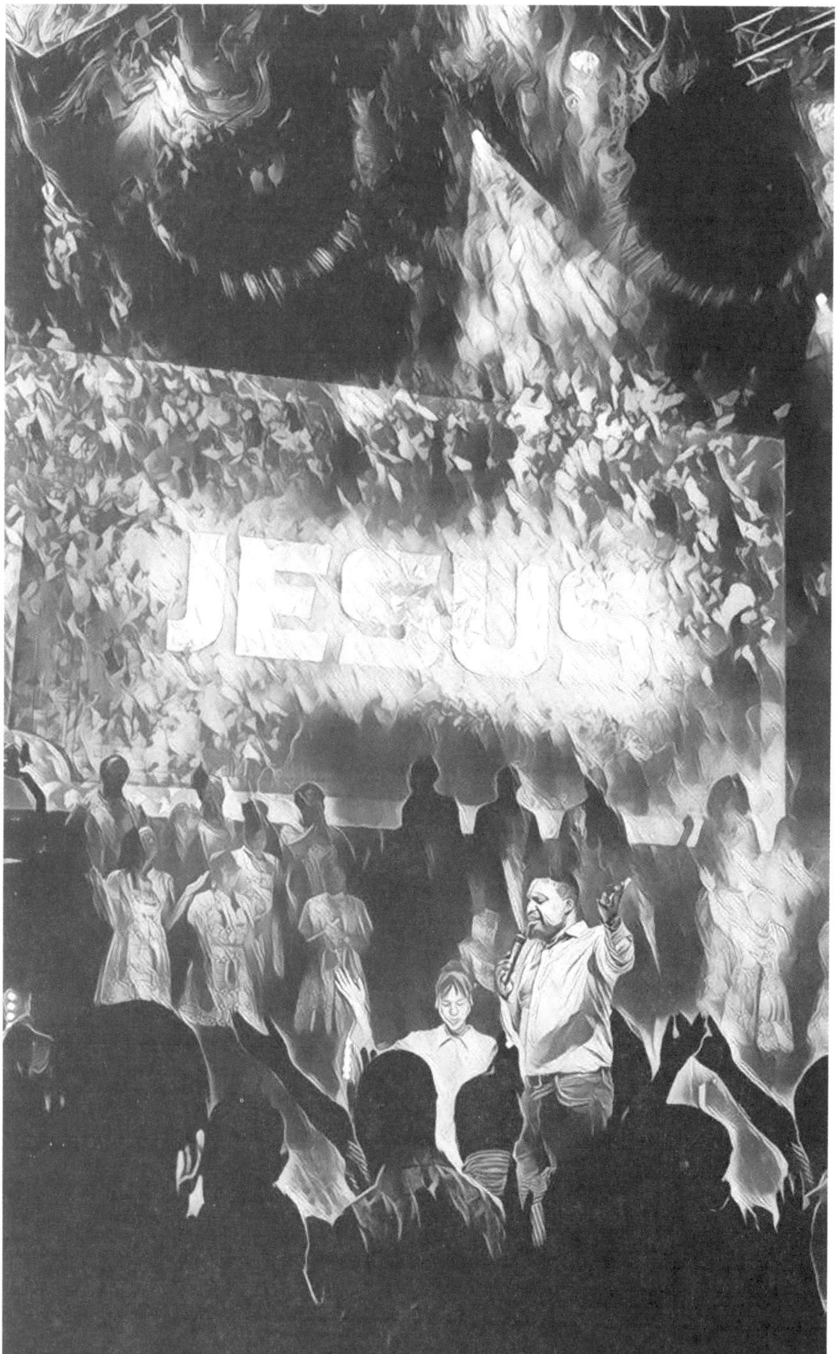
JESUS

> "Missions is not the ultimate goal of the church. Worship is. Missions exists because worship doesn't."
>
> *John Piper*

19
~ Pressing On ~

"Multiplying campuses, growing leaders, and cultural transformation."

The years continued to unfold. The number of people attending what was still, at that time, called Kampala Pentecostal Church, or more affectionately KPC, continued to swell. The lively, contemporary worship drew many. Practical, biblical messages were presented in a passionate but restrained manner. We were careful to avoid anything that would portray the services as showy or professional. Everything we did was done with excellence but covered with worship, wonder and awe to the One whom we worshipped, King Jesus.

It was obvious that Ugandans had a deep love for music and worship. The quality and standard of what was presented at church was very high. This was demonstrated not only in the regular celebration services but the level of excellence in the children's choirs and the other special musical presentations the church made at Christmas and other times. People, especially young Ugandans, were drawn to this. It was, at the time, different from what was being presented in churches across the city.

The church was also unique in having a 'Mzungu' (White Man) for the pastor. I did take some lessons in Luganda, but when people asked me if I was going to learn Ateso, Langi, or one of the other languages in the country, I realised that it was impractical to continue. We were an English-speaking church. Everything we did was in English except for an occasional worship song in one of the vernacular languages. Being English and having a Canadian as the pastor meant that we were not tied to any specific local culture or tradition. We were free to create a church with a new culture.

~ A New Culture ~

There are many good things about each tribe and culture. There are, however, many cultural practices that are inextricably linked with spiritual and religious activities and witchcraft in each people group. Youth often found some cultural practices either offensive, outdated, or undesirable, even if they were being done in a church. Being involved with a church that was fashioning a new culture and throwing off the shackles of undesirable practices was attractive to young people. An example might be the way a church allowed their youth to wear their hair or how they would dress. It was an interesting challenge to integrate the good and the desirable things about African culture with an emerging new culture. The worship music we crafted was neither just African nor completely Western. It was a blend of both, and so it became something unique and new.

My desire has always been to, first and foremost, live out and promote neither African nor Western culture but a Kingdom culture. I did not come to Uganda to build a church that reflects Canadian culture and church practice. Neither did I come to Uganda to build a church that reflects Ugandan culture. I came to Uganda to build a church that reflects Kingdom culture, biblical culture, and Jesus' culture. The church must live by and model Kingdom culture and may integrate into it the desirable and useful aspects of any culture, African or otherwise, as long as they reflect biblical values and culture.

We did this, and it was attractive to the youth who wanted to passionately and effectively live for Christ in a contemporary way. Culture all around the world is fluid and being changed, continuously and aggressively, by the pervasive influence of the international media, arts and entertainment. No culture is exempt from external cultural influences that will provoke change. Not all of those cultural influences are positive. In fact, many are openly negative and openly ungodly. Any cultural norm or value that violates Kingdom and biblical culture should not be practised by the church or, in fact, by society anywhere.

The glorious and perfect message of biblical truth will never change, but the way it is expressed may and will mutate and, in doing so, maybe more relevant, effective and attractive to contemporary society. We do not exist to simply copy and paste worldly culture into the church in order to be relevant, effective and attractive. The test for what is culturally acceptable must be the inerrant, irrevocable and eternal Word of God, the Bible. Church culture must reflect Kingdom culture and may be flavoured by desirable local or international culture only as it reflects biblical values and truth.

This was a very effective factor in attracting young Ugandans to church. The numbers attending Celebration swelled, not suddenly but steadily, until even two services on Sunday morning were not enough to accommodate those coming to worship King Jesus. It was a very exciting thing to finish the first service, allow the celebrants to exit through side and rear doors and then open the opposite side doors, off the parking lot, and watch as thousands of eager people pressed in to get a good seat, near the front, either in the lower auditorium or the balcony. They had been gathering outside, and anticipation rose as they heard the vibrant celebration of people inside. I would stand and weep as I watched precious souls press in to attend church. We would be ready with worship, the Word, expecting a loving work from a good God.

It was obvious that we would need to do something to address the need to accommodate more people at church. One option was to increase the capacity of the auditorium downtown. It would be costly and interfere with regular activities, but it was a possible solution. Perhaps we should build a new modern auditorium that would seat thousands of people. It could be multifunctional and used for other activities during the week. Another option was to open a new celebration point in another part of the city. Most people who came to worship downtown would come by city transport, but as the economy grew, more and more came in their own cars. They would come in from a considerable distance and the four corners of the city.

~ Multiple Campuses ~

As we thought it through, we recognised that the largest number of people at church came from the northern suburbs of the city. We decided that we should plant a second celebration point somewhere in the northern part of the city. We announced it to the congregation and were delighted at the joy and anticipation that it brought to the people. Of course, we needed to find a suitable place for the services. Until we could acquire one, we rented the Odeon Theatre, another smaller facility downtown. There was real excitement the day we launched the second celebration point, and a good number of people living in the northern suburbs of the city made it home. We carried on like this for two years before we were able to buy a seventeen-acre piece of land in Ntinda. We brought in a tent that would seat a thousand people. Pastor Joshua Mugabi and his wife, Christine, gave the pastoral oversight to the new campus, which also grew steadily.

We called the new celebration point KPC North. It was the first of many campuses we would plant over the years. Eventually, there was a KPC East, West, and South. We ran out of compass points, so we called the new campuses by the name of the suburb it was in. We established strong celebration points in all of the Watoto Villages and eventually in Gulu, Entebbe, Mbarara, Jinja and Juba, South Sudan.

~ Leadership ~

Key to the success of planting new campuses was the availability of competent pastors. This necessitated, from the very outset, the ability to raise a generation of new-thinking pastoral leadership. If there is anything that is a core and absolutely integral component of who we are as a couple and as a church, it is that we have concentrated on raising leaders. Leadership development is not a program of the church. It is what we do all the time as a way of life. The true lessons of leadership development take place in the crucible of life, with its ups and downs, its trials and tests, its successes and failures. Leadership is not so much taught as it is caught. The leadership guru, John Maxwell, says that new leaders are modelled, motivated, mentored and multiplied by other leaders. I'm convinced that everything rises and falls on leadership, whether it is good or bad leadership. What the world needs are more good leaders. If we are to change culture, build a better world and bring about social and community health, well-being and transformation, we need a new generation of godly leaders. The place to raise those leaders is in church, where we learn the principles of Kingdom and biblical leadership. It is the role of the church to model and multiply leadership. My role as a lead pastor is to model it in the way I not only lead but live. This is a crucial component of how we change our world for the better.

Why should leadership be taught by "secular" authorities and universities that have totally sidelined Jesus, His Church and biblical culture? Where in the world do we see a good model of leadership in the political arena? Watch a presidential debate in the US elections, or any nation for that matter, and ask if you would allow your children to talk and behave in the way the candidates talk to each other. Are they the models of leadership we want our children to emulate? Business leaders have placed financial wealth as the true goal and test of their leadership skills and, in the process, have turned from true integrity. Of course, I could go on to the other spheres or major influences in society, but that is not the focus of this account.

I know that Jesus wanted us to concentrate on raising a new generation of Ugandan leaders who would reflect godly character while building a new Africa. These leaders would grow up in church or one of our Watoto Villages.

In the next chapter, I want to come back to this thought on raising leaders, especially as it relates to what God called us to do in becoming a cell-based church. But before that, we had another nasty incident that tested our call to be in Uganda.

~ Get On The Floor ~

We heard from Selwyn Hughes that he wanted to visit Kampala and speak at the church. We were always eager to host visitors, especially as so few came due to the insecurity in the nation at the time. Selwyn was from the UK and a well-known, much esteemed, senior church statesman and writer of a very popular devotional, Every Day With Jesus. We would be delighted and honoured by his visit. He wrote back, informing us that he would send someone several months prior to his visit to meet us and make any necessary preparations.

Consequently, I went out a month later and picked up the gentleman who had come to scout out the land. That afternoon as we were sitting around the dining room table after lunch, three gunmen strolled into the room, cocked their rifles with the harsh metallic sound of bullets being forced into the chamber. There was a firm but clear instruction from the man who seemed to be in charge.

"Everyone! Get on the floor under the table. And don't look up. Keep your heads down."

I was seated opposite the gentleman from the UK. It was his very first day in Africa. He looked up at me with a questioning gaze as if to say,

"Is this some kind of joke?"

I looked straight back into his befuddled eyes.

"Get on the floor! Right now! Please!"

He did! All three of us did!

"No talking!" snapped the man in charge.

"And don't look up!' He repeated his instructions.

The following minutes seemed like an eternity. The men dispersed around the house collecting stuff. One of them stayed with us nervously, playing with the hardware on his rifle. The clicking sound was annoying, threatening and scary.

Sellwyn's man folded himself up into a foetal position and trembled. We all lay there, not knowing what would happen next.

After a short while, man in charge came back into the room.

"Where are the keys to the car?"

"In the first cupboard, in the kitchen." I looked up to show him.

"I said don't look up." He was rather firm!

"If you do it again, I'll shoot your head off."

I pointed in the general direction of the kitchen, determined not to lift my head again. I certainly didn't want my head blown off. It would ruin what had started as a good day.

He found the keys. I knew that, not by sight but by the sound they make. They collected the stuff and went out to pack it into our new blue, four-wheel drive Mitsubishi Pajero. We had bought it from a man who worked for the US embassy and was tired of the fear of losing his nice new car every time he drove it out of his gate. I guess he knew what he was talking about, as it seemed we were about to lose it instead.

Gun clicking man stayed with us the whole time.

I heard the engine of the car being cranked. It was a diesel engine, and it was necessary to warm the plugs before starting it. Man in charge, or whoever was trying to do it, didn't seem to be aware of that. The engine continued to turn over, and then the cranking sound started to slow down.

"Oh, oh! If he drains the battery and can't start the car, we are dead!"

The thoughts swirled around in my head. I prayed!

"Please, Lord! Start the engine."

Sure enough, He did. An inner sigh of relief.

Whoever was driving began to back out of the garage. The sound of losing our car to a gang of thieves was wonderful. It meant they might leave us alive, and the ordeal would be over.

We had a very steep driveway. The engine stalled as the driver backed the car up. More cranking. The engine was turning over too slowly. Again, I prayed.

"Please, Lord! Start the engine."

Sure enough, He did. A bigger inner sigh of relief.

Gun-clicking man stepped out of the room. The car door banged. The wonderful sound of our retreating, stolen car receded. It was quiet.

I could hear each of us slowly breathing.

"Well! I think that's it," I said.

We emerged from under the table. My first thought was to telephone the police for help. We had two problems. One, they had ripped the phone out of the wall. We couldn't use it to phone the police. This was long before the convenience of a cell phone. Fortunately, they had ignored the fax machine, which could double as a phone. I called the police.

Problem number two! When you call the police for help, the standard reply is that they are very sorry, but they have only one vehicle available, and it has no fuel. And then, not to worry, they are coming on foot! Wonderful! How long will that take? They weren't sure. Probably a couple of hours. Wonderful again! By that time, the thieves will be in the Congo.

I was rather surprised by the reply I got from the policeman on the other end of the phone.

"No problem, pastor! We'll be there in just a few minutes."

The President had decided that national development would require national security. He had had enough of these gangs of thieves roaming the city, causing death and chaos. So, he established rapid response teams of police and soldiers to react quickly to just this kind of scenario. You would see them dashing around town in specially outfitted pickup trucks, helmeted, fully armed and decked out in military clothing.

The police arrived in eight minutes! With politeness, they asked the necessary questions about what had happened and what vehicle the thieves had made their getaway in. I answered their questions. There was a buzz on the police radio. A policeman spoke into it.

"Excuse us, please. The vehicle has just been seen heading into town. We will be back." Off they went in a cloud of dust.

We waited! Nervously!

An hour later, they returned. The same policeman who spoke to me the first time was beaming from ear to ear.

"Now, what's up?" I thought.

"Well! They won't be bothering you anymore." The smile widened even further.

It was my turn to smile. "Why? What happened?"

"Oh, they're all dead!"

"Excuse me!"

'We caught up with them." He shrugged.

"They refused to stop, so we shot the driver and the passenger who was in the front seat. We took the other one to the police station. He confessed but also died. We will make a report. You can come and pick up your vehicle tomorrow."

I thanked them profusely and went inside to have a cup of coffee and encourage our guest from the UK. It turned out to be a day he'll never forget. Selwyn later did come to Kampala and had a very fruitful time of ministry at the church.

The next morning, we went to the police station, stopping along the way to pick up a newspaper. One of the lead stories was "Pastor Skinner robbed. Police kill thugs in shoot out." There were 22 bullet holes in the car. Inside was a mess of blood and what seemed to me like spatters of brain matter.

It dawned on me a few days later that a good number of the people who had come against us had ended up dead. The commander in the barracks in Masaka, who had driven our car, was killed when the advancing forces of the new government liberated the town. The gang of thugs that terrorised our community and had tried to invade the house while I was picking up the car were later killed by the police. The so-called "prophet" had dropped dead at his home. Now, the men who had stolen the car had been killed in a shootout. I was left again with a sense of holy awe for an amazing God.

I also decided that I didn't want to get on the wrong side of God.

PRESSING ON

~ Reflect and Discuss ~

As you reflect on your own story and engage in discussion with others, consider the following:

1. Importance of Church Forming Culture:

    • Reflect on why it is important for culture to be formed by the church rather than by secular society. Consider how the values, beliefs, and practices of a culture shape individuals and communities.

    • Discuss how a culture formed by the church aligns with biblical principles, fosters spiritual growth, and promotes values such as love, justice, compassion, and integrity.

2. Practical Steps to Develop Godly Christian Culture:

    • Explore practical ways to actively work towards developing a godly Christian and biblical culture. Reflect on the role of teaching, discipleship, and modeling in shaping the values and behaviors of individuals within the church community.

    • Discuss the importance of intentional efforts to integrate biblical principles into all aspects of life, including family, education, work, and social interactions.

3. Role of Leadership in Cultural Development:

    • Consider the importance of leadership in developing a new culture within the church and broader society. Reflect on the influence of leaders in setting the tone, vision, and direction for the community.

    • Discuss how effective leadership involves leading by example, cultivating a culture of accountability and transparency, and empowering others to participate in the process of cultural development.

During your discussion, offer support, encouragement, and prayer for one another as you seek to align your lives and communities with God's principles and values. Reflect on the significance of building a culture that reflects the character of Christ and fosters spiritual growth and transformation. Commit to being active participants in shaping and promoting a godly Christian culture in your spheres of influence, trusting in God's guidance and empowering presence every step of the way.

~

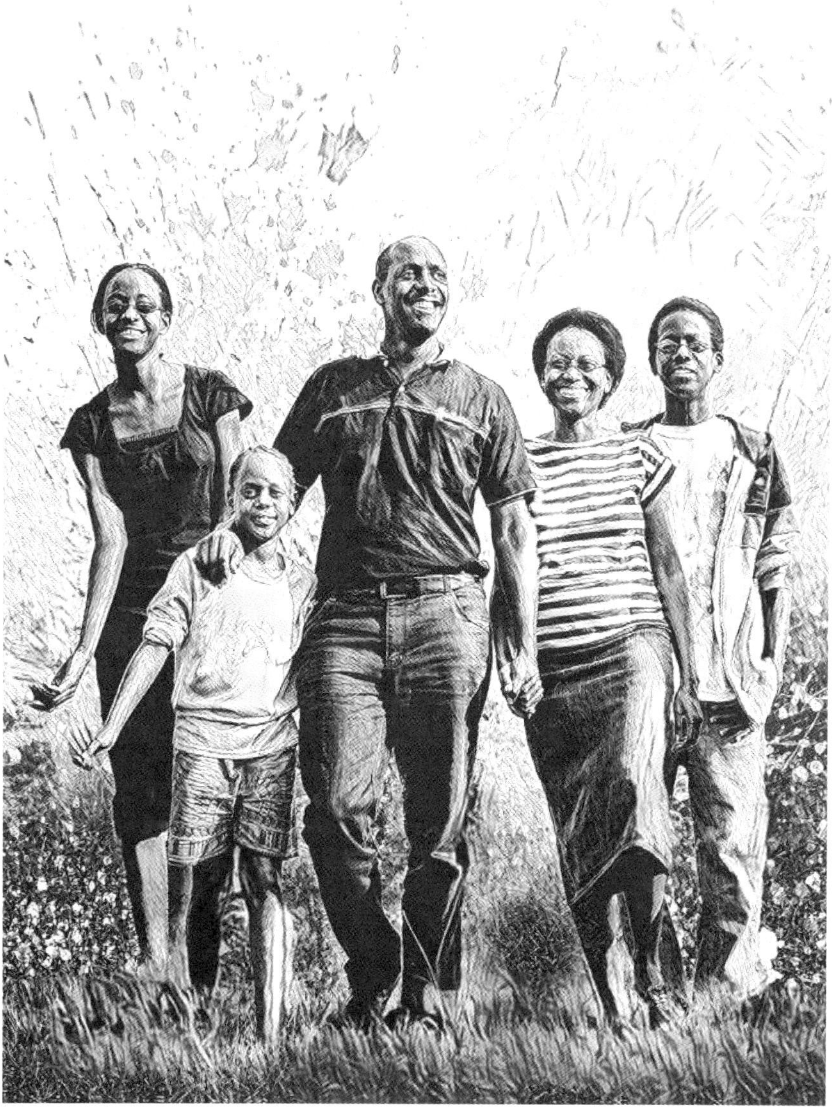

"Akwaagala, Akwaagula no bujama bwo."

"He who loves, loves you with your dirt."

Baganda Proverb

20
~ Doing Life Together ~

"You can't clap with a single hand."
African Proverb

We were well into what God had called us to do in Kampala. The church was planted, growing and meeting in multiple locations. A wonderful ministry to rescue vulnerable children had started. Children's choirs were telling the story around the world.

In a time of devotion one morning, Father God spoke clearly to me.

"Who do you think you are anyway?"

"I'm sorry! I don't understand what you mean?"

What He had said had taken me by surprise.

"I said, who do you think you are anyway?"

I was still befuddled.

"I'm sorry! I don't know what you mean by that?"

His reply took me by surprise again.

"You think you pastor these thousands of people."

I assumed that was what I was supposed to be doing.

"I do!" I answered.

We had about five thousand people attending church. What he said this time changed my world forever.

"No one can pastor more than ten people! Even my Son Jesus only pastored twelve. Who do you think you are."

In that moment, I knew that we were to become a cell church. We had started "Home Fellowship" meetings with a cell format. They were small groups designed to encourage church members as they met in their local neighbourhood. There were not many groups, and we hadn't made it a priority. It wasn't backed by a firm determination to make it a vital component of the church. I knew now, with absolute certainty, that it was to be a priority.

To be honest, I didn't have a clue how to make this a reality. So, I told the Lord that I was delighted to do whatever he wanted me to do. It was just that He would have to show me what and how we could be a cell-based church.

A few weeks later, we were on a family holiday in Kenya, staying at a nice beach hotel. I looked across the swimming pool and saw a face I knew. It was Don Matheny, the pastor of a young church in Nairobi. I went over, and we had a chat. We spoke of what the Lord was doing in our respective cities and churches. It was obvious that He was at work in East Africa. I shared with him my latest conversation with the Father and that we were to transition the church into a cell church. I confessed that I had no idea how to make it happen.

"No problem!" he said. "Three years ago, God said the same thing to me, and we transitioned. I'd be happy to help in any way I can."

The next months were a time of learning and discovery. Books on the subject came into my hands. We spent time together with the church in Nairobi and picked up many things we should and shouldn't do. A team of pastors from the church in Nairobi visited us in Kampala to interact with our leadership team and discuss the ins and outs of transitioning a program-based church into a cell-based church.

We learned that there is a difference between being a cell church and a church that does cells as one of the things they do. The goal of a cell-based church is that everyone who comes to the church is in and committed to a small group. The support for the members is provided in the small group. We celebrate weekly on Sundays in a large corporate gathering but meet in small, intimate, relational groups mid-week. What we learned changed the way we did church.

We took a full year to discover and understand the systems and structures of a cell-based church before implementing the transition. We shared the vision for a cell-based church with the people of the church. We taught from the pulpit in our celebration services about what it meant to be a cell church. We invited congregation members to ask questions and query what we were doing and why. One of the things we were prepared for was an exodus of people who may not understand or agree with what we were doing.

As I began to understand the cell-based church, it was evident that there were several models. One was promoted by a very large church in South America. As I looked into the details, I felt a check in my spirit about adopting that model. It was successful in growing the church, but legalistic and controlling.

The other was a five-by-five model. There was a much more relaxed and relational network of churches and leaders implementing this model. It was much more sensitive to people, their time and commitment and was being used successfully in several parts of the world. I felt a confirmation in my heart to go down this route. We began to interact and connect in this network without it being controlling or cloying. It was helpful, supportive and encouraging.

Five members would make up a cell, which was led and cared for pastorally by a cell leader. Five cells make a Section, with a sectional leader taking pastoral leadership care for that group of cells and their leaders. Five Sections would make up a Zone, five Zones a Region, and five Regions a District. Each Celebration Point or Campus was a District. Each leader in the structure provided pastoral care to only five to twelve other leaders or members.

A cell is a group of about five or six members of the church who live in the same neighbourhood. They meet weekly in a host home. The point is to grow the cell until it is no more than twelve people and then multiply it into two groups. The follow-up from the Sunday celebration service is handled by the cell. Discipleship is taught with a specific set of materials provided by the church. Members of the small group mentor new believers. Each group meets, usually on a Wednesday evening, for fellowship, worship, and a discussion of the message from the celebration service of the previous Sunday. There is an intentional effort to practically implement what had been learned from the sermon and discussion. The group aims for the pain by caring and praying for those in need in the group. The conclusion of the meeting is always about reaching family, friends and neighbours with an invitation to the small group through the personal relationships of the members.

We implemented "Focus Ten." Each cell member drew up a list of the ten people they wanted to see come to Christ and join the church and the cell. They were to pray for the people on their list throughout the day as they came to mind. The cell would take time to pray specifically for those on the member's Focus Ten list. The prayer was to ask the Lord to bring circumstances into the lives of those being prayed for that would draw them to Christ. Each member would pray for a God-appointed opportunity to share Christ with the people on their list. As a result, tens of thousands of people were being prayed for consistently by members of the church.

Cells are effective in seeing many come to Christ and integrate into the life of the church.

~ A Multitude of Leaders ~

One of the critical things necessary for the success of this transition was the training of leaders. Any group, nation, church, business or organisation is only as successful as the integrity and skill of its leadership. To succeed, we need more than a clear vision. We need trained, godly leaders.

We invited those who would like to become cell leaders to enrol in a cell leadership school. It was a one-year training class. Seven hundred and fifty people signed up for the training. At the end of the year, about two hundred and fifty had remained consistent to the classes.

On the launch date, two years after God had laid it on my heart, we started two hundred cells. On a Sunday, we transitioned by placing members in their cell groups, praying and believing that the Lord would bless us as we followed what He called us to do. There was the normal growth and eventually multiplication of cells, as well as those that didn't last. We persisted and loved the people, the leaders and Jesus with more passion.

Looking back, it has been a colossal success with multiplication into thousands of cells. Pastoral care for an unlimited number of people is taking place. New believers are integrated into a caring fellowship in their immediate neighbourhood. It is a thrill to see so many of the church activities, such as weddings, funerals, baby dedications, graduations and other activities, succeed as members are surrounded by cell members who genuinely care for each other.

During the COVID crisis and the consequent shutdown of the church for two years, we saw continued successful church ministry take place through cells.

Key to all of this is the leadership training. A trained leader leads every cell. Each leader mentors two other leaders so that when the cell grows and multiplies, the new cell is led by the older leader and the older cell is led by the younger leader. Each section, zone, regional and district leader raises other leaders so that unlimited multiplication takes place at every level. As a result, we are continually training and upgrading the leadership skills of thousands of church members who are actively involved in the practice of leadership.

What is exciting is that leadership principles that work in a cell group are the same leadership principles that work in the community at large. Leadership is leadership! I began to realise that God was helping us to raise leaders who would not only lead cells but become leaders in the careers, callings and occupations that God had called them into in the city and country. This, too, is a critical component of bringing transformation to the city and the nation.

~ Caring For Community ~

And then, God did several more things that expanded the impact of the cells in the community.

The Lord began to impress on us as leaders that a cell group was not just a holy huddle on a Wednesday evening that would bless and provide pastoral care to the cell members. There was more. Each cell was to reach out to and serve the needs of their neighbourhood with the practical love of Jesus.

In a time of devotion, one day, I whispered to Jesus that I loved Him and that it was an honour to serve Him.

"You don't serve me, Gary."

I was shocked by His reply.

"I've been serving you all my life. I exist to serve you."

I was confident in my answer but didn't know what to say next.

I felt impressed in my spirit to read, in Acts 17, what Paul had told the Greeks in Athens when he saw the statue to the unknown god.

I opened my bible and read.

> "The God who made the world and everything in it is the Lord of heaven and earth and does not live in temples built by human hands. And he is not served by human hands if he needed anything. Rather, he himself gives everyone life and breath and everything else."
>
> *Acts 17:24-25 (NIV)*

"No, Gary! You don't serve me. I'm God, fully self-contained. I don't need anything."

I didn't know what to say next.

I felt prompted to read what Jesus told his disciples in Matthew 25. The context is the return of Jesus. No one knows of the day or hour of His return. The parable of the ten virgins is about being prepared for the bridegroom's coming. The parable of the bags of gold is about using what God has given into our hands and multiplying it for the glory of the master whose it is and who placed it on our hands. Then it's the sheep and the goats being divided, the unfaithful on the left to lose it all in eternal hell, and the others on the right to inherit the Kingdom. Why?

> *"For I was hungry, and you gave me something to eat, I was thirsty, and you gave me something to drink, I was a stranger and you invited me in, I needed clothes and you clothed me; I was sick and you looked after me, I was in prison and you came to visit me.'*
>
> *"Then the righteous will answer him, 'Lord, when did we see you hungry and feed you, or thirsty and give you something to drink? When did we see you a stranger and invite you in, or needing clothes and clothe you? When did we see you sick or in prison and go to visit you?'*
>
> *"The King will reply, 'Truly I tell you, whatever you did for one of the least of these brothers and sisters of mine, you did for me.'"*
>
> *Matthew 25:35-40 (NIV)*

And then Jesus spoke to me again.

"Gary! The only way you can serve me is to serve people."

My world turned upside down. A word from Jesus revolutionised my perspective on life and leadership. It all came down to this! We are called to be servants.

~ Relentless Service ~

My purpose, your purpose, our purpose, is to serve people and, in so doing, serve God. It does not matter who you are or what station you hold in life; we are only as successful as our service to others. Serving people is where we discover meaning and fulfil our service to God. The words on the emblem for Uganda are "For God and My Country." Our service to God, which is a priority, can only be realised when we first serve our country.

We are called to serve. Leaders succeed when they serve. Servanthood is the culture of the Kingdom.

Small groups are not just a place for followers of Jesus to gather, be encouraged and be ministered to. Cells are the launch pad for taking the love and solutions of Jesus into the community. Every single Christian is to be active in reaching out in loving service to people. This is not a program of the church; it is the purpose of the church.

No Christian is exempt from a life of service. Every Christian is called to a life of service. Christians are to see their career and calling in life as an opportunity to serve. Politicians are to serve the people they lead. Doctors are to serve their patients. Teachers are to serve their students. Businessmen are to serve their clients. We are all called to be servants. The Church is to raise up and train servant leaders who inundate and invade every sphere of society with the culture of servanthood. Everyone has a role to play in building a healthy community, not by taking but by giving, not by being served but by serving others.

This was revolutionary to me as I led the church. Ministry is not what one man does behind a pulpit on Sunday; it's about what we all do every day in our community.

~ Our Vision~

Each step that we took as we were planting and building the church was a step taken after clear instruction from Jesus. He put a vision in my spirit, and we were to walk in obedience to that call. The vision was to plant an English-speaking church in the heart of Kampala. But the components of what kind of church we were to be unfolded and clarified the vision as time passed.

It was also essential that I share this vision with anyone who was part of the church. Without vision, nothing happens; people perish, and they cast off restraint. Vision focuses people on specific goals and objectives that are reached as we press forward. Nothing of great value happens without vision. That's just the way it works.

People follow visionary leaders. Successful leaders are visionary leaders. If you don't have a vision, then you are not a leader. I had a vision, but it needed to be clear, attainable, faith-filled, and a vision people understood and were willing to follow. We wrote down a vision statement that would reflect what God had called us to be as a church. Here is the statement:

> "We are an English-speaking, cell-based community church, celebrating Christ, growing and multiplying as each one reaches one, touching those around us with the love of Jesus, bringing healing to the city and the nation."

I spent years preaching and teaching what this vision is and the individual components of the vision. Why English? What is a cell-based church? What does it mean to be a community-based church? What does it mean to celebrate Christ? What role does generosity have in the celebration of Christ? What is the process for growth and multiplication? What is the role of each follower of Christ in reaching others? How do we practically demonstrate the love of Jesus to community? What role does the church play in community transformation?

As the vision became more and more clear to the members of the church, they participated by their involvement and generosity. People willingly gave of their time, their talent and their treasure. The vision statement was memorised and integrated into the life of the church and the lives of the cells and the members.

Clear vision was critical to the success, growth and maturity of the church.

~ Seed Projects ~

Serving the community is not just about inviting neighbours to attend the cell but to take the cell to the community. It's about serving the community by identifying their needs and coming compassionately alongside them to address and solve those problems. It wasn't just about meeting our needs but the needs of others around us.

So, we started cell seed projects.

Seed projects are compassionate acts of beneficial kindness that address the real needs of the community.

It begins with identifying the needs of the community. That wasn't very challenging. We are faced with those critical community issues every day as members of the community. Every cell was encouraged to prayer walk, as a group, through their immediate neighbourhood. They were to ask God to show them the problems of the community. They were to ask God what problem they were to address as a cell and with the community. Once they identified the problem, they were to approach the leadership of the community and offer to work on a solution to the problem alongside the community.

The city of Kampala is divided into thousands of small communities, each one led by an elected Local Chairman, many of whom are corrupt and inept. The cell leader and some members of the cell would make an appointment with the local chairman and ask, not as members of KPC but as members of the local community, how they could serve the chairman and the community. The official was usually confused by such a question. People usually approach the chairperson to get something from them, not offer something instead. The cell leader would mention a community problem that needed to be solved and offer to work with the chairperson and with the community to address the problem. It might be a marketplace that is clogged with sewage from a blocked drain. It might be overgrown hedges or broken lights that rendered a specific location unsafe as young ladies made their way home in the evening. It might be a police post or a local school that hadn't seen paint in years. It might be the lack of clean water because the community water well was broken. The list is endless.

The cell would then lead, with the support and engagement of the community, to set a date, time and place for a 'seed project.' The cell would work with the community to address an agreed-on community project. The cell didn't do something for the community. It did it with the community. They performed the seed project as members of the community, not members of the church. The church, working with communities all over the city on a specific date, would literally do hundreds of community projects. We were very specific not to promote the church in the process, just to work with and love the community. Projects would often end with a simple drink and a bun.

By the process of osmosis, believers emanated with the love of Christ, who lives in them. The community would come to be aware that this was the church at work. The impact of cells loving and serving the community and meeting real needs has had a powerful impact on the city. The city knows about the rescuing of vulnerable children through Watoto. The city also knows about the impact of loving service through community projects. The church is about loving people, about loving the city.

I sensed that Jesus wanted us to do one more thing through the cells. AIDS was having a seriously negative effect on the city. Families were suffering the loss of family members or heads of the family as parents or spouses died. Jesus wanted each cell to identify an AIDS-affected family and just love and serve them. The cells responded magnificently to the pain of thousands of families surrounding them with loving care. And, of course, people found not only love but found Christ and were transformed by the gospel.

One Sunday, I attended a celebration service at the south campus. It was a special day, so food was being served after the service. As I was approaching the table to be served, one of the pastors pointed out one of the ladies who was helping in dishing out the food.

"Let me tell you her story when we are seated."

He told me how a very simple and ordinary young lady who was a cell leader had called on her cell to do what pastor Gary had asked them all to do. They were to find a family affected by AIDS and just care. They all knew of a single woman in the community who was HIV+ and living alone. They decided to visit her and see how she was coping. They arrived at the small, modest little house and knocked on the door. There was no answer. They knocked again. Still no answer. Calling gently, they opened the door to the house and were assaulted by a foul smell. They went in and found the woman alone, lying in her vomit and excrement in the grip of the disease. They got down beside her, took her hand, lovingly prayed and then helped clean her up and began to care for her. She recovered, gave her life to Christ and came to the place that had loved her in her pain, to the church. She found family; she found purpose. She was the lady serving the food. She also became a living witness to the love of Jesus as the people in the neighbourhood heard her story.

And her story is one of many.

The love of Jesus transforms people. This powerful love is demonstrated through ordinary people who do extraordinary things for God by serving people.

And they do it in cells, in small groups.

~ Reflect and Discuss ~

As you reflect on your own story and engage in discussion with others, consider the following:

1. Role of Cells in the Life of a Local Church:

    • Reflect on the role that cells, or small groups, can play in the life of a local church. Consider how cells provide opportunities for deeper fellowship, spiritual growth, accountability, and support within the church community.

    • Discuss how cells can serve as avenues for discipleship, prayer, Bible study, and ministry involvement, fostering a sense of belonging and connectedness among members.

2. Importance of Leadership in Growing Strong Small Groups:

    • Explore the importance of leadership in growing strong small groups within the church. Reflect on the qualities of effective small group leaders, such as relational skills, spiritual maturity, and a heart for discipleship.

    • Discuss how strong leadership can create a nurturing and empowering environment within small groups, facilitating meaningful interactions, fostering growth, and addressing the needs of group members.

3. Serving God by Serving People:

    • Reflect on the biblical principle that the only way we can serve God is to serve people, as emphasized in Matthew 25:35-40. Consider how Jesus identifies Himself with the marginalized, needy, and vulnerable in society.

- Discuss how serving others is not only a commandment but also a privilege and opportunity to express love, compassion, and obedience to God. Reflect on how acts of service reflect the character of Christ and advance His kingdom purposes on earth.

During your discussion, offer support, encouragement, and prayer for one another as you explore these questions and seek to deepen your understanding of the role of cells in the church, the importance of leadership in small group ministry, and the significance of serving others as an expression of devotion to God. Commit to actively participating in the life of your local church, engaging in small group fellowship, and seeking opportunities to serve and minister to others in Jesus' name.

~

311

> "Every believer has received grace gifts,
> so use them to serve one another as faithful stewards
> of the many-colored tapestry of God's grace."

The Apostle Peter - 1 Peter 4:10, (NIV)

21

~ Strategic Alliances ~

"One log doesn't light a fire."
African Proverb

The church was growing. The Watoto Children's Choirs were travelling, telling the story of hope and redemption. Sponsors were being raised. Homes on the Watoto Villages were being built by teams who were coming from countries around the world. Things were progressing well.

One Sunday morning, in the middle of a celebration service, I sensed the incredible presence of Jesus. There have been several times in my life when it was clear that He was right there in the room with me, uniquely and specially. Each time, I knew He was telling me something important. His presence was so real, so powerful, I could not remain standing up. I had to get down on my face. In those days, I was still wearing a suit and tie. It didn't stop me from kneeling down and then laying prostrate, flat on my face on the dusty platform, my arms extended forward. I lay quietly, waiting. The congregation was raising a worship song to heaven. I waited! Marilyn noticed and thought to herself.

"What is he doing lying on that dusty floor in that nice suit? How am I going to clean it? There is no place to get a suit cleaned here."

And then Jesus spoke to me.

"Gary! I want to do something in this place that the whole world will hear about."

That was it! The acute awareness of His presence slowly evaporated, and I stood up. We continued and finished the service. On the way home,

Marilyn asked the inevitable question.

"What were you doing lying on the floor in your nice suit?"

I told her what had happened as Jesus' presence overwhelmed me, and He spoke of doing something great here that the whole world would hear about. She didn't say it out loud, but the thought hit her.

"Here! In this place? You can't be serious!"

I have to admit that while I knew what Jesus had said to me, I thought the same thing. Wow! He wants to do something here, in this mess of a place.

I mulled this over in my heart. If God was going to do something that the whole world would hear about, then we needed some strategic alliances. We needed personal relationships with others that would advance the cause of the marginalised, the vulnerable and especially the fatherless children. So, we did what we knew to do! We prayed. It was in the blue room, up in the corner of the building, where there was a small childcare office. We asked the Lord to lead us to key people who would come alongside us in what He had called us to do.

Looking back, I can tell you that Jesus answered that prayer. The choirs were doing well. They were helping us develop new relationships with churches and pastors around the world, but I sensed there was more.

As missionaries sent out by the Pentecostal Assemblies of Canada, we were always welcome to attend the bi-annual General Conference of the fellowship. We hadn't attended one for 14 years and, to be honest, didn't have any desire to do so. At least, not yet. But I couldn't get away from this niggling feeling that we were supposed to attend the next one. I told Marilyn that I thought we should go to the next conference. She asked where it was going to be held. I told her that it would be in Saint John, New Brunswick. She wondered if they had any decent shopping in the small, out-of-the-way city on the eastern side of Canada. Of course, she was willing to do whatever was necessary. So, we attended the conference.

After one of the sessions, Bill Morrow, the General Superintendent of the fellowship, a man who was also one of my classmates from Bible School days, saw us and invited us over.

"Gary! Come and meet the speakers for the conference."

He introduced us to Brian and Bobbie Houston, pastors of the amazingly influential Hillsong Church in Sydney, Australia. We greeted them, and Bill told them what we were doing in Uganda. He included that we were caring for fatherless children and had choirs that travelled telling the story.

"Are you the pastors of those beautiful children that are in Australia right now?" It was Bobbie asking the question.

We did have a choir in Australia, and yes, they had just been in Sydney.

"Oh! They were amazing. They came and visited our church on a Saturday evening."

Bobbie asked Marilyn to sit with her at the ladies' banquet she was to speak at as a part of the conference. She and Bobbie just connected.

The truth is that our Watoto office had tried to see if the Hillsong Church would host the choir, but it hadn't come together. As it turned out, the choir had a concert cancelled on the Saturday they were in Sydney. Marilyn had taught the choir team leader that if they had a cancellation, they should get the kids dressed up nicely and just go and attend a good local church, enjoy the service, be blessed and be ready for anything. So, the team leader decided that, as they had always wanted to see Hillsong, they should attend that evening. They had a few hours before the service, so they went and walked around the nearby shopping mall. Brian and Bobbie happened to be at the same mall and noticed the children walking through the mall and wondered who they might be, probably a choir from Africa. That evening, Brian looked down from the platform at the Hillsong Church and noticed the same kids sitting in the service. He asked the question.

"Hey! Who are you children anyway? Are you a choir from Africa or something?"

The team leader confirmed that they were.

"Come on up and give us a song," Brian said.

Now, if you know Brian, that's not like him at all. The choir was ready, came up and did a song. The church was moved and loved it.

After the service, Brian asked the team leader if they could come on Father's Day Sunday, just a few weeks away and sing again. The team leader said that he would check it out and let him know. The Australian Watoto office called to let us know what was happening. Marilyn asked if the choir already had a booking for Father's Day Sunday. They did, but it was a small local church. Marilyn informed them that they could not cancel a previous engagement. Hillsong would have to wait for another tour a year or so later. And now, here we are in Canada, and the Lord has brought us together.

The conference ended, and we all headed to the airport only to find that most of the flights had been cancelled due to bad weather. Brian and Bobbie noticed us and asked if we were going back into town and if we would like to ride back together, which we did. They let us know that they were going to be in Uganda in just two weeks. They were bringing a team out to see some of the sponsored children with another childcare organisation. We asked if we could meet them in Kampala at the end of their trip and take them out for dinner. They were delighted, and it was set up. Two weeks later, we hosted them for a meal. They had just returned from the western side of Uganda and were quite traumatised by a terrible car crash they had witnessed. They went to the airport and returned to Australia. We got on with our lives again, not giving much thought to what had happened.

A month later, I got an e-mail from Bobbie to Marilyn. She didn't have Marilyn's address and wanted to know if Marilyn would speak at her Hillsong Women's Conference called Colour. I wrote back to Bobbie on Marilyn's behalf, accepting the invitation and then went and informed Marilyn that she was going to speak at the conference in Sydney.

"What are you talking about? What conference? Where? With who?"

You have to understand that Marilyn is an amazing person and incredibly capable, but she had never spoken at a church before.

"I've never spoken in my life before. I can't do this." She wasn't exactly delighted at the prospect.

"I would never have accepted the invitation!" She was getting a little worked up.

"I know, that's why I wrote back on your behalf and said you'd come. I knew you wouldn't accept, but I know you have to do this. In fact, I know you can do this, and you'll do great. I believe in you."

It didn't help settle the tension.

"Well, you will have to write my sermon."

"You're a big girl. You can write your sermon, and I know you have something powerful to say to those ladies."

The tension remained.

Some months later, Marilyn boarded a plane at Entebbe on her way to Sydney to speak at the Hillsong Colour Conference. Thousands of women, gathered from all around the world, listened in raptured silence as they heard the story and the heart of God for the vulnerable women and children of Africa. They stood at the end and gave Marilyn, my precious little package of dynamite, a standing ovation. Marilyn will tell you that they were not standing for her but for our amazing Jesus and His magnificent plan of reaching hurting people with His love.

Marilyn was invited back to speak at the conference for the next number of years. Invitations from churches all around the world filled her inbox, and I must tell you, God gave us the strategic alliances that we had prayed for in the blue room. So much support financially and in other ways has come to Watoto through the amazing network of relationships that have been forged because the Lord put us on an international stage for the specific purpose of standing up and speaking on behalf of those who cannot speak for themselves and for highlighting His passionate love for the hurting of our world.

> *"Speak up for those who cannot speak for themselves,*
>
> *for the rights of all who are destitute.*
>
> *Speak up and judge fairly;*
>
> *defend the rights of the poor and needy."*
>
> *Proverbs 31:8-9 (NIV)*

Over the years, Hillsong Church demonstrated its heart not only for building strong local churches but caring for the vulnerable and marginalised in our world. They provided the resources to build dozens of homes, came alongside Marilyn in reaching thousands of vulnerable women in Uganda, keeping tens of thousands of girls in school, provided surgical intervention for hundreds of mutilated women in war-torn northern Uganda, and provided the financial resources to purchase a strategic piece of land for a church facility in the middle of the city of Gulu, northern Uganda. No one did more to help us than Brian and Bobbie Houston and Hillsong Church. They introduced us to a host of amazing people who also came to stand beside us and partner in this great cause that is a key component of the English-speaking church God called us to plant in Kampala.

~ Her Majesty, the Queen ~

One of the Hillsong conferences that Marilyn spoke at was in London, England. The venue for the conference was the iconic Royal Albert Hall, just meters away from the London Geographical Society, where the great missionary David Livingstone was commissioned and sent to Africa.

Marilyn spoke so capably and then took her seat at the front of the hall. The seats at the Royal Albert Hall are owned by the rich and famous, and one of the special seating areas is the Royal box reserved for the British Royal Family. As Marilyn took her seat, one of the hosts leaned over and told her that as she went up to the stage to speak, someone had entered the Royal box. She thought nothing more of it.

Several months later, while we were in South Africa, Marilyn received an e-mail message on her phone. The subject line read: Buckingham Palace. She rolled her eyes at what she assumed to be spam but read the message anyway. It was an invitation from the palace on behalf of Queen Elizabeth II. The Queen would be holding a special function at Buckingham Palace for distinguished members of the British Commonwealth and had invited the Watoto Children's Choir to sing at the event. As the founders of the choir, the Queen invited us to join the choir at the function and that she would like to meet us personally at the event. We replied that we would be honoured to be present.

On the day of the event, I hailed one of London's famous black taxis.

As we got in, I said to the driver as deadpan as I could and in the most distinguished voice I could muster,

"Buckingham Palace, if you please."

I winked at Marilyn, whispering, "I've always wanted to say that."

On our way through the crowded streets of London, we prayed quietly.

"Lord, would you give us a chance today to witness for you and to speak of your fame."

The taxi dropped us off at the main gate of the palace, where we showed the invitation to the Queen's Royal Guard. We walked across the huge open area in front of the palace, our feet crunching on the cold gravel. At the massive front entrance to the palace, we were again required to show our invitation. This time, a gentleman in formal dress, who we learned was the Master of the Royal Household, stepped forward and greeted us.

"Rev. and Mrs. Skinner, I've been expecting you. Welcome. Come with me, please. I'm taking you to the Royal Music Room, where the choir will join you. They will sing for Her Majesty, and then she would like to meet you. Follow me, please."

Marilyn and I looked at each other and smiled. This was fun! We entered the huge front foyer with its grand staircase. It rose perhaps 15 steps and then divided with one staircase leading left and the other right. At the top of the staircase on the right, the children's choir was singing as the guests entered and were taken up the left-hand staircase. The Master of the Royal Household led us up past the choir, and we smiled and winked at them. We were led down a massive hallway, the walls covered with artwork and hanging tapestries. We turned left into the Music Room, where the choir stand was all setup, ready for the choir. Some of the choir adults were in the room. We hugged and were then given a crash course on how we were to interact with the Queen. We were instructed to hold our hands a certain way, bow a certain way, and if she spoke to us, we were to call her "Ma'am", but most important, do not touch the Queen.

The choir soon joined us in the room, as all the guests had arrived and were now waiting for the Queen to meet them in a large reception chamber down the hallway. The Queen entered the Music Room, accompanied by Prince

Philip. She approached the choir, smiled and greeted them. She spoke to them for a few moments, and then they sang for her. She smiled again and thanked them. She then walked over to where we were standing, watching the proceedings with fascination and pride.

The Queen smiled and spoke to us.

"Mr. And Mrs. Skinner, welcome. Thank you for the choir. Please, may I ask you why you do what you do?"

I remembered the prayer in the taxi. This was the moment I was given to share with Her Majesty Queen Elizabeth II of Great Britain and Northern Ireland about the work Jesus had called us to. I took just one minute to tell her of the great love of Jesus for all mankind but that He had a special place in His heart for the hurting, the poor, the marginalised and the broken of His world. If there was an even more special place in his heart, it was for the fatherless children, left alone and destitute. The Lord had commissioned us to reach them and love them on His behalf. My heart nearly stopped as she reached out and took my hand. She looked me in the eye and, with sincerity, said, "Thank you, Mr. Skinner. God bless you."

The Queen turned and exited the room and made her way to the waiting British Commonwealth dignitaries with Prince Philip and us in tow. While there, Prince Philip approached us and engaged in some conversation. When he was done, another well-dressed woman walked up to us. She spoke directly to Marilyn.

"Hello, Marilyn. Welcome. How are you?"

Marilyn replied that she was well and honoured to be at the palace.

"You wouldn't know me, but I heard you speak at Royal Albert Hall last year."

"Oh! Wonderful." Marilyn smiled.

"I was in the Royal Box when you spoke. When you had finished, Bobbie Houston asked us all to consider how we could help you and the children. As I thought about it, it occurred to me that I work for the Queen. So, I said to myself, 'I'm going to go back and tell Ma'am to consider inviting you and the choir to Buckingham Palace! Today is the result of that meeting.'"

Jesus told his disciples,

> "On my account, you will be brought before governors and kings as witnesses to them and to the Gentiles."
>
> *Matthew 10:18 (NIV)*

We were never pursuing these ends or trying to control the outcome. We simply were trusting that if we were faithful, God would create opportunities for us to honour and glorify him.

The Watoto Children's Choir had the honour of singing for Queen Elizabeth on three different occasions. Once at Buckingham Palace, and then, on the occasion of her visit to Uganda and, finally, at her Diamond Jubilee in 2012, a huge nationwide celebration marking the 70th anniversary of the Queen's coronation.

At this Jubilee celebration, the Queen invited some of the children to meet her in Windsor Castle. On that occasion, Lydia, one of the young girls in the choir, broke all protocol and hugged the surprised Queen. The following day, a prominent newspaper wrote an article with a photograph of the hug. The same newspaper sent a journalist to Uganda a week later and did a much larger article about the little girl who hugged the Queen. They visited the Watoto Village, where Lydia lived.

As I reflect on all of this, I must confess that God has always been true to His word. He has stood beside us through every situation, proving Himself to be faithful. We asked him to provide us with strategic alliances that would advance the cause of the vision He birthed in our hearts to plant an English-speaking church in Kampala.

He certainly did it!

~ Reflect and Discuss ~

As you reflect on your own story and engage in discussion with others, consider the following:

1. Developing Strategic Friendships:

    • Discuss the importance of strategic friendships in advancing a cause or mission. How can we cultivate such relationships within our communities?

    • Consider the friendships and alliances in your life that have helped you achieve your goals. How have these relationships influenced your journey of faith and the outcome of your aspirations?

2. The African Proverb:

    • Discuss the concept behind the African proverb, "One log doesn't light a fire."

    • How does Proverbs 27:17 agree with this concept of friendship?

3. Working With Others:

    • Why is it essential to work with others to achieve significant goals?

    • Reflect on a project or mission you were a part of that required collaboration. What were the key factors that made it successful or challenging?

~

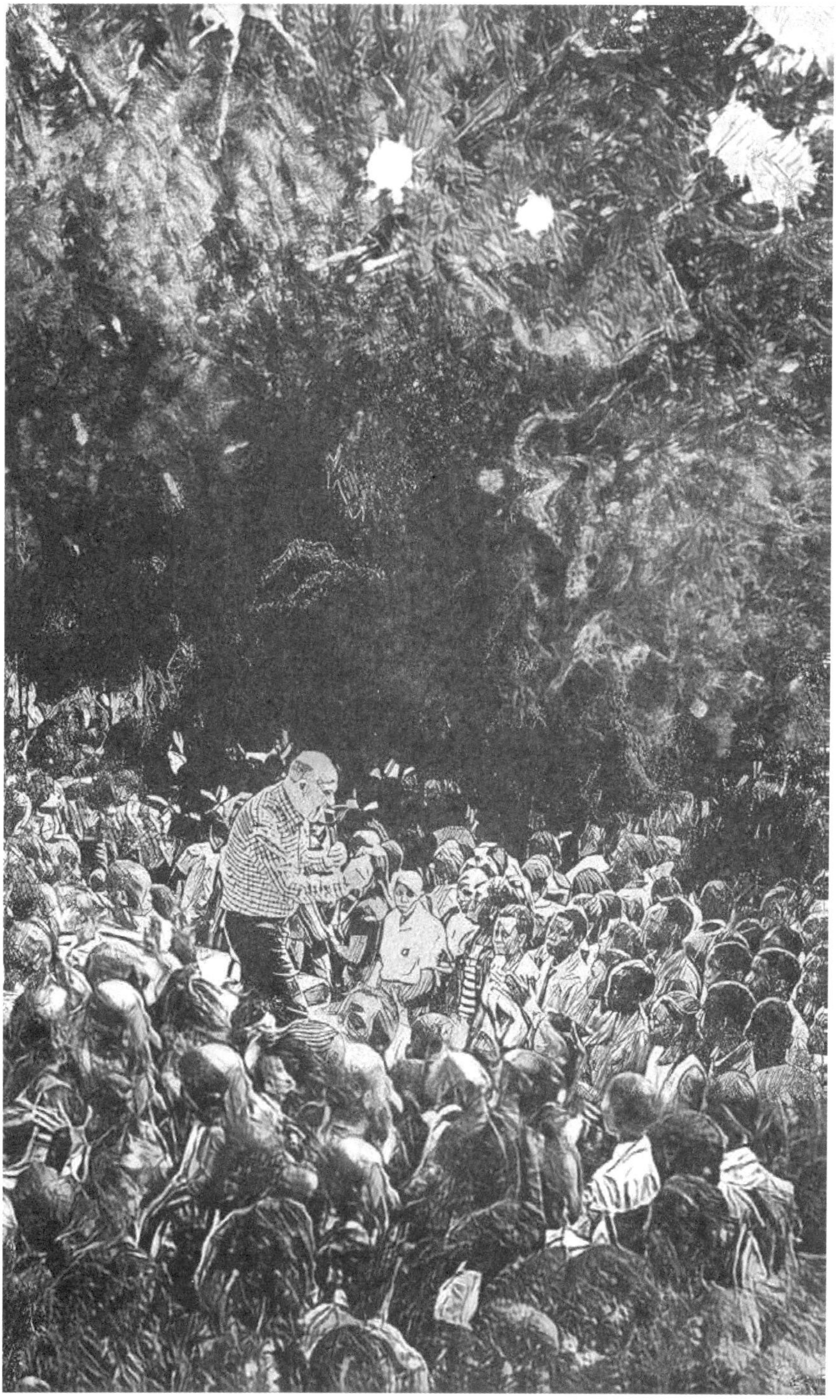

> "The true measure of our love for God
> is how we love those He loves."
>
> *Jack Hayford*

22

~ Some Good Things ~

"Love makes a way."

People without Christ are lost!

Jesus made it very clear that He is the only way to the Father. Jesus, God's only Son, entered human existence to model what life can be but, more importantly, to die on the cross as the sacrifice necessary to satisfy the justice of God in His righteous requirement of full payment for sin. Nothing we do can ever win salvation. Jesus is our salvation. He paid the penalty on our behalf, on the cross. This is the gospel message, the good news about Jesus. Every person on earth should hear this gospel.

Planting and building a church is not just about attracting people to dynamic celebration services; it's about confronting them with their sin and their need for a Saviour and calling them to repentance and surrender to the Lordship of Christ. Then, we draw them into vibrant, meaningful fellowship.

~ A Dramatic Presentation of Eternity ~

As I wondered how we could present the gospel more effectively, I was drawn to a powerful gospel drama called Heaven's Gates and Hell's Flames. Rudy and Karen Krulik, Canadian friends, had developed this dramatic portrayal of people being confronted with the absolute necessity of surrendering to Christ. Rejection of Christ meant eternal damnation in the lake of fire. Surrender to Christ meant eternal life in God's presence, in heaven. The drama was being presented by multiple teams around the world, with huge numbers of people responding to the call to surrender to Christ.

We contacted Rudy and asked if he and Karen would come and present the drama in Kampala at the church. Happily, they agreed. The actors for the drama are Christians in the local church, trained over a week prior to the event. An elaborate set is built in the church, with lighting and dynamic sound effects. We planned to run the presentation over a week.

On the first day, a good crowd filled the auditorium, and many came forward at the end of the presentation to receive Christ. Wonderful! The next day was chaos! So many people had heard of the power and impact of the presentation that large crowds arrived early to witness the gospel presented in such a powerful way. We managed to control the crowd, but it was push and shove. By the third day, it was almost out of control. Thousands gathered early, and when the doors opened, the crush was crazy. We were able to keep control of the crowds that came, and it was certainly worth it as, over the week, well over a thousand people had received Christ. It was a massive success.

Our cell groups provided the follow up, and hundreds of people joined the church, connected to the cell in their community, and the people of the church were delighted at having been able to participate in such a compelling and effective demonstration of the gospel. We knew that we had to do it again another year.

Over the years, we have been able to stage the drama a dozen times. Most tragically, Karen was killed in a motorcycle accident the week before we were to present the drama the second time. But the legacy of her work with her husband Rudy is immense. Each year, we were able to refine the script to make it more appropriate to a Ugandan audience. We were able to ensure safe crowd control. Three presentations each day for eight days meant that thousands watched a very dramatic portrayal of the most important decision every one of us has to make. Every show was packed out, with a detailed system of church volunteers overseeing the smooth transition between presentations. At the end of each presentation, I had the honour of watching and then leading hundreds of people in a prayer of repentance and surrender to Christ. The response was so massive that we literally did not have enough room at the front of the church and would fill the platform as well with souls receiving Christ.

Each year over ten thousand people would come forward in response to the gospel call. There were so many coming to Christ that we knew we could not manage to integrate them all into the church. We encouraged them to find a church near to their homes, meet the pastor and witness to him of what had happened. I received calls from pastors thanking me for presenting the drama and sending people to their local church. One pastor had so many first-time visitors the following Sunday that he was shocked and enquired where they all had come from. They told him of the drama and their acceptance of Christ.

Local schools would arrange with the church to bring entire classes of children to see a presentation. One ten-year-old boy came with his class and responded to the invitation to receive Christ. He became part of the church youth, was discipled, became active in the church ministry, was selected to serve as a youth missionary to the UK for two years, returned and became the pastor to the youth of the church, and then became a pastor of one of the church campuses. His name is Julius Rwotlonyo, and when it was time to hand the mantle of leadership of this great church over, Julius and his wife Vernita became our successors. "Heaven's Gates and Hell's Flames" has been a significant tool to help us build the church.

~ Hope For Africa ~

We held the "Hope for Africa Conference" and invited anyone interested in seeing what we were doing, especially in caring for the vulnerable of the community, to join us at the conference. I felt that if we could inspire others to realise the importance of not just celebrating Christ but caring for community, it would accomplish what we wanted to do. We had a wonderful variety of guests who joined us for the conference from other parts of Africa and from around the world. Some of them returned to their churches and began to implement some of the things they had seen in Kampala.

~ We Changed Our Name ~

Kampala Pentecostal Church was planted. It was now a multi-campus cell-based church. Watoto Childcare Ministry was rescuing some of Uganda's most vulnerable children. Dozens of teams from churches all around the world came every year to help build homes, schools and infrastructure for the Watoto Villages. Most of the churches that sent teams were from evangelical churches that did not have a Pentecostal legacy. Some of the teams confessed that they were concerned about attending a Pentecostal church while in Uganda, as they assumed they were wild, out-of-control services. Of course, they were amazed and delighted to witness KPC at worship.

I had intentionally directed the church away from the traditional concept of titles and positions that, in my opinion, were outdated and smacked of a style of leadership and ministry that I felt the youth were not attracted to. I wasn't the Senior Pastor. I was the Pastoral Team Leader. We didn't have chairmen, secretaries and so on of boards. Our board of Elders became a Team of Elders. Those who worked at the church were a team and not merely a staff. We wanted to fashion something fresh and new but authentic. The very name Kampala Pentecostal Church painted us with a certain brush. I felt we needed a new coat of paint.

Many visitors came to Kampala to visit and share in the building of the Watoto Villages. They would be asked what church they were visiting. They knew of the choir but not so much of the church. Their reply was often, "the Watoto Church." I suppose we became known by what we do, so we proposed the name to the people of the congregation. There was a great discussion and very little dissent.

The Church celebrated its twenty-fifth birthday with a Big Party. It was held over most of a whole week. Special guests joined us from all around the world and we all rejoiced in the goodness of King Jesus. It was at the party that we took on our new name, Watoto Church. The church and the city very quickly accepted it.

~ Life for Abandoned Babies ~

The people of the city still faced many social problems. One of them was the abandonment of babies. Some of the children who were coming into our Watoto homes came from organisations that rescued abandoned babies. As we became more aware of the scope of the problem, I felt that we were to establish a Watoto Babies Home to provide care for the most vulnerable abandoned babies.

There are a variety of reasons a mother may abandon her newborn child. Addressing those issues is the responsibility of the entire community. Where possible, the extended family network in Africa cares for biological children who are orphaned or born to unwed mothers. The breakdown of the cohesion of the family and the social implosion due to HIV infection, war, poverty and urbanisation results in the abandonment of children. While the government assumes the responsibility to address these issues, the simple truth is that they do not have a track record of success in this matter. The church has classically been openly active in providing care to the poor of the community. While there are incidents of inadequate care provided, this is not usually the case. The church has done a stellar job of taking up the matter and delivering great service to the vulnerable. I felt that, as a church, we were also to be involved in rescuing abandoned babies in our city.

As we drove daily from home to the church, we passed a large house near the downtown core. There was a sign posted showing that it was for sale. I determined that I would go in and enquire about it as it would be perfect for a Babies Home. When I did go in, I was told that it had just been sold. I was disappointed, only to find a few weeks later the sign was back up. I went in immediately and negotiated with the Asian owner to purchase it. I had no idea where the money was going to come from to buy it, but I was so confident that it was the right venue that I persisted. Two generous donors from different parts of the world provided the funds we needed. It all came together at the last minute.

What a joy to fix, repair and renovate it from its original purpose as a police club to a rescue centre for children who have been sadly rejected. We painted it in lively colours with cute murals on the walls.

We called it the Bulrushes. The first baby that came in was a boy, so we called him Moses. Just as Moses had come out of the bulrushes to become a great leader, we dreamed that these little abandoned infants would come out of our bulrushes to become leaders in building a new Africa.

The babies we have rescued come to us from a variety of sources. Some come from police stations where a desperate mother has abandoned them. Others come from hospitals where a mother, after giving birth, just leaves her newborn baby in the ward. Some are found abandoned in a banana plantation or a garbage dump. Once a diligent effort to find the baby's family becomes futile, these precious little bundles of life are brought to Baby Watoto. Here the process of nurture and care takes place. Volunteers from around the world have come on an internship to assist us in the care of the babies.

Some of the babies come to us malnourished and at the point of death. Through generous donations from friends of Watoto, we have one of the best neonatal care facilities in the country, saving little children from an early grave and giving them an opportunity to become what God created them to be. One of the great thrills of life for us is to meet a young man or lady who is happy, healthy, whole and active in service to the Lord, only to find out they were rescued as a baby, passed through one of the Babies Homes, was integrated into a Watoto Village, graduated and is now fulfilling their purpose in life.

Today, when Marilyn and I get the chance to see a Watoto Children's choir presentation somewhere in the world, it thrills our hearts to realise that three-quarters of the children on the platform are children who were rescued as babies and have begun their life journey of discovery and purpose, at Watoto.

~ Reflect and Discuss ~

As you reflect on your own story and engage in discussion with others, consider the following:

1. Effectively Winning People to Christ:

    • Reflect on ways you can effectively win people to Christ in your city. Consider utilizing creative outreach methods, such as drama, community events, evangelistic campaigns, or personal testimonies, to share the gospel message.

    • Discuss the importance of building authentic relationships with non-believers, demonstrating Christ's love through acts of service, and engaging in intentional conversations about faith and salvation.

2. Addressing Social Issues in Your Community:

    • Reflect on the social issues prevalent in your community that the Church can address to bring healing. Consider issues such as poverty, homelessness, addiction, mental health, racial injustice, or educational disparities.

    • Discuss how the Church can be a catalyst for positive change by providing practical assistance, advocacy, and support to those affected by these issues, as well as by promoting social justice, reconciliation, and unity.

3. Taking Practical Action:

    • Reflect on practical steps you can take to help solve these problems in your community. Consider volunteering with local organizations, participating in outreach programs, advocating for policy changes, or starting initiatives within your church.

- Discuss the importance of prayer, discernment, and collaboration with other believers and community stakeholders in addressing social issues effectively and sustainably.

During your discussion, offer support, encouragement, and prayer for one another as you explore ways to more effectively share the gospel and address social issues in your community. Commit to taking practical action steps and trusting in God's guidance and provision as you seek to bring healing, hope, and transformation to your city in the name of Christ.

∼

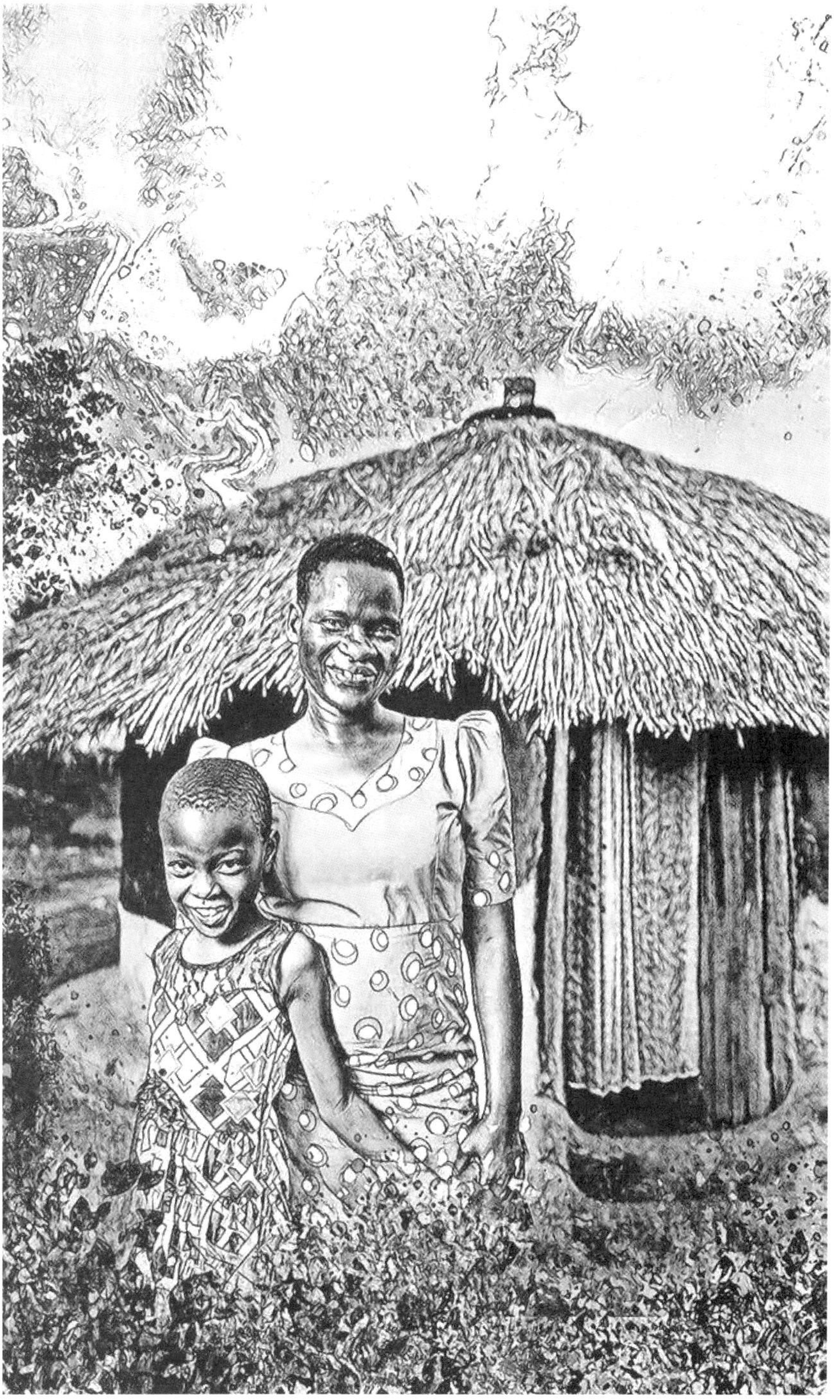

"We must be convinced that in living for ourselves,
we live for nothing; in living for others, we live for God."

Ignatius of Loyola

"Hope has two beautiful daughters;
their names are Anger and Courage.
Anger at the way things are, and Courage to see
that they do not remain as they are."

Saint Augustine

"Whoever oppresses the poor shows contempt for their Maker,
but whoever is kind to the needy honors God."

Proverbs 14:31 (NIV)

23

Celebrating Christ, Caring for Community

"The church is Christ's body, in which he speaks and acts, by which he fills everything with his presence."
Ephesians 1:23 MSG

Even though we had lived in Kampala for decades, I never became accustomed to the poverty, social disorder, chaos and the plethora of community problems that confronted and assaulted me every time we drove through the city. I was disgruntled by the ineptitude and inability of the government to address these pressing matters adequately. Corruption was the order of the day. I sensed real frustration at the community's lack of will or power to solve its problems. The common thinking was that the government was to solve the problems, but, of course, they were not doing it.

I was disgusted by the conduct of members of the community who openly and flagrantly ignored what I thought was proper social decorum and behaviour. Garbage was disposed of wherever someone found a convenient space. Plastic bottles and shopping bags blocked drainage channels, creating open sewerage to flow onto broken-down streets. Traders set up shop anywhere it was convenient, blocking traffic flow and pedestrian movement.

Traffic congestion had become a major problem, as more and more vehicles were registered due to the growing economy. Very little new road infrastructure was being built. Public transport was solved by thousands of minivans converted into small buses. There was no order to traffic flow. Everyone did whatever they could to move forward, ignoring any system of lanes or traffic rules. One lane became three, and if that wasn't enough, the vehicles began to use the sidewalk, pushing aside pedestrians. Movement was so slow that small motorcycles imported from Asia began to flood the streets, compounding the traffic disorder even more.

If the minivans were a problem, the motorcycles were a disaster. Any remaining sense of order evaporated completely. The motorcycles were a convenient mode of rapid transport as they wove through the stalled traffic, completely ignoring, and flagrantly disregarding all sense of order or traffic regulations. The motorcycles were called Boda Bodas, as they were introduced decades ago to get people to the border crossing between Uganda and Kenya. They had now taken over the city as a rapid means of transport in a congested city. The police took no notice of them as they totally discounted any traffic regulations. In fact, they flagrantly ignored and violated them, turning the sidewalks into motorcycle highways.

The problem became so bad that the large government hospital opened up a massive ward designed to treat only victims of motorcycle mayhem. Death due to motorcycle accidents soared. I remember watching a motorcycle speed by us with a mother sitting behind the driver while holding desperately onto her infant baby. They swerved in front of us to pass another vehicle, hit a pothole, and the mother and infant flew off the seat and rolled down the street in front of us. The motorcycle driver kept going. He didn't want to be involved in any repercussions, so off he sped leaving mother and child to the consequences.

One of our beautiful young Watoto girls grew up on one of the Watoto villages, went on to university, graduated and on the first day of her new job, took a motorcycle taxi to get there. A passenger minivan hit the motorcycle, and she was killed. No consequences to any of the drivers or compensation to the girl's family was forthcoming. A payoff to corrupt traffic officers solves a lot of personal problems but leaves the community in chaos. Unfortunately, I could go on with more stories just like this one, stories of ordinary citizens of Uganda, that should cause anyone with a sense of moral responsibility to wonder how life can be allowed to go on like this in a supposedly modern and developing capital city. That's certainly how I felt, and I must confess there were numerous times I wept.

In a time of devotion, I was complaining to God about the flood of community problems. I wondered how we could just go on building a great church and ignore the plight of the community.

Jesus said to me,

"Gary! So, who owns the community."

I immediately thought, as perhaps many of us automatically do, that the government owns the community. I was rebuked by another immediate thought that I think came from Jesus.

"That's a dumb answer!"

Another thought followed it.

"Well, I guess the people own community."

Same response. It was a dumb answer.

And then I felt Jesus emphatically say, "Gary! I own community! I own everything!

The scripture flashed through my consciousness.

> *"The earth is the LORD's, and everything in it, the world, and all who live in it..."*
>
> *Psalm 24:1 (NIV)*

"So, Gary!" It was Jesus again. "If the community has problems, whose problems are they?"

My natural inclination was to follow the same kind of thinking as before. The government owns the problems, or the community owns the problems.

Then Jesus again, "If I own the community and the community has problems, they are my problems."

Okay! I guess God has a problem and needs to come up with a solution.

Jesus again! "So, Gary! If they are my problems, then who am I going to give them to? I am going to give them to my people!"

It was a moment of revelation that would go on to provoke in me a deep search to understand the church's responsibility as we live in the community.

We had already started to get every small group to become active in serving the community. The matter of God's ownership and consequent care for the community shook me. We simply could not get on with building a church but ignore the plight of the city. The city belongs to God. Christians cannot simply abandon society to the whims of the world. We cannot be so heavenly-minded that we are no earthly good. We dare not separate life into compartments of spirituality or secularism. All of life is sacred, created by God. Jehovah God is the sovereign owner of all of life. We are to be his prophetic voice announcing to the city the will and way of God. We are to speak up against injustice and corruption. We are to raise Christian civic leaders who will enter the marketplace of life with godly solutions to bring the Shalom wholeness of God into society. We are to model the culture of Christ by the way we live in community. We are to declare and work to establish the sovereign rule of Christ over all community life.

Every facet of community life is addressed in the scripture. Every career and calling must be a means of working together to bring about community health. These thoughts flooded my mind and my spirit. I knew I was to search the scripture and come to an understanding of the role of the Church in community development.

Another thing I felt we wer to do was to establish a school of community leadership. I actually wanted to call it a school of political leadership. It was designed to train Christians to run for and serve in basic low-level community leadership. From there, some would step up to other levels of city and possibly national political and civic leadership.

I realised that what was needed was the training and equipping of followers of Christ not just for political but business, educational, medical, and judicial leadership, in fact, leadership in every arena of life. The Church must teach Political Science, Medicine, Law or other skills through Christian University and other Christian tertiary institutions. However, leadership skills are taught and modelled by the local church because leadership belongs to God. He has the perfect model of and principles of leadership. If he is calling us to serve, then he is calling us to lead.

We established the School of Community Leadership and have taken hundreds of Christian men and women through training in servant leadership. They have adopted leadership skills into their careers. Some have run for city and national political office. Some have succeeded and entered parliament and other senior levels of leadership. Some have been appointed to significant postings in the city and national leadership. Community transformation is taking place.

It became abundantly clear to me that planting a church is not just organising church services on Sunday or a weekday. It's not only about bringing people to Christ; it is about helping people live for Christ. We don't go to church; we are the church. The church is people. We are to be the church, not just in a building on Sunday, but be the church, God's people, every day in the community, serving God by serving the community.

We do gather together in corporate celebration on Sunday, the Lord's Day. We gather to worship but also to witness to the sovereignty of God over our lives and nation. We gather to be prepared and equipped to go into the world and be Christ in our community.

My role as a pastor is to equip God's people for what he has called us to do in serving the people around us. This is precisely why God called us to Kampala.

> *"So Christ himself gave the apostles, the prophets, the evangelists, the pastors and teachers, to equip his people for works of service, so that the body of Christ may be built up..."*
>
> *Ephesians 4:11-12 (NIV)*

Planting a church is not about just the number of bums on pews on Sunday but serving hands in the community on Monday. This is what church is about.

I was blown away by the Message translation of Paul's letter to the Ephesians.

> *"God raised him (Jesus) from death and set him on a throne in deep heaven, in charge of running the universe, everything from galaxies to governments, no name and no power exempt from his rule. And not just for the time being but forever. He is in charge of it all, has the final word on everything. At the center of all this, Christ rules the church. The church, you see, is not peripheral to the world; the world is peripheral to the church. The church*

> *is Christ's body, in which he speaks and acts, by which he fills everything with his presence."*
>
> *Ephesians 1:20-23 MSG*

Jesus is in charge of it all, He is over and above everything. He is Lord! There is no higher authority. Why? He created it all! He owns it all! He has the final word, once and for all, over everything! All of life comes under His sovereign reign.

How does He live out this authority? Through the church. How does He demonstrate His love for the community? Through the church. How does He bring His flawless character and culture into society? Through the church. The church is crucial, central and pivotal over all of life.

> *The church is Christ's body's, in which he speaks and acts, by which he fills everything with his presence.*
>
> *Ephesians 1:23 MSG*

We prepare God's people to establish the rule of God in the core of community by serving Him through their respective careers.

God helped me to see this more clearly when He called us to plant a celebration point in Gulu and then in Juba, South Sudan.

~ Reflect and Discuss ~

As you reflect on your own story and engage in discussion with others, consider the following:

1. Basis for All of Life Belonging to God:

Reflect on the biblical truth that all of life belongs to God. Consider passages such as Psalm 24:1, which declares, "The earth is the Lord's, and everything in it, the world, and all who live in it."

Discuss how recognizing God's ownership of all things shapes our perspective on stewardship, responsibility, and purpose in life. Reflect on the implications of this truth for how we use our time, talents, resources, and relationships.

2. Impact of Christ's Sovereignty on Daily Life:

   • Reflect on how the sovereignty of Christ affects daily life. Consider how acknowledging Christ as Lord and King influences our decisions, priorities, and values.

   • Discuss how the sovereignty of Christ provides comfort, assurance, and guidance in times of uncertainty, adversity, and change. Reflect on the peace and confidence that come from trusting in God's ultimate authority and control over all things.

3. Practical Demonstration of Christ's Rule in Society:

   • Reflect on practical ways to demonstrate the rule of Christ in society. Consider how Christians can be salt and light in the world by advocating for justice, mercy, and righteousness.

   • Discuss the importance of living out kingdom values such as love, compassion, humility, and integrity in our interactions with others, as well as actively engaging in efforts to address systemic injustices and promote the common good.

4. Meaning of "Serving God":

- Reflect on what it means to "serve God" in various aspects of life. Consider how serving God involves obedience to His commands, devotion to His purposes, and alignment with His will.

- Discuss how serving God encompasses both acts of worship and acts of service, as well as how every aspect of our lives can be lived out as an offering to God. Reflect on the joy and fulfillment that come from living a life surrendered to Christ's lordship.

During your discussion, offer support, encouragement, and prayer for one another as you explore these questions and seek to deepen your understanding of God's sovereignty, the implications for daily living, and the call to serve Him faithfully in all areas of life. Commit to living in light of these truths and being ambassadors of Christ's kingdom in the world.

~

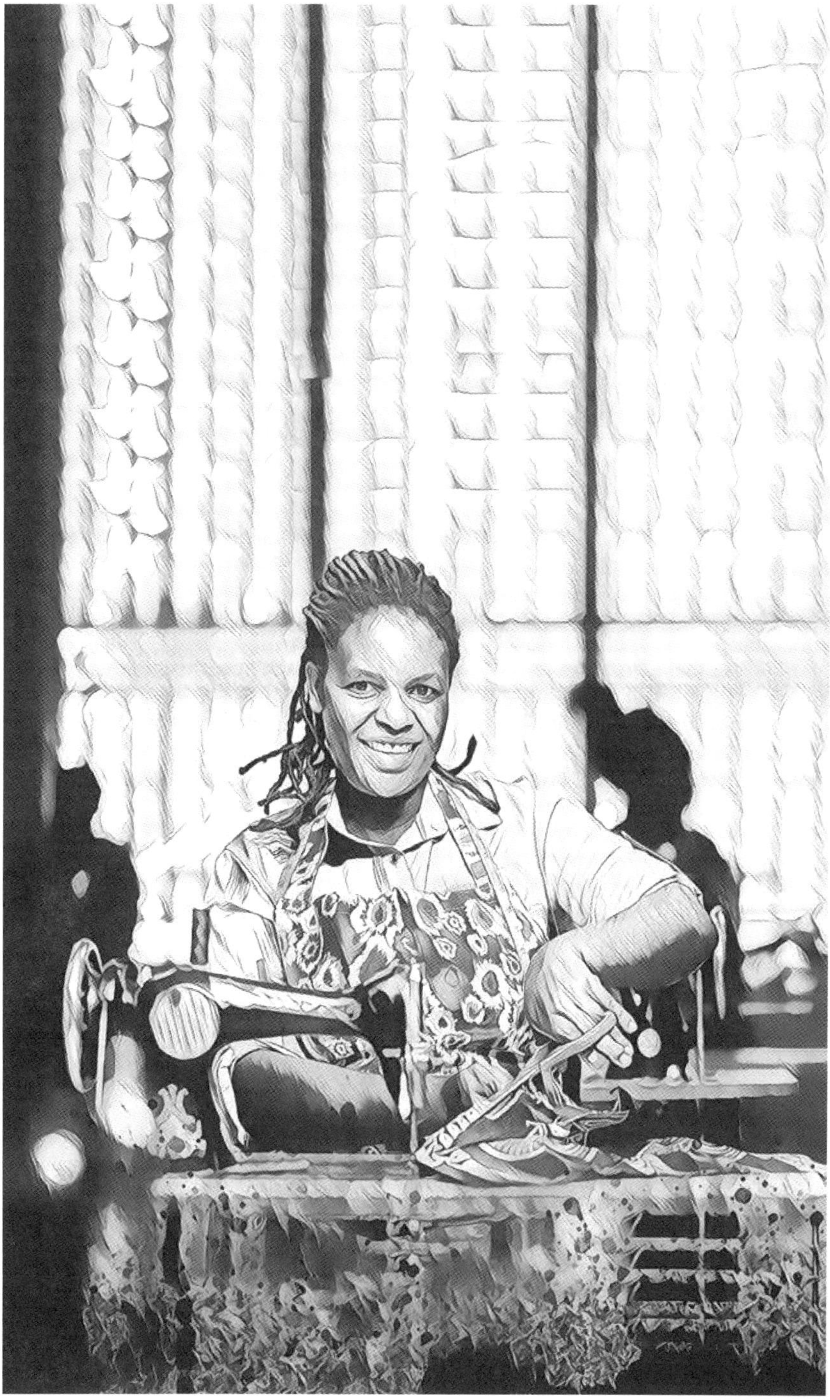

"Do all the good you can, by all the means you can, in all the ways you can, in all the places you can, at all the times you can, to all the people you can, as long as ever you can."

John Wesley

24
~ Project Gulu ~

"Restoring faith, hope and love in northern Uganda."

Paul teaches us in Ephesians 6:12 that,

"...our struggle is not against flesh and blood, but against the rulers, against the authorities, against the powers of this dark world and against the spiritual forces of evil in the heavenly realms." (NIV)

In Uganda, a million people were slaughtered under the brutal regimes of Idi Amin and Milton Obote. In Rwanda and Burundi to the southwest of Uganda, the age-old bitterness between rival people groups resulted in the most rapid genocide and slaughter of civilian population in the history of the world. The people of Eastern Congo on the border of Uganda experienced ruthless rebel warfare that has resulted in the death of six million people, with six million more displaced in a decades-long humanitarian crisis. In Sudan to the north of Uganda, the same physical and spiritual slavery and domination by evil leadership and demonic wickedness plagued the people.

All these conflicts are the consequence of Satanic spiritual forces being unleashed from hell against the people of Central Africa through ungodly leadership. There is no political way to resolve this crisis. The solution is a spiritual one. The answer is to align our national ethos and culture with Biblical and Christian culture. Jesus is the hope of the world, and Jesus brings healing to nations in direct proportion to the establishment and health of the Church in the community.

In northern Uganda, a series of quasi-political cultural leaders rose to prominence, who were controlled by evil spirits and openly used the practices of witchcraft in the pursuit of political gain. One was a woman called Alice Lakwena and then, more recently, Joseph Kony. Northern Uganda was kept in a state of civil war throughout the 1990s and into the early 2000s.

For twenty years, the Lord's Resistance Army, under the rule of Kony, abducted 30,000 children from their homes in rural northern Uganda. They were forcefully drafted into an army of child soldiers who were compelled to commit the most heinous and senseless slaughter of other human beings. Ranging throughout northern Uganda and South Sudan, many of the children were led back to the villages they were born in and forced to slaughter family members.

Two of our extended family Watoto children, one a boy and the other a young girl, were among those abducted. For several years, we prayed for them, believing that somehow, they would return home. We never heard from the boy again, but news reached us that the girl had escaped and returned to her home just outside Gulu, the largest city in northern Uganda.

We felt compelled to go to Gulu and meet and help her. In an armed convoy of government soldiers, Marilyn was escorted to Gulu. She visited some of the refugee camps where more than a million civilians had fled to escape the inevitable raid of the rebel soldiers and the abduction of their children. Each morning, at sunrise, families would walk to their rural homes and tend the crops and animals. At dusk, they would return to the relative safety of the urban centres and sleep anywhere they could find a place to lay their mats. Wall-to-wall sleeping children crammed into every usable space.

Marilyn visited with the leaders of the refugee camps. She witnessed the social chaos and the breakdown of order and civil integrity. The camps registered some of the highest rates of HIV infection and mortality in the world. Drunkenness, theft, and physical and sexual abuse were rife. Marilyn heard the stories of children who lived in these UN Internally Displaced Peoples Camps. They had escaped or been released from the rebel army but were not able to return to their families because of the atrocities they had been forced to commit against them. The children, not yet out of their teens, had murdered, raped and mutilated innocent villagers. The level of trauma the children faced was incomprehensible. They carried scars, some seen and some invisible.

PROJECT GULU

Marilyn went to see Jane (not her real name,) the young Watoto girl who had been abducted. Jane met her and led her into the mud and grass thatched hut where, in the middle of the night, she and her siblings had been taken from her family. She told of how she had watched the rebels beat her mother and aged grandmother, and then been forced to run throughout the night, collecting other children along the way. In the middle of the wearying trek, some of her youngest siblings had tired and could not go on. The soldiers forced Jane and the other children to beat their brothers and sisters to death and then were made to run on.

On reaching the rebel camp, the soldiers threw their shirts in a pile, and the girls were told to pick up a shirt. Jane became another "wife" for the soldier who owned the shirt that she held in her hands. She had to wash his clothes, cook his food, carry his equipment and service him sexually. She was fourteen years of age when she was ripped away from her home and family. The following year, she gave birth to a baby by the soldier, an older man. For two years, they moved from camp to camp and fought in skirmishes and battles with government soldiers. The heinous practices of human sacrifice, cannibalism, and sexual abuse that Jane had to observe, endure, and participate in are too much to include in this record.

Jane told of how she would lie awake in the middle of the night and gently sing a song she had learned in Sunday School.

> *My only hope is you, Jesus, my only hope is you.*
>
> *From early in the morning 'til late at night,*
>
> *My only hope is you.*

She managed, one day during a battle, to escape and trudged for four months through the bush until she was found by government soldiers and returned home. Her grandmother had died while she was away, and then, her baby died. She and Marilyn wept as she told her story.

"All I ever wanted was to be a normal girl, go to school and become a nurse."

Marilyn promised her that she would make sure that happened. Jane graduated from school, studied social work and now works with refugees on the border of Uganda and South Sudan. She has experienced counselling, healing and a new life.

We had thought that we would help the most vulnerable of the children by bringing them to Kampala. God spoke clearly to Marilyn.

"I don't want you to take the children to Kampala. I want you to plant a church here in Gulu and "make the community livable again."

This phrase was from a passage in Isaiah 58 that God had put into our hearts when we had first come to Uganda.

> *"If you get rid of unfair practices,*
>
> *quit blaming victims,*
>
> *quit gossiping about other people's sins,*
>
> *If you are generous with the hungry*
>
> *and start giving yourselves to the down-and-out,*
>
> *Your lives will begin to glow in the darkness,*
>
> *your shadowed lives will be bathed in sunlight.*
>
> *I will always show you where to go.*
>
> *I'll give you a full life in the emptiest of places—*
>
> *firm muscles, strong bones.*
>
> *You'll be like a well-watered garden,*
>
> *a gurgling spring that never runs dry.*
>
> *You'll use the old rubble of past lives to build anew,*
>
> *rebuild the foundations from out of your past.*
>
> *You'll be known as those who can fix anything,*
>
> *restore old ruins, rebuild and renovate,*
>
> *make the community livable again."*
>
> *Isaiah 58:9-12 MSG*

PROJECT GULU

She phoned me immediately to let me know what the Lord wanted us to do. My spirit leapt in confirmation. At the next meeting of our pastoral team, I passed on the news that Jesus wanted us to plant a church in Gulu. There was a resounding yes from the entire team.

Knowing that demonic spiritual control over the region was the real issue, churches and Christians engaged in serious spiritual warfare. The nefarious powers of darkness were broken. They lost their ability to continue to operate in the area. The LRA moved its primary activity to the eastern Congo, where it continued to create mayhem.

I asked Julius Rwotlonyo to give oversight to the planning of the Gulu church plant. We decided to make a visit with the pastoral team to Gulu to connect with the community and pray.

Norbert Mao, the governor of the Gulu region, agreed to see us. He welcomed us warmly into his office and informed us that he knew of Watoto Church as his wife attended one of the campuses in Kampala. He had been there for the first time recently when his wife had been baptised.

"We've come knowing that God wants us to plant a church here in Gulu, but that's not the only reason. We know that God loves Gulu and wants to make the community liveable again. So, we've come to ask this question, 'How can we serve you and the people of Gulu?'"

"Wow! I've never been asked that before," he replied.

And then, without hesitation, he answered the question.

"There are three things I need help with. First, the abducted children who have returned home. Second, our hospital and third, the women on the streets of our city."

He then went on to explain. There were former child soldiers who had returned home, but because of the brutality against their communities and families and because they returned with children borne to rebel soldiers, they were not welcomed back. A five-million-dollar fenced-in rehabilitation centre had been built with aid money from a European country. It housed six hundred former child soldiers, and all efforts to help rehabilitate them were failing. The children were in desperate need.

"I think we can do something about that," I said.

He asked if we had seen the government hospital. It was in complete disrepair; the medical store was empty, and the staff was demoralised and ineffective.

"I think we can do something about that as well."

He told us that there were thousands of women in the city who were struggling to raise their children alone. Some were former child soldiers, others abandoned women or women who had lost their men to war. They were active by any means to try and meet their children's most basic needs.

"Yes! We can do something about that, too."

We launched the Gulu campus several months later with a burning passion to introduce a revolution of love to a broken city. Joe and Jackie Ogwal, who had led Watoto Children's Choirs for several years and were now on our pastoral team, were the pioneer pastors at Gulu. Over two thousand people attended the launch service with about eight hundred worshippers continuing to gather weekly immediately thereafter.

One of the first things we did was to contact Dr. Robi Sonderegger, a friend in Australia who is a clinical psychologist. He had visited Uganda, spoken at the church and expressed interest in helping with trauma rehabilitation in Uganda. He had a colleague who was a clinical psychotherapist and was ready to move to Uganda and assist us in addressing the need for counselling to the huge number of deeply distressed people in the Gulu region.

A few months later Carl and Julie Gaede relocated to Uganda. They trained our youth in trauma counselling and took on the responsibility of regularly visiting the rehabilitation centre and helping the former child soldiers deal with the rejection, nightmares and trauma they lived with. It was a long ordeal that required patience, persistence and love. We witnessed hundreds of desperate, formerly abducted children who had been forced to commit unspeakable atrocities take on a journey of healing and restored mental health with the support of the church youth. Many were integrated back into society to rebuild their lives.

It was not just former child soldiers who were traumatised. It was the entire community that was grieving at the state of their community and the effect of the war. Parents and grandparents were emotionally crushed by the abduction of their children and their failure to protect them. We were able to organise trauma counselling for entire village communities in rural northern Uganda. Announcements and invitations were made for any who needed help. The entire village would gather under the spreading boughs of the largest tree and listen to the power of love, forgiveness and acceptance. Tens of thousands of people were helped overcome bitterness and grief over what had taken place. Thousands received Christ. Churches were strengthened.

We built a Watoto Village outside Gulu, which became home for the children who had no home or family to return to.

We put together a musical tour with some of the children telling their stories of hope, healing and health to the world. We called it the "Restore Tour. Child Soldier No More."

On the tour itself, we found Jesus' restoration at work. We noticed some underlying tension between two of the girls on the trip. We discovered that the father of one of the girls, a rebel commander, had forced the other girl to watch while he brutally killed her grandmother. These two young girls, victims of horrific evil, were travelling, interacting and even presenting their story together. The team was able to facilitate a difficult but immensely healing conversation between the two girls. They hugged and sobbed together, one saying to the other, "I forgive your dad for killing my grandmother."

It is one thing to talk about the teaching of Jesus to love your enemies and forgive as God forgives, but it is something else entirely to face a situation like this at its most extreme and to respond with the fullness of Christ's love. Forgiveness and healing are possible when the power of the Spirit of Jesus is at work.

God brought to the community of Gulu a spirit of radical forgiveness, restoration and healing and Watoto Church is honoured to be a part of that story.

I wasn't sure how we were going to help with the request to rehabilitate the hospital. We prayed and asked God to intervene.

Some months later, after speaking at a conference in Australia, I was asked to meet with a gentleman from the local church. He told me that for ten years, he had a very strong sense that God was getting him ready to serve in Uganda.

He asked, "Is there any way I can help?"

"What do you do?" I asked.

"I am a hospital administrator," he said.

I smiled. "Oh yes. I think we could use your help."

For two years, Matthew and Tanya Cross worked with the church, the government, and other aid organisations, restoring the Gulu hospital to full working order. Buildings, infrastructure, systems and staff were put into place to make the Gulu Hospital effective again. A prominent Ugandan newspaper did an article with photos showing how soldiers had traded in bombs and bullets for brooms and brushes as they worked with the community to rehabilitate the facility. It was a collaborative effort by many, for which we are grateful. Joyce Meyers' ministry gave generously to the restoration, sending much-needed medical equipment to supply the hospital requirements.

~ Restoring Dignity to Women ~

The third request was to help the suffering women of Gulu.

Marilyn, in particular, felt God tugging on her heart. He spoke to her.

"Marilyn! Don't get too comfortable! I have something else for you to do."

Marilyn swallowed, "What is it, Lord?"

"I want you to restore dignity to Uganda's most vulnerable women."

She knew what she had to do. Her heart was moved as she remembered the women she had met in northern Uganda as well as those in Kampala. They needed real help. She knew that it was the responsibility of God's people, the church, to reach out with the love of Jesus to these women. We were to introduce a new facet of Watoto's ministry. We were to rescue and restore dignity to women who had been abused and discarded.

Living Hope Ministries was established so that we could come alongside women to improve their lives and the lives of their children. There were three things that we began to focus on. We would embrace, empower and engage with them.

To embrace them meant giving them both a physical and personal hug. Many needed immediate material help so, they received a welcome package of food and household items. Women who had been rejected, abandoned and abused are embraced. They're taught to understand, appreciate and accept their God-given value and worth. They learn that each person is precious, created in the image of God and loved so much that Christ died for them and has a beautiful purpose for their lives. Embracing the women is the first step to healing. It's uplifting, liberating and empowering.

To empower them is to give them the skills they need to enable them to sustainably generate personal income through skills training. It's providing them with the knowledge and wisdom to raise their children with dignity and purpose. This is done through discipleship classes, trauma rehabilitation, skills training, and basic literacy programs.

To engage with them means that, once trained, we provide them with the capital and coaching support they need to start and grow their own income-generating businesses and practise healthy financial habits as a way of life. It means walking with them as they contribute to the welfare of the community and other needy women around them.

The city of Gulu provided us with the very same facilities that had once housed the children who walked into town each night to sleep securely and avoid being abducted. We created a training centre in the heart of Gulu to carry out this wonderful work. The facility also became a hub for making craft items that would earn an income for the women and be sold by the children's choirs on their tours around the world.

~ Facial Reconstruction ~

We learned that some of the women who had escaped or been released from the LRA had been horrifically disfigured by the gruesome practice of facial mutilation. When a woman in LRA captivity displeased a rebel soldier, disobeyed a commander or fought with another woman, she would have her lips, nose and ears cut off with razor blades. This would be done as a means of discipline or to instil fear and submission in the other women.

To see a woman who had been subjected to this kind of gruesome injury was heart-wrenching. The gargantuan trauma of betrayal, rejection, abuse and rape was compounded by the violent removal of the very things that made a woman attractive. The scars were physical and worn on their faces for all to see. But the scars were also mentally and emotionally devastating. These they carried in their hearts, hidden away so that no one could see. Most were so ashamed of their appearance that they would never appear in public, choosing rather to spend their lives secluded deep in a rural village so as not to be seen.

Marilyn determined to find a way to intervene in the lives of these precious women surgically. With the help of the Hillsong Sisterhood, she was able to finance a program of reconstructive surgery. Skilled Plastic Surgeons came voluntarily to Kampala and performed surgeries to repair the faces of the neediest women.

Working with the local community and community leaders, by radio advertisements and word of mouth, hundreds of women responded for help. Watoto provided reconstructive surgery for every woman who needed it.

What a thrill it was to be at the bedside of a woman whose bandages were tentatively removed, to watch as she looked into a mirror and saw a new face. One woman wept and said,

"I am beautiful again."

~ Keep a Girl in School ~

And then, Marilyn was confronted with another issue that carried tragic consequences. She learned that young girls who reached puberty would drop out of school for the simple reason that they did not have the menstrual pads necessary for their monthly period. As the months passed, the girls would fall further and further behind in class until they were forced to drop out of school. This would inevitably end up in early marriage and the massive loss of their precious human potential. The provision of a girl's monthly needs could reverse that decision and the trend in northern Uganda.

Watoto Church started "Keep A Girl in School," a sponsorship initiative to provide as many girls as possible with the items they needed so they could stay in school. The dropout rate in schools plummeted to virtually nil because a church cared for the real needs of the community.

Today, each month, a team of volunteers visits the school and personally hands a package to each girl. The package contains menstrual pads, a new pair of panties and a bar of soap. To witness the joy of the girls as they realise they do not have to drop out of school is a delight. The schools invited the church to hold monthly assemblies so we could teach the girls the important subject of God's plan for sexual health and well-being. Girls were often teased by the boys when they knew they were going through their monthly cycle. The boys felt left out of the care being provided, so the schools asked us to hold assemblies for the boys separately. We taught them about the wonder of God's gift and plan for their sexuality.

I used to often joke with people as I shared the story of the church's intervention in the community by saying,

"Who would have thought that handing out menstrual pads is a work of God and an important ministry of the Church."

I would also say that ministry is not what one man does behind a pulpit on Sunday but what we all do every day in the community.

~ Meeting the Monsters of the LRA ~

Marilyn and her friend Bobbie Houston were visiting Gulu and working together in their passion and commitment to come alongside the women of the area.

One day, Christine, one of our amazing Watoto leaders who helped us set up the entire Gulu operation, walked into the room.

"There are some people here who want to meet you," she said.

Her tone was grave. "The government has just given some of the top LRA leaders amnesty. They are in the next room."

"What?" Marilyn felt her tension rise at Christine's words.

Christine continued.

"They've heard we care for women and children. They want our help."

Marilyn and Bobbie looked at each other and then back to Christine. You could have heard a pin drop in the room.

"I don't want to meet these people," Marilyn thought. "I'm here to help the victims, not the perpetrators."

What were they to do? A group of murdering, raping, child-abducting warlords were in the next room, waiting to meet them. Steeling themselves, the three women walked through the doorway into the room. Three men stood and reached out their hands. Marilyn, Bobbie and Christine reached back and shook hands with the three men.

The man who spoke first introduced himself as Kony's second in command. The second man said that he was the general in charge of planning the LRA's battles. The last "trained" the children for combat.

Marilyn didn't know whether to throw up, run out the door or slap them in the face. She did none of those things. She tried to smile while remaining as calm as she could.

"We have something to show you," they said and led Marilyn and the others outside.

Three groups of young women and children of every age and size sat on the grass in front of them. The first two groups were the wives and children of rebel soldiers and LRA leaders. They were led to the third group. A sign taped onto the wall of the building read, "To God be the Glory."

"And here, madam," one of the men said, "are Joseph Kony's wives and children."

Marilyn fought back the temptation to gasp out loud. Sitting before her were the wives and children of one of the most infamous warlords in the world. They were the innocent victims of a brutal system of evil and witchcraft. Most of the women had been abducted themselves, their children born in the bush, running for their lives from battle to battle. They needed shelter and care. With reluctance but with open hearts, Marilyn and her friends agreed to help.

On the short plane ride back to Kampala, Marilyn wrestled with God.

"Lord," she prayed fervently, "These are the masterminds of this whole wicked operation. I don't want to help them!"

She knew Jesus' teaching about loving our enemies, but this all felt too real.

The little plane pushed on through the turbulence. Marilyn's Bible was open on her lap. The pages turned, and Marilyn looked down at it. It was the Book of Job. She read the first verse she saw on the page in front of her.

> "(God) is not partial to princes, nor does He regard the rich more than the poor, for they are all the work of His hands."
>
> *Job 34:19 (AMPCE)*

Marilyn knew at that moment that just as there was no amount of good Marilyn could do to deserve God's love, there was also no amount of evil these men could do to keep God from loving them.

"But God, I don't think that's fair." Marilyn protested. "I actually think you should love me a lot more than these men. Lord, please, they don't deserve my help."

The plane bumped in the turbulence again. The pages of her Bible folded back a few turns. Marilyn's breathing stopped as she looked down and read.

> *"He will deliver even one who is not innocent, who will be delivered through the cleanness of your hands."*
>
> *Job 22:30 (NIV)*

Marilyn breathed in and felt a fresh baptism of compassion flow through her. She knew that the revolution of Jesus' love was being ignited in Gulu, and it required this sort of radical grace and forgiveness.

A few weeks later, we heard that Kony's former second-in-command had come to church at our Gulu celebration point and surrendered his life to Christ and His Lordship. Marilyn was overwhelmed with a new realisation of the power of the gospel to transform and heal anyone and any situation. She became more aware of the healing impact of forgiveness. She identified with the deep inner struggle that the women and children she was rescuing were going through, who, in the face of extreme evil, had chosen the love and forgiveness of Christ as their way of life.

This man is today a radical follower of Jesus, totally transformed by the love of Christ. You will find him on Sunday morning greeting worshippers as they enter the church services in Gulu. Many know who he is; some have suffered at his hand, but they have released the miraculous forgiveness of Jesus to flow through their hearts and extend grace and mercy to those who do not deserve it.

Watoto Church is not the only force of God's goodness in Gulu. God works through all of His Church and His people wherever they may serve Him. But it is this sort of radical Jesus love that brought Gulu back from the brink of the darkest despair imaginable. Today, the region has been radically reborn. The LRA is gone, and the land is peaceful and prospering. A generation of once-invisible children are living as productive citizens and loving husbands, wives, and parents.

~ School of Agriculture ~

Another wonderful development is the four-hundred-and-fifty-acre piece of farmland, just twenty kilometres south of Gulu, bought with the donation of a faithful Watoto partner. What will be the best agricultural college in East Africa is near completion. Bobi Agribusiness Institute is being developed under the oversight and work of Brent Smith, who, for decades, has given himself tirelessly to help fulfil the Watoto dream.

Watoto children who have a heart for agriculture, and eventually other young Ugandans will study and work on the farm, earning a degree in Agribusiness from an American University, graduating debt-free and going on to help transform the agricultural sector of the Ugandan economy.

Transformation and healing to nations will happen when the Church begins to exercise and operate in its God-ordained place in society. We must inculcate into our national systems and structures Biblical values. We must enshrine them into our legal and ethical structure. We will know the truth, and the truth will set us free.

~ Reflect and Discuss ~

As you reflect on your own story and engage in discussion with others, consider the following:

1. Role of the Church in Community Development:

    • Reflect on the role of the Church in community development. Consider how the Church can serve as a catalyst for positive change by addressing social, economic, and spiritual needs in the community.

    • Discuss the importance of the Church's involvement in initiatives such as poverty alleviation, education, healthcare, housing, job training, and family support. Reflect on how the Church can empower individuals and families to thrive and flourish in all areas of life.

2. Identifying Wounded People in the Community:

    • Reflect on who the wounded people are in your community that the Church can help. Consider individuals and groups who may be marginalized, vulnerable, or experiencing various forms of suffering and hardship.

    • Discuss how the Church can reach out to the wounded and offer compassion, support, and practical assistance. Reflect on the importance of listening, empathy, and building relationships with those in need.

3. Practical Ways to Help Care For Community:

    • Reflect on practical things you can do to help your church fulfill its goal of caring for the community. Consider volunteering your time, skills, and resources to support various outreach programs and initiatives.

- Discuss opportunities for involvement in areas such as food distribution, clothing drives, medical clinics, educational programs, mentorship, counseling, and advocacy. Reflect on how you can contribute to building a stronger, more compassionate community through your active participation.

During your discussion, offer support, encouragement, and prayer for one another as you explore ways to actively engage in community development and support the mission of Watoto Church. Commit to being intentional in your efforts to care for the wounded, marginalized, and vulnerable in your community, and to being agents of positive transformation and healing in Jesus' name.

~

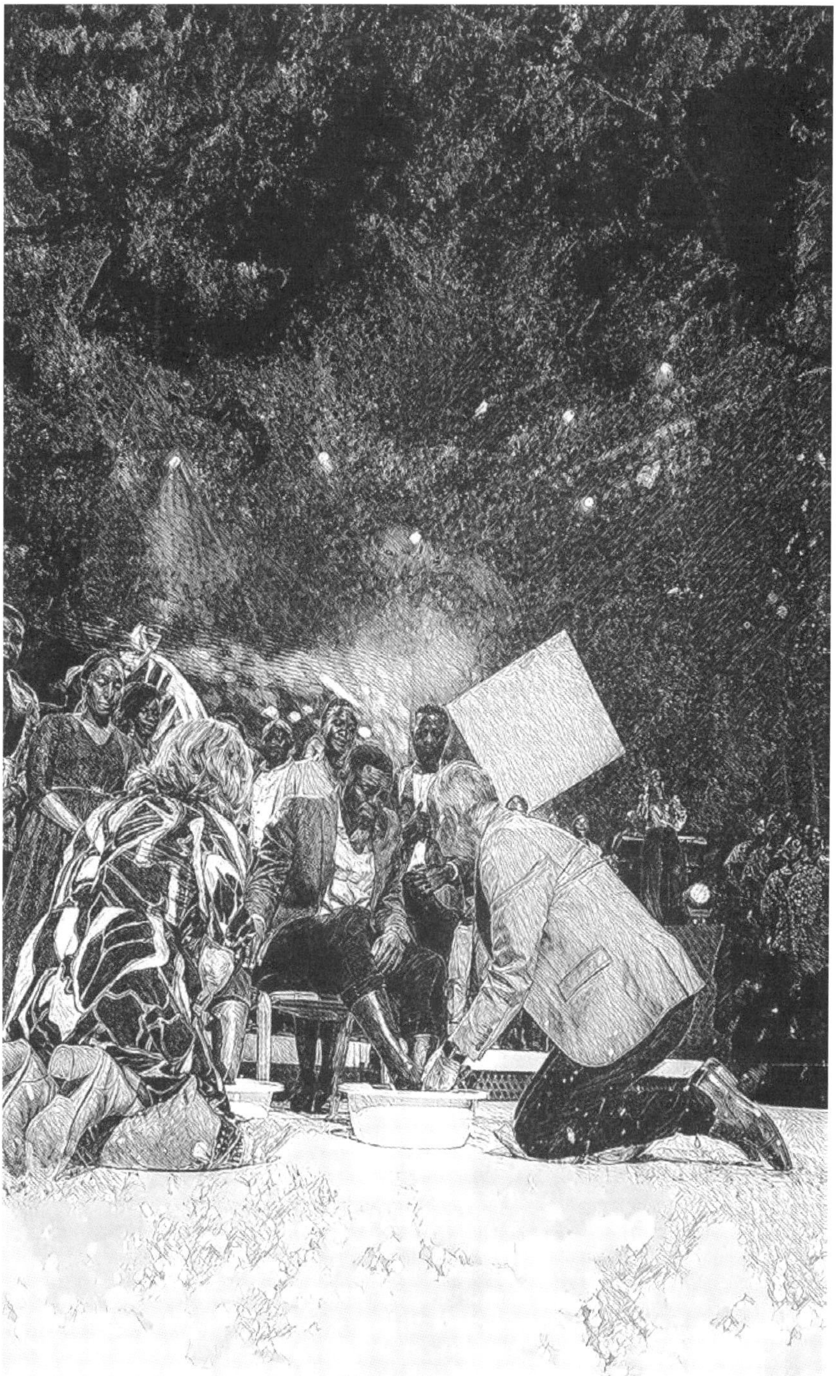

"God does not call us to do extraordinary things,
but to do ordinary things with extraordinary love."

Charles Colson

25

~ Epilogue ~

"In the end, it is love that restores, heals and transforms."

What God had done in Kampala and Gulu was wonderful. People's lives were changed by the presence of Jesus through the Church. The city of Kampala was experiencing healing. The nation of Uganda was experiencing a new beginning.

~ Juba, South Sudan ~

While the work grew in Uganda, the nation of South Sudan was born. The youngest nation on the planet came into being right across the northern border of Uganda. The nation emerged out of generations of warfare and chaos. It is one of the least developed nations in the world. Many of the social and national conflicts and challenges that we faced in Uganda were now being experienced by the people of South Sudan. One thing made it worse. Islam from North Africa dominated and oppressed the "Christian" south. Some of the tallest and most noble-looking people in Africa were enslaved by the Islamic regime in Khartoum and by generations of witchcraft, Animism and superstition.

The people of the new nation were determined to throw off the shackles of the Islamic past. They want to be a Christian nation with development and a new start. And then God did it again. He called us to plant an English-speaking church in the heart of Juba, the capital city of the nation of South

Sudan.

So, that is what Watoto Church was determined to do.

~ My Miracle Missions Offering ~

The Lord spoke to me. Again!

"Gary! I want you to ask the people for an offering."

Each year, the church had been giving a missions offering that amounted to about thirty thousand dollars. It was not an insignificant amount for a church in the middle of Africa and from a nation that is considered one of the poorest in the world.

So, I thought, no problem. But then God made his intentions a little more clear.

"I want you to ask the people for an extravagant offering. Not only that! I want you to give it all away."

Okay! I realised that something was up and wondered what it might be.

"I want you to ask the people for an offering of a million dollars."

A number of years earlier, I had sensed that God wanted us to give a special offering to Israel. Wayne and Anne Hilsden, friends of ours who pastored the King of Kings Assembly in Jerusalem, would be the recipients through which Watoto Church could sow into what the Lord was doing in Israel. We set a goal of twenty-five thousand dollars as a gift to Israel. Wayne and Anne visited us, led us in some amazing Jewish worship and we gave. We took our friends to the national game park the next day. While watching the most amazing herd of giraffes, we received a call from the church to let us know that we had given fifty thousand dollars. We were all so excited we frightened off the giraffes.

Now God was asking for a million dollars!

The next time we met as a pastoral team, I let the pastors know what I felt God was asking us to do. They never batted an eye. It was a confident affirmation. Faith in a God of miracles had brought us this far. Anything is possible. Why not? So, we determined to walk in submission and obedience to what the Lord had asked us to do.

I spent several months teaching the biblical message of the power of generosity and asked the people to prepare by setting aside a special mission offering. We were going to give it all away, spending none of it on Kampala. We set a date for our first "MMO," our "Miracle Mission Offering." The congregation was excited, and everyone prepared for the big day. They got their envelopes ready and came to church ready to give. We celebrated our wonderful Jesus, God's extravagant, sacrificial offering and gift to the world, the greatest mission offering ever. And then the entire congregation, children first, then the youth, then the adults jubilated while dancing and trilling up the aisles, worshipping God with an offering, theatrically tossing their envelopes into the massive baskets.

In that one offering, the wonderful people of Watoto Church, God's redeemed people, a people of faith and obedience, people I love so much that my buttons burst when they are mentioned, gave not a million dollars but one million, two hundred thousand dollars.

Wow! Fall on the floor. Get up! Say whaaaat! Hold your head in your hands and exclaim, "Excuse me! How much!"

One point two million. I'm dead serious.

And that in a country considered poor. An equivalent offering from a church of similar size in the USA, considering the economic data of the population, would be a seventy million dollar offering.

We planted Juba and gave the rest away to help plant and strengthen churches in other parts of Africa and the world. For the last decade, we have continued to see the faithful generosity of God's people, as consistently, every year, a million-dollar mission offering has been given by the church as an act of loving worship to our amazing King Jesus to grow His Kingdom.

Joe and Jacky Ogwal, who were our pioneer pastors in Gulu, moved with their family up to Juba and pioneered again. They are some of my heroes.

Victor and Miriam Obina followed them, and through the trials, war and conflict remained steady. What an amazing, servant-hearted couple. Many of the things we have been doing in Uganda are now being replicated in South Sudan. God is at work through His people in South Sudan. I think it's Africa's day to rise and shine!

With the blessing of the Pentecostal Assemblies of God Uganda, we have planted campuses in Entebbe, Mbarara and Jinja, all being led by wonderful young Ugandan pastors, their wives and little families. The future is bright.

~ Transition ~

It was the American statesman Benjamin Franklin, who said,

"… in this world nothing can be said to be certain, except death and taxes."

One other certainty, however, is change. Unfortunately, change is something we resist most. Successful people, however, learn not only to accept change but to welcome and manage it. I heard that there are three kinds of people. Those who make things happen, those who watch things happen, and those who say, "What happened?"

Each of us need to do something noble and valuable with our lives but with the firm recognition that we have a limited time to accomplish what we're doing and then our time will be up. None of us can continue what we are doing forever. Change is inevitable. To bury one's head in the sand while ignoring the impending, is folly. Wisdom calls for the intentional preparation for, what will most certainly transpire, the end of our tenure.

Paul knew that his time of powerful apostolic ministry would end. He prepared his spiritual son Timothy for that eventuality. He encouraged Timothy in the ministry God had called and entrusted to him and said,

> "…the time for my departure is near. I have fought the good fight, I have finished the race, I have kept the faith. Now there is in store for me the crown of righteousness, which the Lord, the righteous Judge, will award to me on that day…"

2 Timothy 4:6b-8 (NIV)
EPILOGUE

Jesus had a transition plan. He spent three years in the most powerful ministry the world had ever seen, while at the same time preparing a group of followers to carry on once he had returned to heaven.

And so, as I entered my mid-fifties, I became acutely aware of the need to prepare for the unavoidable transfer of the leadership of Watoto Church to someone else. To be totally honest that was not going to be difficult, it just required intentionality.

I had spent decades preparing young men and women for leadership in church ministry. I was literally surrounded by them. I not only sought them out, but trained, equipped, empowered and released them into ministry. I lived my leadership as an open book. I mentored, motivated, modeled and watched on a daily basis as they practiced effective servant leadership. In a very real sense, I was multiplying myself in them. I was getting them ready for the day when I would pass the mantle of leadership on to them. The most challenging part was to get those I was leading to accept the fact that we needed to start talking about transition and getting ready for it. Followers don't resist the reality that they will one day take over, they just don't want to offend you by acting too excited about it.

Marilyn and I were in this together. She was skillful and intentional in her mentorship of the pastoral leadership of the church. She too, lived her life as an open book, hosting weekly meetings she called M&M's, Moments with Marilyn. As I interacted with the leadership it was evident that these times of meeting with Marilyn were precious to them. They were becoming effective leaders of character and integrity. She was also having significant influence in the maturity and development of the pastor's wives. Serving in leadership of a local church and preparing the next generation of leaders to carry on was not something I did alone, as a professional pastor, it was what we did as a couple, as Mom and Dad to the family of faith we called Watoto Church.

~ Cathedral Vision ~

I am left with an awareness that while we have been able to see so much accomplished in the decades that we have served in Uganda, there is still a great deal more to do, and the responsibility for that falls on the shoulders of the next generation. This wonderful vision the Lord has put in my heart, and I've been able to pass on to the people of Watoto, is such a huge vision that there is no way that I will see it fulfilled in my lifetime. I call it Cathedral Vision.

In the centuries past, there was a need for a Cathedral to be built in a specific community. It was the place where God met the people through the power of his preached word. Corporate worship was returned to God in the thanksgiving and wonder of the community to God for His goodness. It would tower above the community and provide the foundation for the life, ethics and stability of the people of the city.

Someone would be given the vision for the Cathedral. There was an ongoing process that would literally take, sometimes, two hundred years before the completion of the Cathedral. It would be planned, drawn up, financed, and building started. Those who had the vision and were tasked with seeing it accomplished would not live long enough to see its completion. It might take several generations before the vision was realized. Future generations would then enjoy the magnificence of the great building, raised for the glory of God.

God is a God of the generations. His goodness extends to each generation. Each generation needs to have its own interaction with God and build on the legacy of those who have gone before.

That's the way I look at Watoto Church. I have laid the foundation; another will build on it, and another follow behind him. The vision will come to pass if we keep on being faithful, doing the things God calls us to do.

I leave you with the words of a pastor and preacher whose visionary transformational leadership has inspired many.

> *"God does not need your strength; He has more than enough power of His own. He asks for your weakness; He has none of that Himself, and He is longing, therefore, to take your weakness and use it as an instrument in His own mighty hand. Will you not yield your weakness to Him and receive His strength."*
>
> *Charles Haddon Spurgeon*

In all this, we bear witness to the fame and glory of God.

EPILOGUE

~ Reflect and Discuss ~

As you reflect on your own story and engage in discussion with others, consider the following prompts:

1. Financing the Building of God's Kingdom:

    • Reflect on the various ways God provides resources for His Kingdom work on earth. This can include financial generosity, but also the investment of time, talents, and relationships.

    • Discuss practical ways to align your life with God's means of financing His Kingdom. This may involve being faithful stewards of your finances, using your skills and abilities for ministry, and cultivating a generous and sacrificial spirit.

2. Understanding Cathedral Vision:

    • Explore the concept of Cathedral Vision as described in the text. Discuss how it relates to the long-term vision and mission of the Church.

    • Consider how Cathedral Vision applies to your personal journey and the work you feel called to do in advancing God's Kingdom.

3. Embracing Weakness as God's Instrument:

    • Reflect on the idea that God can use our weaknesses as instruments in His hands. Share personal experiences where you've seen God work through your weaknesses or limitations.

    • Discuss ways to surrender your weaknesses to God, allowing Him to use them for His glory and purposes. This may involve humility, dependence on God's strength, and trusting in His sovereignty.

During your discussion, encourage one another by sharing stories of God's faithfulness and provision in your lives. Take time to pray for each other, asking God for wisdom, strength, and boldness to live out His Kingdom purposes. By engaging in open dialogue and mutual encouragement, you can deepen your understanding of these concepts and grow together in faith.

~